These articles have been published in the Indian Historical Quarterly and the details of the articles is given below for reference:

Issue	Year of Pub.	Page Nos.	Page Nos. in the present book
Vol. 24 (1-4)	1948	251-258	1-8
Vol. 13 (1-4)	1937	549-580	9-32
Vol. 14 (1-4)	1938	110-113	33-36
Vol. 14 (1-4)	1938	114-120	37-42
Vol. 15 (1-4)	1939	90-100	43-50
Vol. 35 (1-4)	1959	45-56	51-60
Vol. 18 (1-4)	1942	60-62	61-64
Vol. 1 (1-2)	1925	18-30	65-74
Vol. 1 (1-2)	1925	201-213	75-84
Vol. 1 (1-2)	1925	369	85-86
Vol. 32 (1-4)	1956	223-248	87-110
Vol. 32 (1-4)	1956	329-337	111-118
Vol. 6 (1-4)	1930	757-772	119-134
Vol. 21 (1-4)	1945	245-270	135-160
Vol. 9 (1-2)	1933	499-502	161-164
Vol. 10 (1-4)	1934	785-796	165-176
Vol. 4 (1-4)	1928	405-416	177-186
Vol. 31 (1-4)	1955	52-67	187-202
Vol. 32 (1-4)	1956	290-296	203-210
Vol. 3 (3-4)	1927	561-570	211-220
Vol. 32 (1-4)	1956	148-162	221-234
Vol. 9 (3-4)	1933	981	235-236
Vol. 6 (1-4)	1930	171	237-238
Vol. 4 (1-4)	1928	559-562	239-242

Facets of Buddhist Thought and Culture: 3

Buddhist Sects And Philosophies

Collection of Articles from the Indian Historical Quarterly

Compiled by
Dr. Mahendra P. Mittal

Introduction by
Prof. S. R. Bhatt

Originals
(an imprint of Low Price Publications)
Delhi-110052

Distributed by
D.K. Publishers Distributors (P) Ltd.
4834/24, Ansari Road, Darya Ganj,
New Delhi-110002
Phones:2 3278584, 23278368, 23261465,
e-mail: dkpd@del3.vsnl.net.in
visit us at: www.dkpd.com

Articles first Published in the Journal from 1925-1963
First Published as a book
With an Introduction 2003
ISBN 81-7536-270-7

Published by
Originals
(an imprint of Low Price Publications)
A-6, Nimri Commercial Centre,
Near Ashok Vihar Phase-IV,
Delhi-110052
Phones: 27401672, 27452453
e-mail: lpp@nde.vsnl.net.in
visit us at: www.lppindia.com

Printed at
D K Fine Art Press P Ltd.
Delhi-110052

PRINTED IN INDIA

Introduction

Prof. S. R. Bhatt

The systems of philosophical thought that grew up in Indian cultural soil have been varied and variegated having several schools and sub-schools though all of them centre around the Vedic thought delineating their viewpoints for or against the basic tenets of the Vedic wisdom. Among these systems, Buddhism occupies a very distinct and significant position making not only innovative contributions but also indepth analysis of various philosophical issues. It has provided a new orientation and a fresh impetus to approach the nature of Reality and also towards the understanding of the empirical world. Loid Buddha who initiated the non-substantialist approach to Reality by way of a contrast to "*ātmavāda*" or "substance ontology" of the Vedic tradition, argued for the constantly changing nature of the world of experience and on this basis advocated a distinct way of life rejecting the idea of permanence or abidance as the sole criterion of Reality.

Buddhist thought, thus, has centred around no-substance ontology. Gautama, the Buddha, was led to philosophizing by an intense longing for the eradication of suffering. He visualised that all suffering is due to '*tanha*', (longing) and that all longing is due to attachment to the false notion of permanence. His philosophical enterprise was exclusively geared towards eradication of suffering. He, therefore, propounded the four Noble Truths. These are

i. Sarvam duḥkham

ii. Duḥkha samudaya

iii. Duḥkha nirodha

iv. Nirodha gāmini pratipadā

All important Buddhist doctrines flow from these four Noble Truths. Whether we take into account the metaphysics, epistemology, axiology and value theory, eschatology, social and political thought, ethical and cultural deliberations, in every sphere of philosophizing Buddhist thought stems from and pivots around these four Noble Truths which provide a foundation to the entire Buddhist thought and culture.

(1) History of Buddhist thought

The Early Buddhist thought is contained in the Tripiṭakas which are Suttapiṭaka, Vinayapiṭaka and Dhammapiṭaka. These are composed in Pāli language and they are regarded as *'Buddha-vacana'*, since Buddha gave his discourse in Pāli language. Though Buddha did not himself write anything, his followers subsequently put in writing his ideas, thoughts and practices. Several Buddhist councils (*Saṅgitis*) were held in ancient times in India to compile and edit the *Buddha vacanas*. In these councils particularly in the first council, the task of systematisation and editing of *Buddha vacanas* was undertaken and the canonical Buddhist literature was produced. In this enterprise Bhikṣu Mahākāssapa along with Upāli and Ānanda played leading role. Arising out of the canonical literature a large amount of non-canonical literature was also produced. By the time of King Asoka Buddhist thought was quite extensive and rich in contents. However, because of its extent and variety there was a scope for differences of opinion and numerous interpretations came into existence among the adherents of Buddhism. Thus many schools and sub-schools of Buddhism came on the scene.

(2) Schools of Early Buddhism

It is learnt that differences of opinion in the Buddhist fold cropped- up during the time of Buddha himself. His own cousin Devadatta differed with him. Buddha was also aware of the fact that his views might be subjected to multiple interpretations. He, therefore, insisted that Dhamma and Vinaya piṭakas should be regarded as supreme authorities for all settlement of disputes concerning his views. From the very fact that various councils were held and different voices were raised with regard to the authoritative exposition of the *Buddha vacanas* it was natural that varying schools were likely to be cropped up. The original literature and its basic tenets are regarded as authoritative and sacred by all followers of Buddhism, but they widely differ with regard to their interpretations. The first schism in the history of Buddhism appeared between the Theravāda (Sthaviravāda) and Mahāsāṅghika. The Sthaviravādins were more orthodox and conservative particularly in the content of the ethical norms. The Mahāsāṅghikas were more liberal and advocated relaxation of the stringent rules. Even within these two sects the split went on widening and in the course of time many sub-sects came into existence. It will not be possible to go into details of the doctrines and practices advocated in all these schools and sub-schools and their distinctive features for which good amount of literature is already available, we may only name them. They are as under:-

1. The Staviravādins or the Theravādins
2. The Mahīśāsakas
3. The Sarvāstivādins
4. The Haimavatas
5. The Vātsiputrīyas
6. The Dharmaguptikas
7. The Kāśyapīyas
8. The Vaibhāṣikas
9. The Sautrāntikas or the Saṅkrāntivādins
10. The Mahāsāṅghikas
11. The Bahuśrutiyas
12. The Caityakas
13. The Mādhyamika School
14. The Yogācāra School

This diversification of Buddhism and Buddhist thought resulted in newer understanding, innovative interpretations, novel expositions and widening of the spheres of thought. This was not only due to the ingenuity of the subsequent Buddhist thinkers who were brilliant in their ideas and highly sophisticated in their expressions, but their fierce exchanges of ideas in dialogues and debates with thinkers and scholars of other philosophical traditions also contributed to this enrichment. The point is that, the multiplication in the form of schools and sub-schools is not to be treated as a negative development but as an asset in so for as it resulted in substantive addition to Buddhist literature. Special mention may be made here of the exchanges of thought between Buddhist thinkers on the one hand and Vedāntic, Nyāya-Vaiśeṣika, Sāmkhya-Yoga and Mīmāmsā thinkers on the other.

Philosophically many new schools of Buddhist thought came into existence and a vast literature wạs produced. It would be voluminous work to give an exposition even of their seminal ideas, salient features and significant delineations, however, a brief reference to important Buddhist works and thinkers may be helpful. The Buddhist literature was composed both in Pāli and Sanskrit. Apart from the Pāli Tripiṭakas a special mention can be made of important works like *Abhidharma Kośa, Jataka Kathās, Mahāyāna Sutras,* works of thinkers like Buddhaghoṣa, Aśvaghoṣa, Nāgārjuna, Buddhapālita, Bhāvaviveka, Asaṅga, Maitreya, Vasubandhu, Dinnāga, Dharmakirti, Śāntarakṣita, Kamalaśīla, Ratnakirti etc.

(3) Schools of Buddhism outside India

During the time of Aśoka and thereafter, Buddhism spread far and wide in Asia and parts of Europe. Several important schools came up in all those countries where Buddhism made its appearance. Most of the schools were initiated and led by Indian monks who went to those countries to preach and teach Buddhism. However, the contribution of the local thinkers and scholars is not to be minimised because they also provided native orientations and internal inputs. That is why we may make a rough distinction like Indian Buddhism, Tibetan Buddhism, Chinese Buddhism, Japanese Buddhism, Korean Buddhism, etc. Broadly speaking a popular distinction is put forth between Hīnayāna and Mahāyāna, Tantrayāna constituting an important component of the Mahāyāna. In countries south of India, Hīnayāna has dominant following and in the countries north of India Mahāyāna is more popular. In all these countries there are distinct schools and sub-schools of Buddhism. There is need to have cataloguing of all these schools and sub-schools with their differential characters and specific philosophico-religious positions. However, we may make a broad reference to different schools in China and Japan.

In China the important schools are as under:-

(1) The Ch'an (Dhyāna) School

(2) The Vinaya School

(3) The Tantra School

(4) The Vijñanavāda School

(5) The Sukhāvatīvyūha School

(6) The Avatamsaka School

(7) The Mādhyamika School

(8) The Tien-t'ai School

In Japan mainly under the Chinese influence many schools of Buddhism developed among which the following are well-known:-

(1) The Tendai Sect

(2) The Shingon Sect

(3) Pure Land Buddhism

(4) Zen Buddhism

(5) The Shin Sect

(6) The Nichiren Sect

In contemporary times Zen Buddhism has attracted world wide attention and recognition. The peculiarity of Zen Buddhism is that it has given rise to a unique mode of meditation which is efficacious both for material prosperity and spiritual enhancement. It has resulted in a symbiosis of the empirical and the trans-empirical modes of existence. Added to this is the Tibetan exposition of Buddhist modes of thinking and living sphereheaded by the present Dalai Lama which concentrates on universal interdependence, universal responsibility and universal compassion. In Korea also Won-hyo and many other thinkers worked on the Buddhist doctrines of Middle path and expounded the principle of universal harmony. Though there is no distinct school named after Won-hyo, his interpretations admit of a distinct identity. He has influenced Korean thought and mode of living on the pattern of Buddhist culture. There are many such Buddhist schools and sub-schools in Thailand and Vietnam etc. It should be possible to deal with them separately in a different volume.

Fundamental Doctrines of Buddhism

Gautama, the Buddha, was a "realized " person. He was a practical thinker who concentrated on amileoration of the imperfections and miseries of empirical life and existence. As stated earlier, his doctrines are popularly known as four Noble Truths. They are regarded as "Noble" (*Ārya*) in the sense that they are undeniable hard facts of life which every empirical existence has to undergo and from which there is no escape. These Truths pertain to a right approach to Reality (*Samyakdṛṣṭi*) and right way of living (*Samyakśīla*). They are elaborated in the form of Eight-fold Noble Path (Aṣṭāngika Mārga). All doctrines and practices of Buddhism emnate from them.

The starting point of Buddhist thought is the fact of Suffering (Duḥkha). Suffering symbolises and represents the evanscence and essencelessness of all phenomena resulting in dependent existence, conditioned living, limitations of experiences and imperfections of life. The cumulative effect of all these is (Duḥkha) suffering. From this, by way of corollary of this basic tenent of "Sarvam Duḥkham", the following doctrines result:

1. Sarvam anityam or Sarvam kṣaṇikam
2. Sarvam anātmam
3. Sarvam anisvaram, and finally
4. Nirvāṇam śāntam

Sarvam anityam - the most significant and distinctive doctrine advocated by the Buddha is the view of flux in Reality. There is nothing which is immutable, eternal and abiding. The objects of experience are products of various components known as '*Skandha*'. Each *Skandha* has its own flow and it is like a stream or a burning lamp which gives impression of permanence but which is constantly and incessantly fleeting. All objects have origination and conditioned production. This is known as *pratītya-samutpāda*, i.e. dependent and inter-dependent origination.

Sarvam anātmam - It stands for non-substantial approach to Reality and life. In the phenomenal world there is nothing that is permanent, eternal and abiding which can be regarded as soul or self. It is due to (*mithyā-dṛṣṭi*) false view that a permanent abiding substance is experienced. There is no soul in any living being which exist eternally, the immorality of which is aspired for. It is our wishful thinking that there should be a self which exist for all times.

Sarvam aniśvaram - The denial of permanence in Reality implies not only the rejection of a permanent individual soul but also rejection of the idea of God as the Creator and Sustainer of the world. Buddhist tradition is a part of *Śramaṇa* culture which advocates self-reliance and self-effort to achieve *mokṣa* which is the *sumum bonum* of life. It denies any transcendental help from a supra-human source like God.

Nirvaṇam śāntam - The empirical life is a life of '*Samsāra*' in which there is a constant flow of experiences which are ultimately misery-mongering. They stem from longing and attachment to the mutative world and its fleeting objects. They motivate beings to act and this gives rise to volitions and desires which remain unfulfilled and give rise to suffering. Cessation of suffering is possible only if the worldly state of *karma* and *samsāra* is terminated. The existence in *karma* and *samsāra* is of the nature of birth and re-birth in this life and life here after. This is practically known as *Bhava-cakra*, the cycle of birth and death. This *Bhava-cakra*, also known as *pratitya samutapāda,* consists of twelve elements so linked together that the succeding follows from the preceding. Though differently explained by the various schools of Buddhism, it is always expressed as: 1. Ignorance 2. Action 3. Consciousness 4. Name and forms 5. The Senses 6. Contact 7. Sensation 8. Craving 9. Attachment 10. Becoming 11. Birth 12. Old age, disease and death. The goal of all existence should be to stop this cycle. This is known as *Nirvaṇa* which is described negatively as annihilation of the sense of 'I' or ego and positively as peace or bliss.

Buddhism lays great emphasis on proper knowledge and good conduct. Knowledge always leads to good conduct. *Prajñā* and *karuṇā* are the two facets of the same *bodhi*-situation. *Prajñā* without *karuṇā* is lame and *karuṇā* without *prajñā* is blind. Knowledge without conduct is futile and useless. A person having knowledge without practice is compared to a donkey who carries burden of sandal wood without knowing its value or utility. As the donkey bears the burden of sandalwood but has no share in the wealth of his load, similarly a person without practice merely bears the burden of his knowledge. He can not enjoy spiritual progress, which is the real fruit of knowledge. Instead he indulges in evanescent and fleeting worldly affairs which invariably end up in pain and suffering and a feeling of vanity of life.

One of the most fundamental doctrines of Buddhism is the notion of *Kāraṇa sāmagri* which implies that the world does not come into existence out of a single cause but due to a conglomeration of several causes (*hetu*) and conditions (*pratyaya*). The karmic force operates in an autonomous manner and is the formative principle of the universe. It is cumulative effect of individual and collective volitions (*cetanā*). The concept of *karma* plays the most important role in Buddhist ethics.

The concept of *Dharma* has been the unique contribution of Indian thought and its Buddhist analysis has been deep and subtle. It has both constitutive and regulative aspects. It is a rich and complex concept and its ethical implications need to be worked out separately. Similarly the concept of *Dharmakāya* is highly pregnant from ethical point of view. It is not a cold and lifeless metaphysical principle but an inexhaustible fountainhead of love and compassion. It is the ultimate Reality that underlies all empirical phenomena. All particular existences acquire their meaning only when they are thought of in their oneness in the *Dharmakāya*.

The *Bodhisattva* is representation of *Dharmakāya*. He is a *kalyāṇamitra* (friend working for welfare) of all beings. His *citta* and *caryā* are ideals of our emulation. His qualities of *sarvasattvānukampā* (compassion for all beings) and *sarvajīvadayā* (kindness for all beings) have universal value and perennial significance. The *Bodhicaryāvatāra* of Śāntideva gives an elaborate treatment of the nature, role and function of *Bodhisattva* in this universe. The Buddhist doctrine of *karuṇā* (compassion) calls for a trans-valuation of values through a paradigm shift based on enlightened view of Reality and life. It calls for a global ethics of obligations, and not of rights, of responsibility and not of capriciousness, of care and concern and cosmic fraternity.

The Buddhist ethical code springs from *karuṇā* and it touches each and every form of existence. It therefore provides a solid basis for ecological concerns. Instinctive love and respect for and protection of nature and environmental awareness have been deeply rooted in Buddhist tradition as a part of general Indian tradition. Similarly the flow of *karuṇā* is not confined to human beings alone and has to be extended to all creatures. All life is sacred, meaningful and valuable. Indian ethics not only regulates human conduct in relation to one's own self and in relation to other fellow human beings but goes a step further to bring in human conduct in relation to all living beings and natural environment. Every existence has instrinsic worth and it must be given due respect.

While concluding it must be stated that pursuit of excellence (pāramitās) and striving for betterment of life have been perennial human concerns and aspirations. Freedom from imperfection and consequent suffering has been the main motivating factor for all human enterprises. But this has to be a global vision and a universal realization without any prejudice to any section of the universe. This should be the implication of the Buddha's saying, "*Bahujana hitāya bahujana sukhāya*". This realization requires propagation and practice of global ethics. The principle of universalizability of ethical norms and their adherence without exception should be understood in this sense. The ideal of globalization should not be confined to material sphere in terms of liberalization of trade and commerce. It has to be given a spiritual orientation. Ethics also has to be spiritualistic aiming at universal well-being based on the enlightened principle of selfsameness of all existence. In modern turbulent times the Buddhistic ethics calls for a new value schema which cares for all and tends all.

Contents

Introduction

Chapter

1 Schools of Buddhism in Early Indian Inscriptions - *J N Banerjea* 1

2. Doctrines of the Mahāsaṅghika School of Buddhism - *Nalinaksha Dutt* 9

3. Doctrines of the Mahāsaṅghika School of Buddhism - *Nalinaksha Dutt* 33

4. Doctrines of the Sarvāstivāda School of Buddhism - *Nalinaksha Dutt* 37

5. Doctrines of the Sammitīya School of Buddhism - *Nalinaksha Dutt* 43

6. The Second Buddhist Council - *Nalinaksha Dutt* 51

7. A New Buddhist Sect in Kanheri - *M G Dikshit* 61

8. The Northern Buddhism - *Haraprasad Sastry* 65

9. The Northern Buddhism - *Haraprasad Sastry* 75

10. Notes on Buddhism - *Louis De La Vallée Poussin* 85

11. Place of Buddhism in Indian Thought - *N Dutt* 87

12. Zen Buddhism and Bodhidharma - *W Pachow* 111

13. Buddhist Studies with Special Reference to Tibetan - *Vidhusekhara Bhattacharya* 119

14. Popular Buddhism - *N Dutt* 135

15. Sources of Buddhist Logic - *Durgacharan Chatterji* 161

16. The Four Ways and the Four Fruits in Pāli Buddhism - *I B Horner* 165

17. Growth of Not-Man in Buddhism - *C A F Rhys Davids* 177

18. Interpretation of the "Anatta" doctrine of Buddhism - *R P Chowdhury* 187

19. Scientific Background of the Buddhist Tantras - *B Bhattacharya* 203

20. Saṁsāra or Buddhist Philosophy of Birth and Death - *Narada* 211

21. Buddhist Controversy over the Five Propositions - *Et. Lamotte* 221

22. Saṅkara's Reference to the Buddhist Passage - *Vidhusekhara Bhattacharya* 235

23. Saṅkara's Reference to the Buddhist Passage - *Vidhusekhara Bhattacharya* 237

24. Society for Buddhist Lore - *M Walleser* 239

Chapter - 1
Schools of Buddhism in Early Indian Inscriptions*

J.N. Banerjea

The immediate disciples and followers of Buddha were unanimous in their acceptance of the *fundamental* ideas formulated by him. But differences were soon to rise in the Śaṅgha about the interpretation of many of the tenets (*dharma*) and the rules of discipline (*vinaya*) taught by the Master. This led to the growth of schisms among the brotherhood of the Buddhist monks, and various ācaryas interpreted Buddha's dicta according to their own light. Buddha was himself aware of the possibilities of disunity amongst his followers, and he insisted on them that they should conduct themselves as unified body (*samaggā parisā-Mahāparinibbāna Sutta*). Early Buddhist tradition records that dissensions in the brotherhood, though of a minor character, began to appear even during Buddha's lifetime (division at Kosāmni, and schism of Devadatta), but these were settled by the Master's timely intervention and careful meditation. With his disappearance, however, splits became more frequent and permanent, inspite of the efforts of the elders like Mahākāśyapa and others. These came to a head about a century after the *Mahāparinirvāṇa*, when the second Mahāsaṃgīti was held at Vaiśālī. This was the occasion when a large body of the Buddhist monks separated from the Saṃgha, and formed a school of their own described by the later tradition, both southern and northern, as the Mahāsaṃghika. During Aśoka's time, schismatic tendencies were rampant in the Saṃgha and we find him threatening measures against those monks and nuns who would break up its unity. In his Sāñcī, Kosāmbi and Sarnāth Pillar Edicts he warns them that he would drive them out of the congregation and make them wear white robes, if they persisted in their evil intentions. The tradition about Aśoka's expulsion

---

* Read at All-India Oriental Conference, Darbhanga 1948.

of the schismatic and heretical teachers from the Order is recorded in the *Mahāvaṃśā*, and Buddhaghosa's *Samantapāsādikā*. Aśoka's punitive measures were, however, of no avail, and the schisms which had presumably developed into several schools within Buddhism continued to grow resulting into further divisions and subdivisions within the Buddhist Order.

The edicts of Aśoka do not mention the name of any sect. It can be presumed that he stood by the Theravāda or Sthaviravāda school which appears to have conformed most to the original teachings of the Buddha. Both the southern and northern texts of a much later date, however, refer to a number of schools most of which, according to them, came into being before Aśoka's time. The *Mahāvaṃśa*, one of the earliest southern texts to give us a systematic account of the evolution of these sects, mentions first the names of as many as 17 different schools other than the original Theravāda and the first schismatic school Mahāsāṃghika. The twelve that were connected with the former (Theravāda) were:—the Mahiṃśārika, the Sammiti, the Vajjiputtiya, the Sabbattha, the Dhammaguttika, the Kassapiya, the Saṃkantika and the Sutta, the five associated with the latter were the Gokulika, the Ekavyohārika, the Paṇṇatti, the Bāhulika and the Cetiya. If we are to believe the *Mahāvaṃśa* account fully, all these 17 schools (12 Theravādin, 5 Mahāsāṃghika) had come into existence in the second century after the Mahāparinirvāṇa. Aśoka, thus, had every reason to denounce *saṃghabheda*, one of the principal sins, (*pañcanaatariyāni*), that could be committed by a Buddhist. The schisms continued to multiply, and the *Mahāvaṃśa* says that the other schools which arose afterwards were the Hemavatā, the Rājagiriyā, the Siddhatthakā, the Pubba-Seliyā, the Abara-Seliyā and the Vājiriyā. These six separated from the rest in Jambudvīpa, while the Dahmmarucī and the Sāgaliyā separated from the rest in the island of Laṅka.[1] The northern tradition about the grouping of the schools is preserved in the 90th volume of the *sūtra* of Bstan-hgyur from the works of Vasumitra, Bhavya, Vinitadeva and others. Bhavya first distinguishes the two major schools, the Sthavira and the Mahāsāṃghika. Of these, the first gradually divided into the following 12 factions—the Sthavira proper, also called the Haimavata, the Sarvāstivādina, the Vaibādyavādina, the Hetuvidya also called Munduntaka (or Muruntaka) by some, the Vātsiputriya, the Dhamotariya, the Bhadrāyanīya, the Sammatiya also called Āvantaka by some and kurukullaka by others, the Mahīśāsaka, the Dharmagupataka, the Saddharmavarṣaka (or properly Sauvarṣaka)

1. Geiger, *Mahāvaṃśa* (English Translation), pp. 26-7.

called Kāśyapīya by some and lastly the Uttarīa, also called by some as the Saṃkrāntivādina. The factions into which the Mahāsāṃghika gradually divided itself were the Mahāsāṃghika, the Ekavyāvahārika, the Lokottaravādina, the Bahuśrutīya, the Prajñaptivādina, the Caityaka, the Pūrvaśaila and the Avaraśaila.[1] A comparison of the two accounts mentioned above will show that much there is in common between the two, though the southern tradition appears to be earlier.

The literary accounts of the Buddhist schools were compiled at a comparatively late period, but references to some of them are to be found in a good many Kharoṣṭhī and Brāhmī inscriptions of a very early date, some as early as the first or even second century B.C., and others be longing to the first or second century A.D. Several of the Kharoṣṭhī inscriptions edited by Konow in the *Corpus Inscriptions Indicarum*, vol. II, which range between 100 B.C. and 2100 A.D., mention the Sarvāstivādins (the Mathura Lion Capital inscriptions, the Peshawar, Zeda and Kurrum relic casket inscriptions of the time of Kaniṣka, and the inscribed Tor Ḍheri potsherds) the Kāśvapīyas (the Bedādi copper ladle inscription, and the inscribed jars from Pālāṭu Ḍheri, and the Mahāsāṃghikas (the Mathura Lion Capital and the Wardak Vase inscriptions). The part of an inscription on some jars unearthed at Pālāṭu Ḍheri was read by Konow as *Saṃghe chadudiśe shamanana Bahushutikana Kashyaviyana parigrahe* ("to the order of the four quarters in the acceptance of the Bahuśrutiyaka and Kāśyapiya śramaṇas'); but he was not very sure of reading the name of the Bahuśrutiyas there. If, however, his reading could be accepted without any doubt, then it would follow that the donor of the record was giving equal patronage to the monks belonging to schools arising out of two rival orders, the Mahāsāṃghika and the Theravāda. But this by itself is not at all unlikely, for the Mathura Capital inscription (N) contains the names of the Sarvāstivādins and the Mahāsāṃghikas side by side. Bühler interpreted this passage as '(in honour) of the teacher Buddhila, a native of Nagara, a Sarvāstivāda monk, who knows the wisdom of the famous Mahāsāṃghikas and is eager to explain it.' Bühler thought that the inscription probably meant to praise Buddhila for his proficiency in the doctrines of the two rival schools. Konow read the passage in question in a somewhat different manner, his interpretation of it being,' to the teacher Buddhila from Nagara, the Sarvāstivādin monk, a *khalula* (dialectician?) to teach the foremost Mahāsāṃghikas the truth.' Whichever of the two be the correct reading and interpretation, there is no doubt that reference is made here to a

1. Rockhill, *The Life of the Buddha*, pp. 182-83.

Buddhist elder hailing from a region just outside the extreme north-west of India (Nagara has been located near Jalalabad in the easternmost region of Afghanistan), who was well-versed in the tow opposite schools. The Sarvāstivādins, as we know from these inscriptions, were in possession of the *vihāra* at Mathura (they are mentioned several times in these records), whereas the Mahāsāṃghikas were not. The latter, however, had a settlement in far remote Wardak (ancient Khawaḍa, Known even now as Khawat, about 30 miles to the west of Kabul) in the second century A.D. The Wardak Vase Inscription of the 51st year of the Kaniṣka era engraved during the reign of the Mahārāja Rājātirāja Huviṣka, records among other things that the *vihāra* was built there by one Vagramarega who had made his abode in Khavada, for the acceptance of the Mahāsāṃghika teachers.Konow says that this inscription is the only Kharoṣṭhī record which speaks of the Mahāsāṃghikas as being in charge of a *vihāra*. He further suggests that the monks of this order were not old settlers in this region, but immigrants of a more eastern district (the donor was certainly a new-comer there). From the evidence of the extant Kharoṣṭhī inscriptions, there is hardly any doubt that the Sarvāstivādin school was one of the most important ones is northern India between the first century B.C. and the second century A.D.[1]

The Brāhmī inscription of the same period, if not a little earlier, found in different parts of India, especially central and western, also contain references to several well-known Buddhist schools grouped under one or the main heads. Thus, the Sāñcī and Sonari inscriptions from the Bhopal State, central India, refer to the Haimavata school which according to Bhavya was another name of the Sthavira school (Theravāda). Relics of several Haimavata teachers, Kāśyapagotra, Madhyama and Dundubhisāra, and others were enshrined in and near Sāñcī. The Ācāryas just named were the fist three of the five, viz., Kāssapagota, Majjhima, Dundubhisāra, Sahadeva and Mūlakadeva, who, according to the *Dīpavaṃśa*, were the inspirers and teachers of the school especially associated with the Himalayan region. The inscription on the steatite relic casket no. I found by Cunningham in *Stūpa* no. II at *Sāñcī* reads—*sapusisa-Kāsapagotasa sava-Hemavatāchāriyasa;* another steatite relic casket (no. III) has a slightly different inscription,—*sapurisasa Kotiputasa (Kanutīputrasya) Kāsapaghotasa sava-Hemavatāchāriyasa*. The term, *sava-Hemavatāchāriyasa*, was translated by Fleet as 'the teacher of all the Himavat region' (*JRAS.*, 1902, P. 681). But there is no doubt the N.G.

1. Sten Konow, *Corpus Inscriptionum Indicarum*, vol. II.

Majumdar was right in interpreting it as 'the teacher of the whole community of the Haimavatas.' He thinks that Kāśyapagotra who, according to early Buddhist tradition, was a contemporary of Aśoka (Majjhima was another, perhaps a younger, contemporary), was the founder of the Haimavat school, as he is described in the epigraphs *as Sarva-Haimavatāchārya*. Dundubhisāra's name is found in an inscription on a crystal box recovered from the Sanari *stūpa* by Cunningham. It reads—*sapurisasa Gotiputasa Hemavatasa Dundubhisāra-dāyādasa*; the casket, thus, contained the relics of the saint Gauptiputra, a Haimavata, who was a relation of Dundubhisāra. An inscribed relic casket of the saint Vāci (Vātsī) Suvijayata, evidently a Haimavata, was also found at Sāñcī. Majumdar rightly observes, 'About the end of the second century B.C., the Haimavatas must have set about collecting from various sources the corporeal relics of their former ācāryas from Kāśyapagotra to Vātsī Suvijayata (about 3 or 4 generations) and proceeded to enshrine them in a *stūpa* at Sāñcī. It would be of interest to note here an imprecatory inscription (no. 396) of the first century B.C. found at Sāñcī, which records the 'he who removes any of the components of the *stūpa* to *aññācārīyakula* should have the fate of the perpetrator of the five sins.' In the *Mahāvaṃsā* account of the Buddhist sects, schools of doctrine other than Theravāda are described as *aññācārīyakula*; thus, 'the injunction here is evidently against the removal of any property from Kākanāva (an earlier name of Sāñcī) to a non-Theravāda community like the Mahāsāṃghikas.' The inscription gives further proof that though the Theravādins were prominent at Sāñcī in the early period, by the first century B.C. other rival schools had also their establishments there.[1] An inscription from its Great Stūpa at Sāñcī records the gift of one Avisinā described as *sutatikini(ya)*. The epithet has been interpreted as versed in the *Suttantas*; it might also signify here 'one belonging to the Santrāntika school' which was one of the divisions of the Sarvāstivāda (Mūla-sarvāstivāda and Sautrāntika) according to Bhavya. According to the *Mahāvaṃśa*, the Mahiṃsāsaka and the Vajjiputtaka parted directed from the Theravāda; from the Mahiṃsāsaka originated tow other schools, the Sabbattha and the Dhammaguttika. 'From the Sabbattha sect arose the Kassapiyā, from these arose the Saṃkantika bhikkhus, from these last, the Sutra sect.' It is presumable that the Sutta school of the Ceylonese text and the Sautrānika of the northern tradition are one and the same.

Early inscriptions in Brāhmī script from western India contain a number of references to some well-known Buddhist schools. Thus an

1. Marshall, *Moment of Sanchi*, vol. I, pp. 297-98.

inscription (Lüders' List, no. 1995) from the Karle cave refers to the gift of a pillar with relics by the preacher (*bhāṇaka*) Satimita of the *bhayamita* Dhamutarias (Dharmottariyas) from Sopāraka. Another inscription (List, no. 1105) from the same place records the gift of a village to the mendicant (*pavajita*) friars dwelling in the Vāluraka caves for the support of the school (*nikāya*) of the Mahāsāghiyas (Mahāsāṃghikas). In the 24th regnal year of the Sātavāhana ruler Vāsiṣṭhiputta Puḷumāyi, a foreigner (Parthian) named Harapharṇa built a nine-called (navagabha) hall (*maṇḍapa*) at Karle for the community (*sagha*) of the four quarters as the special property of the Mahāsāṃghikas; the donor describes himself as the son of Setapharṇa, the Sovasaka, living at Abulāmā. Bühler long ago pointed out that Sovasaka may refer to the Sauvarṣaka or Kāśvapīya sect, a branch of the Sthavira school specially associated with the Sarvāstivādins. This interpretation of the term *sovasaka* is far more acceptable than the one according to which it may mean either *suvāsita dravya-vikrayiṇaḥ* (of the sellers of scented objects) or *suvāsākhya-deśajātasya* (of one born in a country called Suvāsa).[1] The name does not occur in the *Mahāvaṃśa* list, but the Kāśyapiyas are mentioned there as the direct offshoot of the Sabbattha (Sarvāstivādin) sect. It is interesting to note here that the son of a Theravāda sectary is solicitous for the comfort of the monks belonging to a rival sect; it might be that he has his personal leaning towards the Mahāsāṃghika school. The Nasik Cave Inscription of the 19th year of Vāsiṣṭhiputta Puḷumāyi records the gift of a *leṇa* (cave dwelling) on mount Triraśmi to be used as the special property of the school (*nikāya*) of the Bhadavāniyas (Bhadrayānīyas). The Junnar Buddhist cave inscription (List no. 1152) records the gift of a cave (*leṇa*) and a cistern (*poḍhi*) by Patibadhaka Giribhuti Sakhuyaru, son of Savagiri Yāśa of the Apaguriyas, and endowment of these establishments and the nunnery of the Dhammuttariyas (Dharmottariyas) in the town. The first part of the Nasik Cave Inscription no. 22 reads *Chetika upāsakiyasa Mugudāsasa leṇa deyadhama;* it means 'a cave, the meritorious gift of Mugudāsa who belongs to the lay worshippers of the Caitika.' Bühler rightly says, "The Cetikas, in Sanskrit Caitikas, are a subdivision of the Mahāsāṃghika school. Mugudāsa apparently attended the *bhāṇa* of some monk of the school, or to use a modern phrase, 'sat under a Caitika'."[2]

Many more inscriptions of the early period from the different parts of India can be cited, which mention the names of well-recognised

---

1. Sarkar, *Select Inscriptions*, vol. I, p. 203.
2. *ASWI*, vol. IV, p. 103 and note.

Buddhist schools. But there occur various names in the early Kharoṣṭhī and Brāhmī inscriptions, some of which may allude to particular Bauddha goṣṭhis or sects, which have not as yet been satisfactorily explained. Konow says, 'there cannot be any doubt that we have throughout to do with Buddhist donors' in the Kharoṣṭhī inscriptions edited by him in *Corpus*, vol. II. If he is right, then such terms as *Vadhitiraṇa sahayaṇa, Vashishuga sahayarṇa, Pipalakhana sahyaṇa or Dronipadrana shaharaṇa* occurring in some of them as the names and attributes of the donors, should denote members, of individual Bauddha goṣṭhis. It is for the learned Buddhologists to say whether any of these has textual basis; Konow certainly could not give any satisfactory literary parallel. The Sāñcī inscriptions contain many such na,es as the Tāpasiyas, Saphineyakas, Vākiliyas, Dhamakas, Magalakaṭiyas, most of them hailing from Ujjaini. N.G. Majumdar observes about them, 'In several instances gifts are made in the name of the family (*kula*) of an individual, or jointly by a particular sect or guild..........These names are not known from any other sources, and it is difficult to say whether they represent particular families or guilds.[1] But here also one is tempted to ask whether we can find in any of these the name of some long-forgotten Buddhist sects. My late lamented friend Dr. B.M. Barua, one of the most distinguished Buddhologists, told me a fortnight before his death that Saphineyakas might be another form of Sabbhineyakas, i.e., 'those who believe that they should be guided by the Sapurisas or the elect' (cf. *Dhammapada*); Vākiliyas might mean those who followed the tradition of Vakkalii (Vāshkali), a famous immediate disciple of the Buddha; Tāpasiyas might denote those among the Buddhists, who set a great store on the performance of austerities. A Junnar Buddhist cave inscription (List, no. 1152) refers to the Apaguriyas; another from the same locality (List, no. 1164) mentions the holy assembly (*siddhagana*) of the Aparājitas; a third again from the same place (List, no. 1169) describes two brothers, inhabitants of Bharukaccha, as the Lāṃkuḍiyas. Who were these Apaguriyas, Aparājitas and the Lāṃkuḍiyas? Can any light be thrown on them from the extensive Buddhist literature of the early and the mediaeval period? A Mathura Buddhist inscription (List, no. 126) records the dedication of a pillar base (*kumbhaka*) by bhikṣus Sūrya and Buddharakṣita, the Prahāṇikas, for the gift of health to all Prahānikas. Who were these Prahāṇikas? Has the term *prahāṇika* any connection with Pāli *pahāna*? *Pahānasutta* of the *Aṅguttara Nikāya* (IV, 7) lays down that the higher life (*brahmacariya*) is for the purpose

1. Marshall, *op. cit.*, p. 297.

of getting rid of the 7 fetters (*saṃyojanāni*). *Aṅguttara Nikāya* (II, 25) expatiates on the characteristics of the god-life (*brahma-carya*), one of which is 'abandoning' (*pahāna*). The Prahāṇikas, thus, might denote a Buddhist order which set the highest value on '*brahma-carya*' with all its duties and obligations.

Chapter - 2

Doctrines of the Mahāsaṅghika School of Buddhism

Nalinaksha Dutt

The doctrines of the several schools of Buddhism are given succinctly by Vasumitra in his treatise on the Schools.[1] This treatise has been rendered from Chinese into English by Mr. Masuda who, with the aid of Chinese commentaries, has not only presented the doctrines in an intelligible form, but has added notes which are exceedingly valuable for the comprehension of the doctrines. He occasionally referes to the *Kathāvatthu* but it has not been possible for him to utilise fully this highly important work for elucidating the doctrines.

The *Kathāvatthu* not only elucidates and corroborates Vasumitra's statements but also furnishes us with a few additional informations relating to the doctrines of several schools. The close, sometimes even verbatim, agreement between the *Kathāvatthu* and Vasumitra's treatise about the doctrines of the schools enables us to state that both the work must be old and authentic and should be regarded as authoritative as far as the doctrines of the schools are concerned. In Vasumitra's treatise and the *Kathāvatthu* we can expect only those doctrines which were matters of controversy. It seems that Vasumitra who was Sarvāstivādin recorded only those doctrines which he considered as contrary to those of his own school while the compiler of the *Kathāvatthu* mentioned only those which he regarded as heresies from the standpoint of a Theravādin. In the present paper we propose to present the doctrines of the Mahāsaṅghikas with its subdivisions as are to be found in Vasumitra's treatise and the *Kathāvatthu*.

1. Transl. from Chinese by J. Masuda in the *Asia Major*, vol. II, 1925, henceforth referred to as Masuda. There are two other translations of the Tibetan version of this work, one by Prof. M. Walleser entitles *Die Sekten des alten Buddhismus* (Heidelberg, 1927) and other a much earlier one by Wassiljew.

The Mahāsaṅghika group

The Mahāsaṅghikas are the earliest to secede from the original school which came later on to be distinguished as the Theravādins (or in Sanskrit Sthaviravādins). The secession happened in the Second Buddhist Council at Vesāli. The cause of the secession is given in the various accounts of the Councils as certain differences of opinion in the interpretation of ten Vinaya rules. These differences might have appeared serious to the Vinayists (*Vinayadharas*), but to us they do not appear to be of much consequence. In view of the various doctrinal opinions attributed to them by Vasumitra and corroborated by Buddhaghosa in his commentary on the *Kathāvatthu*, it is apparent that the Buddhist monks were already divided into two groups, who may well be described as Westerners and Eastereners[1] long before the Second Council, and the dispute regarding the interpretation of the Vinaya rules was made only an occasion to set a seal to the separation that had already taken place.

Mahāsaṅghikas again became sub-divided into several sects of which Vasumitra takes notice of the Ekavyavahārika, Lokottaravāda, Kaukkuṭika, Bahuśrutīya, Prajñaptivāda, and the Śaila Schools,[2] while the deals, according to the testimony of Buddhaghosa, with the heresies of the Andhakas or the Śaila Schools, including the Uttarāpathakas, Vetulyakas, and Rājagirikas, Siddhatthikas, and Hetuvādas. In the following treatment of ours, the Mahāsaṅghikas include all their sub-sects, as we do not think it worth while to distinguish the doctrines of one sub-sect from those of another.

THE DOCTRINES

I. Is Buddha human?

In Vasumitra's treatise the Buddhas are described as *lokottara* (supramundane), and as such he is made of *anāsrava dharmas*[3] (pure qualities without sleep or dream which are concomitants of *sāsrava dharmas*. Buddhas have unlimited *rūpakāyas* (material bodies), powers (*balas*), length of life (*āyu*), etc.

1. Westerners were the monks of Avanti, Kosambi, etc. while the Easterners were those of Vesāli and its neighbourhood. See *Mahāvaṃsa*, IV, 2.

2. Caityaśaila, Aparaśaila and Uttaraśaila.—Masuda, p. 38. These correspond of Pubbaseliya, Aparaseliya and Uttarāpathaka of the *Kathāvatthu* (henceforth abbreviated as *Kun.*).

3. Masuda renders it as "no sāsrava dharmas." The rendering, I would prefer, is "anāsrava dharmas," i.e. Buddhas are embodiment of anāsrava dharmas, vi., sīlaskandha, samādhisk., prajñāsk., vimuktisk. and vimuktijñānadarśanask. not of rūpa, vedanā, saññā, saṅkhāra and viññāṇa which are sāsrava dharmas. See my *Aspects of Mahāyāna Buddhism and its Relation to Hinayāna* (henceforth indicated as *Aspects*), p. 108.

In the *Kathāvatthu* (XVII, 1&2) the above doctrines are attributed to the Vetulyakas, according to whom the Buddha does not live in the world of men neither should he be located anywhere and it is his created form (*abhinimmito jino*) that delivered the religious discourses. The Theravādins account for this heresy by saying that it is due to the literal but wrong interpretation of the passage: *Bhagavā loke jāto loke sambuddho lokaṃ abhibhuyya viharati anupalitto lokenā ti* (Buddha, born and enlightened in this world, overcame this world and remained untouched by the things of the world—*Saṃ. Nik.*, iii. 140). This is supplemented by further discussions in the *kun.*, (XVIII 1, 2 & XXI. 6) relating to the heresies also attribute to the Vetulyakas, viz., *Na vattabbaṃ,"Buddho Bhagavā manussaloke aṭṭhāsī" ti* (It should not be said that Buddha lived in the world of men—XVIII. 1): *Sabbā disā Buddhā tiṭṭhantī ti* (Buddhas exist in all corners of the world—XXII. 6) and *Abhinimmitena desito ti* (the discourses are delivered by created forms—XVIII.2). These show that according to the opponents of the Theravādins the Buddha is omnipresent and as such is beyond the possibility of location in any particular direction or sphere and that all the preaching of Buddhism has been done by the apparitional images of Buddha.

Buddhaghosa with his usual naïvety understood the Vetulyakas as holding the opinion that Buddha remained always in the Tusita heaven, where he was before he came to this world. The discussions in the *Kathāvatthu* as also the terse statements of Vasumitra leave no room for doubt about the fact that the Mahāsaṅghikas (specially their offshoots,—the Vetulyakas and the Lokottaravādins) regarded Buddha as transcendental. Mr. Masuda suggests that the *Sambhogakāya* of Buddha is referred to in the heresies, but the time of emergence of the conception of *sambhogakāya* is still a matter of controversy.[1] From the discussion in the *Kathāvatthu* (XXI.5) concerning "*atthi Buddhānaṃ Buddhehi hīnātirekatāti* (whether Buddhas mutually differ?) it seems that the *Andhakas* (another offshoot of the Mahāsaṅghikas)[2] were still concerned with the *Sambhogakāya* and had not yet arrived at the conception of the *Dharmakāya*. Buddhaghosa says that the Andhakas hold that Buddhas differ from one another in some qualities other than attainments like *satipaṭṭhāna, sammāppadhāna*, etc., the orthodox school holding the Buddhas may

---

1. Masuda's opinion, however, can be supported by the fact that in the *Mahāvastu*, (I. p. 169) Buddha's *kāya* is equated to *niṣyandakāya* rendered into Chinese by *pao sheng* which is also the rendering of *Sambhogakāya* , see my *Aspects.*, pp. 117, 120.

2. *Mahāvastu*, I, p. 168. लोकानुवर्तनौ बुद्धा अनुवर्तन्ति लौकिकीं।
प्रज्ञप्तिमनुवर्तन्ति यथा लोकोत्तरामपि॥

differ in respect of *sarīra* (body), *āyu* (length of life) and *pabhāva* (radiance) but not in regard to the attainments mentioned above. The discussion in the *Kun.* (XVIII. 3) that Buddhas can have no *karuṇā* (compassion), an opinion attributed to the *Uttarāpathakas*, tends to show that the conception of *Śūnyatā* or *Dharmakāya* was being evolved among the Uttarāpathakas. The opinion that the Buddha's body is made of *anāsrava dharmas* also lends support to the above view. In the *Mahāvastu* (I, p. 167-68) the conception of *lokottara* Buddha appears thus:- Transcendental (*lokottara*) are the practices of Bhagavān, and so are his *kuśalamūlas*, his eating, drinking and such other daily actions. He follows the ways of the world just as much as he follows the transcendental ways. He makes a show of standing, walking and other *iriyāpathas*, but he never gets tired. He washes his feet or body though there is no dirt to wash; he cleanses his teeth though his mouth smells like a lotus;[1] he eats though he has no hunger, and so forth. These are all due to his being an embodiment of the effects of good actions.[2] There is nothing in common between Him and the beings of the world. Everything of the great *ṛṣi* is transcendental including his advent into the world[3].

If the transcendence of Buddha be admitted, then it follows as a matter of course that his length of life would be unlimited and that he could not be subject to sleep and ever awake has nothing to do with dream. It is worth noting here that even in the *Pāli* suttas like the Mahāparinibbānasutta[4] there are hints to the effect that a Buddha, if he wishes, can extend his life-limit up to a *Kalpa* or the end of ȁ *Kalpa* thus revealing that the transcendental conception has taken roots in the minds of the Buddhists at a very early date.

In the *Kathāvatthu*[5] the discussion resting with the topic: *Buddhassa Bhagavato vohāro lokuttaro ti* reveals that the Andhakas, to whom the above opinion is ascribed, held that Buddha's actions (*vohāro*) are *lokuttara* and that they are treated as *lokiya* (mundane) and *lokuttaro* (supramundane) according as the object of the action is *lokiya* or *lokuttara*. Mr. Shew Zan Aung prefers to confine the sense of the word "*vohāro*" to "speech", and we think there is good reason

---

1. Cf. *Kun.* XVIII. 4: Buddhassa Bhagavato uccārapassāvo ativiya aññc gandhajāte adhigaṇhātīti—opinion of some Andhakas and Uttarāpathakas.
2. *Mtu.*, I p. 169: वुद्धानां शुभनिष्यन्दानां एषा लोकानुवर्तना। cf. Laṅkā, pp. 28, 34: निष्यन्दवुद्धा।
3. *Mtu.*, I,. p. 159.
4. *Dīgha*, II, p. 103: yassa kassaci cattāro iddhipādā bhāvitā—so ākaṅkhamāno kappaṃ vā tiṭṭheyya kappāvasesaṃ vā.
5. *Kun.*, II, 10.

for it.[1] In Vasumitra's treatise an opinion of this nature is attributed to the Mahāsaṅghikas in contrast to the Sarvāstivādins, viz., the *sūtras* (or discourses) preached by the Buddha are all perfect in themselves (*nītārtha*). Buddhas speak of nothing but dharma (doctrines), as such their teaching is concerned only with *paramārthasatya* (*paramatthasacca*), i.e., not with *saṃvṛtisatya* (*sammutisacca*).[2] The *paramārthasatya* cannot be normally expressed by words. It can be explained only by silence or at the utmost by an exclamation—which idea, I think, is expressed in Vasumitra's treatise by the sentences: "the Buddha can expound all the doctrines with a single utterance and that there is nothing which is not in conformity with the truth in what has been preached by the World-honoured one."[3] In the *Upāyakauśalyaparivarta* of the *Saddharmapuṇḍarīka* it has been shown that for training up deluded beings in his doctrines, Buddha does take recourse to various expedients which are false, i.e., unreal (*saṃvṛti* or *sammuti*), and that through such teachings the deluded beings can be led to the truth—*paramārtha*. So it follows that all his teachings collected in the *Piṭakas* are merely *saṃvṛti* or *sammuti* (unreal) and hence they are not his real teachings, which are repeatedly described in Pāli and Sanskrit texts as *pratyātmavedanīya or paccattaṃ veditabbo viññūhi*[4] (realisable within one's own self only).

According to the Mahāsaṅghikas, Vasumitra says, Buddhas have both, *kṣayajñāna* and *anutpādajñāna* always present in their mind, the Sarvāstivāda holding that all Arhats may have *kṣayajñāna* but a few only have *anutpādajñāna*;[5] the Theravādins, however, do not make such a distinction.

Among the other attributes of this lokottara Buddha, Vasumitra's treatise speaks of his powers (*balas*) as unlimited while the Mahāvastu[6] of his five eyes (*cakṣus*)[7] as uncommon (*asādhāraṇa*) and excellent those of *Pratyekabuddhas*, Arhats and others. This particular topic—*tathāgatabalaṃ sāvakasādhāraṇaṃ ti* has been taken up for discussion

---

1. *Cf. M.V.*, p. 494. व्यवहारमनाश्रित्य परमार्थो न देश्यते।
2. *Paramārtha-satya* means absolute truth while *saṃvṛti-satya* means the so-called truths as used in every day usage by the people in general. For detailed treatment see my *Aspects*, pp. 216 ff.
3. *Asia Major*, II, p. 19.
4. Aspects, p. 198.
5. *Ibid.*, p. 106 fn. 1.
6. By eyes, the text means all the five, viz., *māṃsacakṣu*, *divyac.*, *prajñāc.*, *dharmac.*, and *buddhac.*
7. Masuda, pp. 21, 42.

(a) *Kṣayajñāna* means cognisance of the fact that all the *āsavas* are destroyed;
(b) *Anutpādajñāna* means cognisance of the fact that one will not be reborn again. Cf. *Kośa*, VI, 67; *Atthasālini*, p. 54.

in the *Kathāvatthu* (III. I), but strangely enough the position taken by the complier of the *Kathāvatthu* is not that of a Theravādin but of a Lokottaravādin Mahāsaṅghika as against the Andhakas, i.e., the Śailas schools. In Vasumitra's treatise this topic appears in slightly different form.

The Theravādins do not regard Buddha as *lokottara* but attribute to him almost all the powers and qualities of a *lokottara* Buddha and this discussion reveals one of such instances. The ten special *balas* (powers) of a Tathāgata appear not only in the *Mahāvastu* (i, pp. 159-160) but also in old Pāli works like the *Majjhima Nikāya* (i. pp. 69 ff.).[1] The contention of the Abdhakas is that there is a certain degree of difference between the Buddhas and the Arhats regarding the acquisition of the ten *balas*, and as such, Buddhas and Arhat are not on the same level (*asādhāraṇam*). In the *Mahāvastu* and the Pāli words this view is accepted with this reservation that Buddhas are *sarvākārājña*, i.e., they possess a complete and detailed knowledge of everything, while an Arhat can at the utmost have sectional knowledge.[2] The Pāli school, i.e., the Theravādins hold that as far as *vimutti* is concerned there is no difference between a Buddhas and an Arhat, and that Buddhas are superior to the Arhats only on account of the fact that the former are promulgators of a new law while the Arhats are only followers of the same.[3]

---

1. The ten balas are,—

(*Mahāvastu*) pp. 159-160	(*Kathāvattu and Majjhima Nikāya*)
1. स्थानास्थानं वेत्ति	1. *Ṭhānāṭhānaṃ jānāti*
2. सर्वत्रगामिनीं च प्रतिपदं वेत्ति	2. *Sabbatthagāminipaṭipadaṃ jānāti.*
3. नानाधातुकं लोकं विदन्ति	3. *Anekadhātuṃ nānādhātuṃ lokaṃ jānāti.*
4. अधिमुक्तिनानात्वं वेत्ति	4. *Sattānaṃ nānādhimuttikataṃ jānāti.*
5. परपुरुषचरितकुशलानि वेत्ति	5. *Parasattānaṃ parapuggalānaṃ indriya-paro-pariyattaṃ yathābhūtaṃ pajānāti.*
6. कर्मबलं प्रतिजानन्ति शुभाशुभम्।	6. *Atitānāgatāpaccuppannānaṃ hetuso vipākaṃ jānāti.*
7. क्लेशव्यवदानं वेत्ति ध्यानसमापत्तिं वेत्ति	7. *jhānavimokkhasamādhisamāpattīnaṃ saṅkilesaṃ vodānaṃ voṭṭānaṃ yathābhūtaṃ pajānāti.*
8. पूर्वनिवासं वेत्ति	8. *anekavihitaṃ pubbenivāsaṃ anussarati.*
9. परिशुद्धदिव्यनयना भवन्ति	9. *dibbena cakkhunā satte passati cavamāne upapajjamāne etc.*
10. सर्वक्लेशविनाशं प्राप्तोन्ति	10. *āsvānaṃ khayā amāsavaṃ cetpvimuttiṃ paññāvimuttiṃ diṭṭhe va dhamme sayaṃ abhiññā sacchikatvā upasampajja viharati.*

2. Cf. *Kun. Cy.*, p. 62: Ṭhānāṭhānādini hi sāvakā *padesena* jānant; Tathāgatā *nippadesena* iti. Tāni uddesato sādḥāraṇāni; niddesato asādhāraṇāni— niddesato *sabbākāravisayataṃ* saṃdhāya paṭikkhipati. Cf. *Mtu.*, 1, p. 158. बोधिमूलमुपगम्य चाप्राप्तायां सर्वाकारज्ञतायां पंचचक्षुः समन्वागता भवन्ति। Cf. *Abhisamayālaṅkāra*, ch. 1.

3. This argument is adduced in the *Kun*. See also Sam. *Nik.*, III, p. 66.

II. Are Bodhisattvas average beings?

If, according to the Mahāsaṅghikas, Buddhas are *lokottara*, and if the Buddhas we *puthujjanas* of, are only created forms or the real Buddha, the Bodhisattvas also cannot be average human being—they must also be supramundane. In Vasumitra's treatise the following account of the Bodhisattvas is given: The Bodhisattvas do not pass through the embryonic stages. They assume the form of white elephants when they enter their mothers' wombs and come out of the same by the right side. The above opinion is the natural outcome of the legendary belief that came to be woven round the person of the great man about a century after his actual existence. In the *Lalitavistara*,[1] the Bodhisattva is placed not only in a crystal casket put within the womb but while in that state he is said to be preaching his *dharma* to the heavenly beings that flocked around him. The stories of the white elephant seen by Māyā in a dream at the time of her conception and the birth of the Bodhisattva by bursting through the right side of the mother's womb are too well-known to need any comment. The incorporation of these legends in the doctrines of the Mahāsaṅghikas shows that the Bodhisattva conception of the Mahāyānists was yet in the course of development.

The only doctrine that can be described as Mahāyānic is that Bodhisattvas take birth out of their own free will in any form of existence for imparting Buddhist dharmas to the sentient beings of that particular form of existence[2]—an idea well illustrated in the *Jātakas*, and developed in the later Mahāyāna works like the Śikṣāsamuccaya and the Bodhicaryāvatāra. This topic has been taken up for discussion in the Kathāvatthu (XXIII.3): *Bodhisatto issariyakāmakārikahetu vinipātaṃ gacchatī ti*—but the arguments put forward completely ignore the standpoint of the Mahāsaṅghikas and attempt to show the untenability of the opponents's proposition by treating the Bodhisattva as nothing but an average human adept toiling along the path towards the attainment of *bodhi*.

In the *niyāmokkantikathā* (*Kun.*, IV. 8. XII. 5, 6 XIII. 4) the same attitude is taken by the Theravādins. By *niyāma*, the Theravādins understand *sammattaniyamo* and *micchattaniyamo*, the former being the practice of *brahmacariya* (purity in conduct) and *ariyamagga* (path of sanctification) including, for the Bodhisattvas, the fulfillment of pāramis, leading to nibbāna (i.e., *samyaktva* or *sammatta*), and the latter the commission of heinous crimes (*anantarīyakamma*) leading

1. *Lalitavistara*, ch. VI, p. 73 (of A.S.B. edition).
2. Masuda, p. 21.

to hell (i.e., *mithyātva* or *micchatta*), all other practices being looked upon as *aniyata* (un-predestined).[1] In the sense as expressed above any Śrāvaka can be a sammattaniyāmo and he need not be a bodhisattva. The Theravādins do not recognise the bodhisattvas as superior in attainments to the Śrāvaka, and in the matter of brahmacariya and practice of ariyamagga they do not want to make any distinction between a Śrāvaka and a Bodhisattva.

In the *Laṅkāvatāra* and Asaṅga's *Sūtrālaṅkāra* and such other Mahāyāna works however it is repeatedly stated that a person by the development of *bodhicitta* becomes a *niyata* Bodhisattva, i.e., through the fulfillment of *pārāmis* and practice of the various forms of asceticism he is to become ultimately a Buddha. Siddhārtha Gautama, in one of his previous births as the Jotipāla-māṇava, did, as a matter of fact, develop bodhicitta at the time of Kassapa Buddha and then through several births, he fulfilled the pāramis and took recourse to all possible *sādhanās*, whether Buddhistic or non-Buddhistic and ultimately attained perfection. He even became disciples of Āḷāra Kālāma and Rudraka Rāmaputta whose doctrines are treated as heresies in the *Brahmajāla* and other *suttas*. In the Mahāyāna texts emphasis is laid more on bodhicitta than on brahmacariya and ariyamagga. In the *Kathāvatthu* discussion, the Mahāyānic sense of *niyata* is ignored and the Theravāda sense of *sammattaniyāma* is kept in view. In the *Kathāvatthu* (XIII. 4) it is argued that to speak of a *niyata 'srāvaka* or *bodhisattva* to have become a *sammatt*[2] carries no sense. The difference of opinion really rests on the interpretation given to the word *niyata* in Mahāyāna texts as against that given by the *Kathāvatthu* writer and commentator. Inspite of the above interpretation of *niyāma* and attitude of the Theravādins they contend that Gautama Buddha in his bodhisattva existence did not become a disciple (śrāvaka) of Kassapa Buddha. In support of their contention they cited the passage: *na me ācariyo atthi, sadiso me na vijjati* etc. The Andhakas, strangely enough, took the opposite view and asserted that he did become a śrāvaka of Kassapa Buddha and cited the passage from the *Majjhima Nikāya* (ii, p. 54): *Kassapo, ahaṃ Ānanda bhagavati brahmacariyaṃ acariṃ sambodhāyāti* etc.[3]

According to the Theravādins, the Bodhisattvas as a class of beings as envisaged in the *Sūtrālaṅkāra* and *Laṅkāvatāra* do not exist. This individual, who happens to become the Buddha, is called a bodhisattva in his previous existence just to distinguish him as a being

1. *Kun*.,pp. 78, 143: *Ime dve niyam ṭhapetza añño niyamo nāma nathi.*
2. *Na niyatassa niyamokkamanaṃ tasmā asādhakan ti. Ibid.*
3. *Kun*., p. 288.

superior to an average one, but by calling him a bodhisattva the Theravādins do not attribute to him any special virtues unattainable by a śrāvaka. The Mahāsaṅghikas or the Andhakas do not subscribe to the above view. According to them an individual from the moment he develops *bodhicitta* becomes a *bodhisatta* and is destined (*niyata*) to become a Buddha and follows a career which is quite different from that of a *Śrāvaka*. The career of the former is marked more by love and compassion for the suffering beings than by path-culture while that of the latter has more of path-culture and sādhanā than exercise of *mettā* and *karuṇā*.

III. Are Arhats fully emancipated?

According to Vasumitra, Bhavya and Vinītadeva, the secession of the Mahāsaṅghikas from the Theravādins was due to the five points of Mahādeva. These five points relate to the qualities attainable by an Arhat. According to the Theravādins only one who is fully emancipated is called an Arhat,—he is *anupatto sadattho vītarāgo vītadoso vītamoho khīṇāsavo ohitabhāro katakaraṇīyo nāparam itthattāyā ti* (in possession of the excellent goal free from attachment, hatred and delusion, in short, all impurities, relieved of burden of khandhas, accomplished in all that is to be done and devoid of any further existence). He had further acquired the clear vision about the origin and destruction of things, got rid of all doubts (*kaṅkhā*) about the Buddha, Dhamma and Saṅgha, non-existence of soul and the theory of causation, seen things for himself without the help of others (*na paravitāraṇā*)[1] and attained bodhi which however is *catumaggañāṇa*[2] and not *sabbaññutañāṇa*—the *bodhi* of the Buddhas.[3] The Theravādins do not admit the failings which are attributed to the Arhats by the Mahasaṅghikas, the Bahuśrutīyas, the Śaila schools and the Haimavatas. The failings are thus enumerated in Vasumitra's treatise:

(1) Arhats can be tempted by other;

(2) They have still ignorance;

(3) They have still doubt;

(4) They gain knowledge through others (help).[4]

In the *Kathāvatthu* (II, 1-5) all the above statements are taken up for discussion and appear thus:

1. See *infra*.
2. The catumaggas are sotāpatti, sakadāgāmi, anāgāmi and arhatta.
3. See *Kun. A.*, p. 76.
4. Masuda, pp. 24, 36, 38, 53; cf. JRAS., 1910, pp. 413-423. For the 5th point see *infra*.

(i) *Atthi arahato rāgo?* (II. 1)[1]

(ii) *Atthi arahato aññāṇan*[2] *ti?* (II. 2)

(iii) *Atthi arahato kaṅkhā ti?* (II. 3)

(iv) *Atthi arahato paravitāraṇa ti?* (II. 4).[3]

The Theravādins emphatically deny that an Arhat who is free from attachment *vītarāgo* can be subject to temptation. The opponents, as shown in the *Kun.*, draw subtle distinction between a *Sadhammakusala-arhat* and a *Paradhammakusala-arhat*, the former, according to the commentator is a Paññāvimutto and the latter an *Ubhatobhāgavimutto*, and that the knowledge of the former is confined to his own personal attainments while that of the latter is extended to other's attainments besides his own. In the Pāli texts the *Ubhatobhāgavimutto* is not regarded as superior to the *Paññāvimutto*, the only distinction made between the two is that the former has *samathābhinivesa* and realisation of eight vimokkhas while the latter has *vipassanābhinivesa* and realisation of only four jhānas[4] but as far as the question of *rāga* or *āsavas* is concerned both the classes of Arhats must be regarded as completely free from them, hence the subtle distinction drawn by the opponents is of no avail according to the Theravādins.

The next two points viz., that an arhat may have ignorance (i.e. *aññāṇa* and not *avijjā*) and doubt (*kaṅkhā* or *vimati*) are also vehemently opposed by the Theravādins on the ground that one cannot be an arhat unless he gets rid of *avijjā* and vicikicchā and develops perfect vision free from impurities (*virajaṃ vītamalaṃ dhammacakkhuṃ*) after having dispersed all his doubts (*kaṅkhā vapayanti sabbā*).

The opponents, as presented in the *Kun.*, in this case also draw a distinction between a Sadhammakusala-arhat and a Paradhamma-kusala-arhat, saying that both the classes of arhats may not have *avijjā* in regard to the truths, the theory of causation, etc. or *vicikicchā* about Buddha, Dharma and Saṅgha or absence of soul, but the former

---

1. In the text the wording is "atthi arahato asucisukkavisaṭṭhi?" It perhaps refers to an instance of the Māra gods having removed *asucisukka* of an arhat. The commentator remarks that the impostors passing as arhats may have asucisukkavisa-ṭṭhi and upon that the contention of the Śaila schools is based. The Theravādins take their stand upon the fact that an arhat cannot have rāga and hence they cannot commit asucisukkavisaṭṭhi?

2. *Aññāṇaṃ* is not the same as *avijjā*.

3. For the discussion "Parihāyati arahā arahattā ti" (I. 2), see *infra*.

4. See my *Aspects*, pp. 250, 276; See *Majjhima*, I, p. 477 and *Manoratha-pūraṇi*, III, p. 188; *Puggala-paññatti*.

may have *aññāṇa* and *kaṅkhā*, say, as regards the name and family of an unknown man or woman or a tree. It should be noted here the opponents do not mean *sabbaññutañāṇa* (omniscience) but just *paradhammañāṇa*—an intellectual power attained by the Ubhato bhāgavimutta-arhats, by which they can know many things outside himself. Arguing in this way the opponents maintain that a section of the arhats, i.e., the Paññāvimuttas or Sa-dhammakusala-arhats have ignorance (*aññāṇa*) relating to things or qualities other than those belonging to himself.

The same arguments and counter-arguments are applied in the next discussion relating to *atthi arahato paravitāraṇa*? The word *paravitāraṇā* perplexed our translator Mr. Shwe An Aung.[1] The discussion in the *Kun.*, reveals that the word means that an arhat develops faith in the Triratna or acquires knowledge of the truths, etc. not by himself but through the instruction of his preceptor[2] in whom he had firm faith. The Theravādins oppose the contention of the opponents, saying that an arhat is *vitamoha* and is possessed of *dhammacakkhu* and so he does not require *paravitāraṇā*. The opponents as before contend that a sa-dhammakusala-arhat requires paravitāraṇā while a para-dhammakusala-arhat does not.[3]

Another statement of Vasumitra relating to the Arhats, namely, "one who is kṛtakṛtyaḥ (=Pāli: katakaraṇīyo) does not take any dharma to himself i.e. has not attachment for worldly things" is echoed, I think, in the *Kun.*, (XVII. 1&XXII. 2) in these terms: *atthi arahato puññopacayo ti?* and *arahā kusalacitto parinibbāyatī ti*. The Theravādins agreeing with the Mahāsaṅghikas contend that the citta of Arhats goes beyond *pāpa* and *puṇya*, *kusala* and *akusala*, *kriyā* and *vipāka*, hence, to speak of them as acquiring merits or demerits is absurd. The opponents, the Andhakas, however, contend that the Arhats perform many good deeds, e.g., making gifts, worshipping caityas and so forth, and remain always self-possessed (*sato sampajāno*) even at the time of his parinibbāna, and so he does collect merits and passes away with *kusalacitta*.

Neither the above discussions in the *Kathāvatthu* nor the terse statements of Vasumitra help us much in finding out the real difference between the Mahāsaṅghikas and the Theravādins about the position

1. "Excelled by others." *See Points of the Controversy,* p. 119. Buddhaghosa writes: yasmā tāni vatthuni pare vitaraṇti pakāsenti ācikkhanti tasmā tesaṃ atthi paravitāraṇā ti.

2. Cf. Masuda, p. 24; "gain spiritual perception by the help of others (lit. enlightment through the other)."

3. In Sanskrit *Pratyātmavedanīya*.

of an Arhat. The Mahāyāna works[1] point out the distinction thus: Arhats, who are perfect Śrāvakas, get rid of only *kleśāvaraṇa*, i.e, the veil of impurities consisting of rāga, dosa, moha, sīlabbataoarāmāsa, and vicikicchābut not of *jñeyāvaraṇa*, i.e., the veil which conceals the truth—the veil which can only be removed by realising the Dharma-śūnyatā or Tathatā.[2] It is the Buddha alone who is perfectly emancipated having both *kleśāvaraṇa* and *jñeyāvaraṇa* removed. That the Mahāsaṅghikas appear to be groping to get at this clear distinction will be evident from two other topics discussed in the *Kun.* but not referred to in Vasumitra's treatise. The topics are,—*atthi kiñco saññpjanaṃ appahāya parinibbānan ti?* (XXII. 1) or *arahattappattīti?* (XXI. 3). To these the Mahāsaṃghikas replied in the affirmative, saying that an arhat is *nikkileso* (free from impurities) and does attain parinibbāna or arhatta but as he is not cognizant of all that is *Buddhavisaya* (domain of Buddha's knowledge), it must be admitted that some saññojanas are left in him, which, evidently point to the *jñeyāvaraṇa*.[3]

---

1. See *Aspects*, p.
2. For details, see Aspects, pp. 35 ff.
3. There are a few subsidiary discussions in the *Kathāvatthu* relating to Arhats. These are given below breifly:-

VI. 1. Householders cannot become Arhats—*Theravādins*.
But householders like Yasa, Uttiyo, Setu became Arhats—*Uttarāpathakas*.

IV. 2. No one is born as Arhats—*Therav.*
But there are Upahacca (uppajja)-parnibbāyī Arhats—*Uttarāp*.

IV. 3. All dharmas of Arhats are not anāsava, e.g. their physical body etc.— *Therav.*
But Arhats are anāsavā (free from āsavas)—*Uttarāp*.

IV. 4. In the Arhat stage, only arhattaphala is acquired—*Therav.*
But all the phalas are possessed by the Arhats—*Uttarāp*.

IV. 5. An Arhat is chaḷupekkho—*Therav*.
Rather Arahā chahi upekkhāhi samannāgato—*Uttarāp*.

IV. 10. All saññojanas are gradualy destroyed and not by Arhattamagga alone—*Therav.*
But by the destruction of all saññojanas one becomes an Arhat—*Andhakas*.

XVII. 2. Arhats may have untimely death as arahatghātaka is mentioned in Buddha-vacanas—*Therav*.
But as one cannot beocme an Arhat before the karmaic effects are exhausted, an Arhat cannot have untimely death—*Rājagirikas* and *Siddhatthikas*.

XXII. 3. Arhats do not die when in imperturbable meditation but devoid of kriyā-citta—*Therav*.
But did not Gautama Buddha pass away immediately after arising from the 4th jhāna—*Uttarāp*.

It should be noted that most of the differences of opinion quoted above are more technical than actual and that may be a reason for Vasumitra's passing over them.

IV. Can there by retrogression of Arhats, Srotaāpannas and other Phalasthas?

The following views regarding the possibility of retrogression of Arhats, Srotaāpannas and other phalasthas are attributed in Vasumitra's treatise[1] to the Mahāsaṅghikas and some of their sub-sects: (i) From the gotrabhūmidharma there is in all stages the possibility of retrogression. (ii) A Srotaāpanna has a chance of retrogression while an Arhat has not.

The above two views are discussed in the Kathāvatthu under the topic: *Parihāyati arahā arahattā ti?* (I. 2).

It will be observed that the *Kun.* differs from Vasumitra in regard to the opinion of the Mahāsaṅghikas about the retrogression of Arhats and Srotaāpannas. According to the Mahāsaṅghikas, the *Kun.*, says, an Arhat has retrogression while a Srotaāpanna has not, while Vasumitra takes a contrary view, as above (ii). Vasumitra says that the former opinion is held by the Sarvāstivādins and other schools. Buddhaghosa[2] points out that this opinion is held by one section of the Mahāsaṅghikas and not all, and so Vasumitra may have in view the views "of that section, according to whom the Arhats may retrogress but the Srotaāpannas do not." The Theravādins admit *pattaparihāni* (loss of what is attained) of those adepts who have attained only *lokiyasamāpatti* and not *arahattādisāmaññaphala* while the opponents speak of retrogression of the latter also, but confine it only to those arhats who are *samayavimuttas*. The basis of this contention of the opponents is a passage of the *Aṅg. Nik.* (iii. 173), in which Buddha says that five *ārāmatā* (indulgences) viz., in *kamma* (deed), *bhassa* (desultory talks), *niddā* (sleep) and *saṅganikā* (frequenting societies) lead to the fall of a samayavimutta-bhikkhu.[3] Buddhaghosa infers from the discussion that the opponents assert that the arhats retrogress up to the Sotāpattiphala but no further and that the retrogression happens only in Kāmabhava and not in Rūpārūpabhava, and that also is confined only to the mudindriya or samayavimutta arhats.

The Kathāvatthu refers to another cause for the fall of an arhat, *viz.*, (i) kammahetu arahā arahattā parihāyati (an opinion of the *Pubbaseliyas* and *Sammitīyas*). It means that the fall of an Arhat is sometimes due to deeds of his previous lives, e.g., of having

1. Masuda, p. 27.
2. *Kun., A.*, p. 35: Sammitiyā Vajjiputtiyā Sabbtthivādino ekacce ca Mahāsaṅghikā arahato parihāniṃ icchati.
3. I.e. a mudindriya arhat. According to the Theravādins: avasippatto jhānalābhī *samayavimutto*. Vasippatto jhānalabhī c'eva sabbe ca ariyapuggalā ariye vimokkhe *asamayavimutto* ti saṃniṭṭhānaṃ. *Kun. A.*, p. 38.-

calumniated an arhat. Perhaps this controversy refers to some stories of the life of an Arhat. It also warns the opponents particularly the Pubba and Apara-seliyas and Uttarāpathakas about impostors passing as an Arhat and committing abrahmacariya offences (vide *Kun.*, II. 1 & XXIII. 2).

All the schools advocating the view that arhats retrogress hold, as stated in the *Kun.*, that the Sotāpannas have no retrogression. This, however, contradicts the statement of Vasumitra.[1] All these schools accept that a sotāpanno is *niyato sambodhiparāyaṇo* and hence is not subject to retrogression, but a sakadāgāmī or an anāgāmī may retrogress but not further than the sotāpanna stage, for some of adepts in these stages may have *anusaya* which may develop into subject to retrogression, but a sakadāgāmī or an anāgāmī may retrogress but not further than the sotāpanna stage, for some of adepts in these stages may have *anusaya* which may develop into *pariyuṭṭhāna* and thus bring about the fall—an argument which will be discussed next in connection with the Aṭṭhamakas. In regard to these two stages the *Kun.* corroborates Vasumitra's statement (no. ii).

Regarding the srotaāpannas, Vasumitra further states that

(1) they are capable of knowing their own nature (svabhāva) through their citta and caitasika dharmas;

(2) they can also attain the dhyāna;

(3) they are liable to commit all sorts of offences except the five anantarīyas (i.e. matricide, patricide etc.).

In the *Kun.*, we do not come across any controversy relating to the first two topics. This silence may be interpreted as that the Theravādins accepted the two view. As regards the third topic, we may take into consideration the controversy: "*Diṭṭhisampanno puggalo sañcicca pāṇaṃ jīvitā voropeyyā ti?* (see *infra*). A sotāpanna is a person with right view (*diṭṭhisampanno*), hence, according to the Theravādins, he cannot commit killing (*pāṇātipāta*) or such other offences, not to speak of the five extreme offences like matricide or patricide. Vasumitra perhaps speaks of the opinion of that section of the Mahāsaṅghikas[2] who contemplate the retrogression of the sotāpannas while the *Kun.* refers very likely to the opinion of the other section, according to whom the sotāpannas do not retrogress.

There are in Vasumitra's treatise two other statements, which also relate to the Srotaāpannas. They are,—

1. See Masuda, II, p. 27
2. They are the Andhakas.

(i) When one enters into the samyakatva-niyama, one may be said to destroy all saṃyojanas.[1]

(ii) None of the dharmāyatanas[2] can be known or understood: they can be attained (only by those Aryan pudgalas above the darśanamārga).

The *Kun.* contributes no discussion on the above two points. The Theravādins also cannot but subscribe to these views.

V (a). Do the Aṭṭamakas have anusaya and pariyuṭṭùhāna?

Relating to the Aṭṭamakas, Vasumitra says that according to the Mahāsaṅghikas—

(i) "In the eighth stage (aṣṭamaka-bhūmi) one can remain for a long time."

In the *Kun.* (III.5) the identical problem is discussed in these words:

(i) *Aṭṭhamakassa puggalassa diṭṭhipariyuṭṭhānaṃ pahīnan ti?*

Mr. Masuda's comment on the first view seems to be wide of the mark if not peurile, though he quotes '*Shu-chi* as his authority. The discussion in the *Kathāvatthu* clears up the view thus. According to the Andhakas, an adept who is in the eighth stage i.e., sotāpatti-maggaṭṭha and not yet sotāpanna gets rid of diṭṭhipariyuṭṭhāna, sīlabbata-p. and vicikicchā-p. but not diṭṭhi-anusayo, silabbata-a., and vicikicchā-a.,[3] i.e., the anusayas may become active (uppajjissati) if they receive an impulse. The Andhakas by drawing this distinction between pariyuṭṭhāna and anusaya hold that an aṭṭhamaka may not get rid of the three *anusayas* and consequently remain away from the sotāpanna stage for a long time."[4]

The *Kathāvatthu* also discusses the following two allied views attributed to the Pubbaseliyas and the Uttarāpathakas:

(i) *Diṭṭhisampanno puggalo sañcicca pāṇaṃ jīvita voropeyyā ti?* XII. 7 (Pubbaseliyas).

(ii) *Diṭṭhisampannassa puggalassa pahīnā duggatī ti?* XII. 8 (Uttarāpathakas).

By the first view the Pubbaseliyas mean that a person by having *sammādiṭṭhi* does not get rid of dosa (hatred), hence he can commit

---

1. The three saṇyojanas are *sīlabbataparāmāsa*, *vicikicchā*, *micchādiṭṭhi*.
2. The Dharmāyatanas are *vedanā*, *saṃjñā*, and *saṃskāra*—See *Abhi. Kośa*, p. 46.
3. Anuśaya means that which lies in the mind in a latent state with the possibility of its coming into appearance if it receives an effective impulse. while pariyuṭṭhāna means its actual appearance in the mind without however a corresponding response in the outer world.
4. Aṭṭamakas puggalas have saddhā but not saddhindriya—Andhaka.

the sin of killing—a view wholly rejected by the Theravādins. By the second view the Uttarāpathaka assert that a person with sammādiṭṭhi cannot be reborn in a lower form of existence; the Theravādins point out that it may be so, but he may have *taṇhā* (desire) for objects and beings belonging to the lower forms of existence.

V (b). Are anuśaya and paryavasthāna associated with mind or not?

There are in Vasumitra two statements relating to anuśaya and paryavasthāna which will clear up the above problem further.—

(1) "Anuśayas (dormant passions or latent bias) are neither citta nor caitasika dharmas: and again they never become the object of thought (anālambana)."

(ii) "Anuśaya is different from paryavasthāna (pervading passion) and paryavasthāna is different from anuśaya. It must be said that the anuśaya does not combine (*samprayuj*) with the citta whereas the prayavasthāna does"

Relating to the above topics, the *Kun.* has,

(i) *Anusayā anārammaṇā ti?* (IX. 4)

(ii) *Anusayā avyākatā ti* (XI. 1)

(iii) *Añño kāmarāgānusayo aññaṃ kāmarāgapariyuṭṭhānam ti?* (XIV.5)

(iv) *Pariyuṭṭhānaṃ cittavippayuttan ti?* (XIV. 6)

Mr. Masuda offers the following interpretation from the '*Shu-chi*: The anuśayas are really *bījas* (germs inborn in the mind) of *rāga* and other passions. They remain dormant unless excited by the corresponding impulse. They remain always in the mind, even in kusalacitta, so they are dissociated from the mind and do not require any object (ālambana) for support. When the anuśaya is excited by a suitable impulse, it becomes paryavasthāna (pariyuṭṭhāna) and as such becomes a mental function (caitasika), and then only it becomes an impurity and clogs the way to spiritual progress. The interpretation given above is corroborated by the *Kun. A.*[1] The Theravādins however do not distinguish between kāmarāgānusaya and kāmarāgapariyuṭṭhāna and maintain that as the anusayas are included in the Saṃkhārakkhanadha, they are all sārammaṇa. But according to the Andhakas some saṃkhāras are sārammaṇa (with basis) and some are anārammaṇa (without basis),[2] but not so are the remaining four

1. *Kun. A.*, p. 117: Tattha yesāṃ anusayā nāma cittavippayuttā ahetukā avyākatā ten' eva anārammanā 'ti laddhi seyyathā pi Andhakānañ c' eva ekaccānañ ca Uttarāpathakānaṃ.
2. *Kun.*, p. 407: Saṃkharakkhandho ekadeso sārammaṇo, ekadeso anārammaṇo.

khandhas. The Andhakas further maintain that as a puthujjana having kusalāvyākata-citta is sometimes described as "sānusayo ti" when their anusayas are without any ārammaṇa, it must be admitted that anusayas may be anārammaṇā.

From the above discussion it is apparent that the anusayas, according to the Andhakas, are avyākata[1] i.e. neither good nor bad, and consequently they are citta-vippayutta, and also causeless (ahetuka). The Andhakas in the third discussion assert that anusayas are different from pariyuṭṭhānas, but in the fourth the *Kun.* makes the Andhakas contend that pariyuṭṭhānas are also citta-vippayutta, which, however, appear to be contradictory. Vasumitra says that the pariyuṭṭhānas according to the Mahāsaṅghikas are cittasampayuttas, so we must dismiss the statement of the *Kun.* as unwarranted.

"The world in its variety originates out of actions (*karma*) which accumulate on account of *anuśayas*. In the absence of *anuśayas*, karma is not capable of producing a new existence (*punarbhava*). Consequently the root of *bhava* or rebirth is *karma*, in other words, *anuśayas*." With these words Vasubandhu opens the fifth book of *Kośa*. (See *Kośa*, V, p. 1).

The Sarvāstivādins like the Theravādins regard anuśaya, paryavasthāna and kleśa as same, the only distinction being that anuśaya is the subtle, while paryavasthāna the manifest, state of *rāga*, etc.

The *Kośa* too deals with the problem under discussion, *viz.*, whether or not anuśaya (e.g. *kāmarāgānusaya*) is a dharma by itself dissociated from mind, the *prāpti* of kāmarāga, etc.? The answer of the Sarvāstivadins is in the negative as that of the Theravādins. The former quote as their authority the *Jñānaprasthāna-sūtra*, in which anuśaya is shown to be associated with mind (*cittasamprayukta*). They assert that anuśayas are kleśas, and hence they cannot but be citta-samprayuktas.

In this connection the *Kośa* refers to the opinion of the Sautrāntikas, who hold that *anuśaya* is different from *kleśa* in as much as it is neither associated with, nor dissociated from, mind because it is not a *dravya* apart; it is a *śakti* left in certain individuals by the previously existing kleśas and has the power of reproducing further kleśas. According to the Sautrāntikas, *kleśa* when non-manifest is *anuśaya* and when manifest, an act, it is paryavasthāna (*Kośa*, V, p. 7).[2]

1. The Andhakas, it seems, looked upon the anusayas as vipākacitta and treated the same as avyākata cf. *Dhammasaṅgani*.

2. For exhaustive treatment of Anuśayas, see La Vallée Poussin's *Abhidharmakośa*, V.

VI Can the Aṭṭhmakas have Saddhindriya?

Vasumitra does not mention this view among the doctrines of the Mahāsaṅghikas but it is stated in the *Kun.* that according to the Andhakas, *aṭṭhamakassa puggalassa natthi saddhindriyan ti* (III. 6), i.e., the aṭṭhamakas may develop *saddhā*, *viriya*, etc. but do not acquire *saddhindriya*, *viriyindriya* etc., a distinction which the Theravādins are not prepared to admit. The Andhakas mean that saddhindriya or viriyndriya, etc. is a faculty forming a part of the mind while saddhā or viriya etc. is only a passing phase of the mind.

VII. Is there worldly samyagdṛṣṭi and samyak-śraddhendriya?

Along with the above we may discuss the allied topic worded thus in Vausmitra's treatise,—

(i) There is neither laukikasamyagdṛṣṭi (worldly right view) nor laukikaśraddhendriya (worldly faculty of faith).

The corresponding passages of the *Kun.* are,—

(i) Natthi puthujjanassa ñāṇan ti? (XX, 2);[1] and

(ii) Nathilokiyaṃ saddhindriyan ti? (XIX. 8).[2]

The argument of the Theravādins is that a layman may have pañña and saddhā of a kind which may be different from those of an adept, but *pañña* and *saddhā* that he possesses do develop into *paññaindriya* and *saddhindriya*. It may be that the layman's paññā or ñāṇaṃ is confined to dāna, sīla, cāga, etc., i.e. lokiya affairs and does not extend to the comprehension of lokuttara subjects like truths, maggas and phalas, hence according to the Theravādins there may be lokiya paññindriya and saddhindriya.

VII. (a) Is utterance of dukkha possible in meditation; and (b) Does it help perception of the truths?

The two statements of Vasumitra (i) "The path is realized by utterances" and (ii) "Even in the state of samāhita one can utter words" to which corresponds "*samāpannassa atthi vacībhedo ti*" of the *Kathāvathu* are explained by Buddhaghosa thus: According to the Śaila schools an adept while in the first jhāna (meditation) and on the point of attainment of the Sotāpattimagga in some cases gives out an exclamation like "aho dukkhan ti."[3] This, the adherents of the Śaila schools account for by saying that in the first jhāna, there is

1. Attributed to the Hetuvādas only.
2. Attributed in the Cy. to the Hetuvādas and Mahiśāsakas and they mean all the five indriyas, saddhā, viriya, sati, samādhi and paññā.
3. Cf. *Yasapabbajjā*: Upaddutaṃ vo upassaṭṭhaṃ vo.

vitakkavicāra, and because of *vitakkavicāra* there is *vacisaṃkhāra*[1] i.e., discussion and discriminating thoughts cause vocal activity, hence there is the possibility of a meditator in the first jhāna uttering the word 'dukkha'. The Theravādins contend that as all physical activities of a meditator are set at complete rest, his giving out an exclamation is an impossibility.[2]

Along with the above we should take into consideration the other three doctrines of the Mahāsaṅghikas presented thus in Vasumitra's treatise,—

(i) The words of suffering can help (the process of realization of the path);

(ii) Suffering leads a man to the path;

(iii) Suffering also is (a kind of) food (āhāra); and

(iv) Through prajñā suffering is destroyed and final beatitude is obtained.

The corresponding expressions in the *Kathāvatthu* are as follows:-

(i) "*Idaṃ dukkhan ti*" *vācaṃ bhāsato* "*idaṃ dukkhan ti*" *ñāṇaṃ pavattatī ti*? (XI. 4).

(ii) *Dukkhāhāro maggaṅgaṃ maggapariyāpannan ti?* (II. 6).

Both these statements repeat in a slightly different form what has been stated by Vasumitra. The Andhakas and the Śailas hold that when a meditator realises within his innermost heart that the world is full of suffering and is not worth living, an exclamation like "aho vata dukkham"[3] spurts out of his mouth and then and there his insight (ñāṇa) penetrates into the first truth "idaṃ dukkhan ti", and as a result, he attains (*pariyāpuṇāti*) the Sotāpattimagga. So "dukkha" may be called an "āhāra" in respect of the realisation of the path as also and "aṅga" (limb) of the Sotāpattimagga.

The fourth doctrine mentioned above is, as Mr. Masuda explains, that *dukkha* can be removed not by means of the observance of moral precepts (śīlas) and practise of meditation (samādhi) but by the

---

1. Cf. *Kun.*, IX, 9: Opinion of the Pubbaseliyas: Sabbaso vitakkayato vicārayato vitakkavipphāro saddo ti? The Cy. on it is: Yasmā vitakkhavicārā vacīsaṃkhārā 'ti vuttā tasmā sabbaso vitakkayato vicārayato antamaso manodhātuppavattikale pi vitakkavipphāro saddo yevā ti. Cf. *Majjhima*, I, p. 301.

2. Cf. *Kun.*, XVIII, 8: Samāpanno saddaṃ suṇātī ti. As it has been said by Buddha that sound is a hindrance ot the first jhāna and that one rises from the first jhāna by an external sound, the Pubbaseliyas inferred there from that one in meditation hears sound. Cf. the instance of Mahāmoggallāna in the *MPS*.

3. See fn. 1 above.

knowledge of the truth, causal law, and *anatta* of the things of the world. It is the basic teaching of Theravāda, hence no reference is made to it in the *Kun.*

VIII. Do Indriyas (organs of sense) percieve?

The following opinions are attributed by Vasumitra to the Mahāsaṇghikas:

(i) "Beings of the Rūpa and Arūpadhātu possess all the six sense-perception (ṣaḍvijñānas);[1]

(ii) The five vijñānas conduce both to attachment (*sarāga*) and freedom from attachment (virāga); and

(iii) The rūpendriyas (organs of sense) are nothing but lumps of flesh: the eyes do not see colours, the ears do not hear sounds, the nose does not smell odours, the tongue does not taste flavour, and the body does not feel touch."

The *Kun.* deals with these topics thus:

(i) *Saḷāyataniko attabhāvo rūpadhātuyā ti?* (VIII.7)

(ii) *Pañcaviññāṇasamaṅgissa atthi maggabhāvanā ti?* (X. 3).

(iii) *Pañcaviññāṇā kusalā pi akusaā pī ti?* (X. 4).

(iv) *Pañc' evāyatanā kāma ti?* (VIII. 4)

(v) *Cakkhunā rūpaṃ passatī ti?...pe...kayena phoṭṭhabbaṃ phusatī ti?* (XVIII. 9).

In the discussion relating to the six āyatanas (spheres of the organs of sense), the *Kun.* shows that the Mahāsaṅghikas took literally the expression: *rūpī manomayo sabbaṅgapaccaṅgī ahīnindriyo ti* and assert that there are in the rūpadhātu all the six indriyas and āyatanas with this difference from the Kāmadhātu, that out of the six āyatanas, three, viz., ghāna, rasa and phoṭṭhabba do not exist but their *nimittas* or the subtlest forms exist.[2] In the Abhidhamma texts it is stated that the denizens of the Rūpadhātu have five khandhas and six (and not twelve) āyatanas while those in the Arūpadhātu have four khandhas and two āyatanas (manāyatana and dhammāyatana only).[3]

As regards the second point, the Mahāsaṅghikas on the basis of the statement of Bhagavā, "Idha bhikkhave bhikkhu cakkhunā rūpaṃ disvā nimittaggāhī hoti...pe...na nimittaggāhī hoti...pe...sotena saddaṃ sutvā etc.," contend that a person using the five sense-organs may

---

1. Or ṣaḍvijñānakāya or the group of six sense-perceptions
2. *Vibhaṅga*, p. 405: In Kāmadhātu there are cakkhāyatana and rūpāyatana, sotāyatana and saddāyatana, etc., in all, twelve āyatanas.
3. *Vibhaṅga*, pp. 405-7.

practise *maggabhāvanā*, by not grasping the object seen or heard (nimittaāhī) and directing his mind towards nibbāna. The Theravādins argue that if through pañcaviññāṇa one attains sotāpatti and other maggas, then the pañcaviññāṇa and magga would belong to the same category, but the former is *lokiya* and the latter *lokuttara*, the former is *savatthuko* (have an object as basis) and the latter is *avatthuko* (without any basis). In this way the Theravādins argue that through the exercise of the five viññāṇas one does not attain nibbāna.

The opposite statement, *viz.*, that through the use of five viññāṇas a person may engender rāga (attachment) is self-evident though the Theravādins would not admit that pañcaviññāṇas are *sābhoga* (X. 5). In the discussion (VIII. 4) whether the five āyatanas are associated with desires (kāma), the Theravādins acknowledge that Buddha said that five āyatanas may or may not be kāmaguṇas, and explained the same by saying that a person's organs of sense or the objects of the senses are not by themselves kāmaguṇas (associated with desires) but one, who has saṃkapparāga (desireful intention) and does not dissociate his mind from the objects of sense, is not expected to attain detachment from worldly objects.[1] The Mahāsaṅghikas, I think, hold the identical opinion though it is not so clearly expressed in Vasumitra, it is only the Sarvāstivādins who held the opinion that the five vijñānas conduce to sarāga and not to virāga (Masuda, p. 48).

Relating to the third point the *Kun.* contradicts Vasumitra and says that it is the Mahāsaṅghikas who held the opposite view, viz., the eyes see colours, ears hear sounds etc. by conceiving a pasādacakkhu, a subtle eye, which has not got the power of āvajjana (reflect) like cakkhuviññāṇa but possesses just the power of knowing (paṭijānāti) objects. In this case also, shall we account for the contradictions by saying that the opinion of 'ekacce mahāsaṅghikā' is represented by Vasumitra while the opinion of the 'aññe mahāsaṅghikā' is noticed in the *Kathāvatthu*.[2] The Theravādins and a section of the Mahāsaṅghikas hold that the eyes, ears etc. are mere material conveyers of perception, the cakkhuviññāṇa, sotaviññāṇa, etc. being the actual percipients, in other words, eyes, ears etc. belong to the rūpa-khandha, which is material, while cakhuviññāṇa, etc. belong to the viññāṇa-khandha, which makes a being aware of the things around him.

IX. How many avyākatas are there?

The opinion of the Mahāsaṅghikas that "there is nothing which is indeterminate" (avyākṛta) has been explained by Mr. Masuda as

1. Quoted in the *Kun.*, p. 370 from the *Aṅg. Nik.*, III, 411.
2. See *infra*, p. 579.

that the Mahāsaṅghikas admitted only two natures of things, good or bad and not a third, neither good nor bad. This interpretation does not appear to be sound as in the Buddhist texts the three natures of things are accepted universally. The avyākatas also refer to those problems which Buddha left unanswered as any answer to them whether in the affirmative or in the negative would mislead the enquirer, or treated the question as absurd and unanswerable. These avyākata problems are always mentioned in a stereotyped form in all Buddhist texts whether Hīnayāna or Mahāyāna.[1] Nāgārjuna has utilised these problems in his *Mādhyamika-kārikā* to establish the Mahāyanic conception of Śūnyatā. If we accept Vasumitra's statement as correct, we shall have to say that the Śūnyatā conception was known to the Mahāsaṅghikas, and so to them the so-called avyākata problems were not avyākata (inexplainable), but this way of looking at the statement of Vasumitra seems to me to be too farfetched and so, I think, Vasumitra's statement is not complete. Perhaps it refers to the problem discussed in the *Kun.*: *diṭṭhigataṃ avyākatan ti?* (XIV. 8),—whether a person holding one of the unanswered views can be regarded as avyākata i.e. neither good nor bad. The answer of the Theravādins is that the holder of any one of the views is wrong, hence akusala and cannot be avyākata as supposed by the Andhakas and the Uttarāpathakas.

X. How many Asaṃskṛradharmas are there?

In the Pāli texts, as also in the *Abhidharakośa* (of the Sarvāstivādins) the three asaṃskṛtas are, (i) Pratisaṃkhyā-nirodha, (ii) Apartisaṃkhyā-nirodha and (iii) Ākāśa. The Mahāsaṅghikas increase them to nine by adding the four āruppas[2] and pratītyasamutpā-dāṅgikatva. Excepting the *nirodha* of two kinds, all other asaṃskṛtas of the Mahāsaṅghikas are not recognised as such by the Theravādins, whose argument is whether each of these asaṃskṛtas is of the same nature as Nibbāna, if not, they are saṃskṛtas. Strangely enough the *Kun.* goes so far as to say that ākāśa is not asaṃskṛtas. The attitude taken in the *Kun.* (VI. 2, 4, 6; XIX. 3, 4) is that Nibbāna is *tānaṃ lenaṃ accutaṃ amataṃ* (escape, refuge, infallible and immortal) so

---

1. Sassato loko, asassato loko; antavā loko, anantavā loko; taṃ jīvaṃ taṃ sarīraṃ, aññaṃ jivaṃ aññaṃ sarīraṃ; hoti Tathāgato paraṃ maraṇā, na hoti Tathāgato paraṃ maraṇā; hoti ca na hoti ca Tathāgato paraṃ maraṇā, n'eva hoti na na hoti Tathāgato paraṃ maraṇā.

2. The four āruppas are—
   (i) Ākāśānantāyatana;
   (ii) Vijñānānantāyatana;
   (iii) Ākiñcanyāyatana; and
   (iv) Naivasaṃjñā-nāsaṃiñāyatana.

each of the seven of asaṃkhatas, even every member of the formulae of the Paṭiccasamuppāda, each of the four phalas must be *tānaṃ lenaṃ accutaṃ amataṃ*, otherwise they are saṃkhatas (constituted). The Mahāsaṅghikas interpret, as presented in the *Kun.*, that the asaṃkhata is that which is unchangeable (aneñja) but not tānaṃ lenaṃ, etc. In regard to the causal law, they rely on Buddha's statement: *avijjā paccayā bhikkhave saṃkharā, uppādā va Tathāgatānaṃ anuppādā vā Tathāgatānaṃ ṭhitā va sā dhātu dhammaṭṭhitatā dhammiyāmatā ideapaccayatā,* etc., and point out that by asaṃkhata they do not mean the links separately but the unchangeable law (a) of the origin a thing through a cause, and (b) of the unchangeable nature of dhammas, undisturbed by appearance (uppāda) or non-appearance (anuppāda) or staying (thiti). As for the *āryamārgāṅgikatva*, the *Kun.* explains that Pubbaseliyas regard as asaṃkhata the fact of attainment (*patti*) of a magga or phala by the removal of certain mental impurities (kilesapahānaṃ) and not the maggas or phalas by themselves. This, Vasumitra corroborates by using the term *mārgāṅgikatva* i.e. prāpti of a mārga and not simply *mārga.*[1] In the *Kun.* there are a few other discussions relating to the asaṃkhatas to which we shall revert when dealing with the Mahisāsakas.

The remaining three opinions of the Mahāsaṅghikas, viz.,

(i) There is no intermediate state of existence (*antarābhava*),

(ii) Phenomena exist neither in the past nor in the future, and

(iii) The nature of mind is pure in its origin: it becomes impure

when it is stained by *āgantukarajas and upalkeśas* - are in accord with those of the Theravādins.[2] Both these schools do not admit that between death and rebirth there is any intervening period in which the subtle khandhas wait for the selection of the parents or the states of existences. The *Kun.* says that the opinion of the opponents is formed through the miscomprehension of the meaning of the word 'antarāparinibbāyī.' We shall revert to this topic while dealing with the Sammitīyas, with whom, the commentator says, the Pubbaseliyas agreed.

As regards the opinion that the past and future exist—the cardinal doctrine of the Sarvāstivādins, to be dealt with next, both the Theravādins and the Mahāsaṅghikas are emphatic in their protest against it.

---

1. In the *Majjhima Nikāya*, (I, p. 301) it is distinctly sated that aṭṭhaṅgiko maggo is saṅkhato.
2. Cf. Aṭṭhasālini, p. 68: Cittaṃ āgantukehi upakkilesehi upakiliṭṭhaṃ.

The third point raises an important problem that is to say whether the mind at the beginning was pure or not. The Theravādins are decidedly of opinion that pubbakoṭī (beginning) and aparakoṭī (end) of beings is unknowlable, and as such they have not gone into the question whether the mind is pure at any time before the attainment of *vimutti*. This doctrine of the Mahāsaṅghikas obtained its full development in the idealistic philosophy of Yogācāra in which the Ālayavijñāna is pointed out as the storehouse of pure consciousness which gets contaminated with worldly objects through the indriyavijñānas and mentally creates a world around it. It is by the removal of this mental creation that a person regains the *ālayavijñāna* in its pure original form and becomes an emancipated being—a Buddha.

Doctrines mentioned in the Kathāvatthu and not in Vasumitra's treatise

The *Kathāvatthu* attributes to the Mahāsaṅghikas and their sub-sects a few other doctrines not noticed in Vasumitra's treatise. These are briefly as follows:-

(i) Restraint (*saṃvara*) or unrestraint (*asaṃvara*) of the organs of sense should be treated as action (*kamma*). The Theravādins regard it as non-action, their contention being that an action should be defined as the actual functioning of the five organs of sense initiated by mind (*cetanā*). *Kun*. XII. 1.

(ii) All actions (*sabbaṃ kammaṃ*) are accompanied by results (*savipāka*). The Theravādins contend that as *cetanā* is the source of all actions,[1] and as there are *avyākata* (neither good nor bad) and *avipāka* (unaccompanied by any result) *cittas*,[2] there must be also avyākata avipāka kammas, hence all actions are not necessarily accompanied by results.—*Kun*. XII. 2.

(iii) Sound and other āyatanas (spheres of the organs of sense) are also results of actions (*kammassa katattā uppannaṃ*). In short, all non-materials (*arūpadhammā*) are products of actions (*kammasamuṭṭhānā*).—*Kun*., 3 & 4.

All the three views mentioned above should, I think, be attributed to that section of the Mahāsaṅghikas who hold that eyes see colours and so fourth (see above p. 575). As Vasumitra does not take notice of the opinion of this section of the Mahāsaṅghikas, he had no occasion to refer to the above three views.

---

1. Cetanāhaṃ kammam vadāmi—*Atthas*., p. 135.
2. See *Dhammasaṅgaṇi*.

Chapter - 3

Doctrines of the Mahāsaṅghika School of Buddhism

Nalinaksha Dutt

Continuation of the chapter 2

(iv) Acquisition of moral purity is not mental (*sīlam acetasikan ti; sīlam na cittānuparivattī ti*). *Kun.* X. 7, 8.

The Mahāsaṅghikas imply by the above opinion of theirs that purity in speech (sammā vācā), actions (sammā kammanto) and means of livelihood (sammā ājīvo) is a corporeal property and as such is non-mental and requires no ārammaṇa (basis).[1] The M. mean that the observance of sīlas transforms the bodily constituents of a being in such a way that it can no longer commit any wrong, i.e. cannot be *dussīla*.

(v) The collection of sīlas (merits) is not associated with mind (*Cittavippayuttaṃ sīlopacayaṃ*). *Kun.* X. 9.

Buddhaghosa explains this as due to misapprehension of the sense of the passage in the *Saṃuyutta Nikāya* (I. p. 33): ārāmaropā vanaropā ye janā...tesaṃ sadā puññaṃ pavaḍḍhati (the merits of those who plant park and woods increase at all times).

(vi) *Maggasamaṅgissa rūpaṃ maggo ti.*[2] *Kun. X. 2.*

(vii) *Maggasamaṅgī dvihī sīlehi samannāgato ti.*[3] *Kun.* X. 6.

A maggasamaṅgī is an advanced adept who has reached one of the maggas, i.e., sotāpattimagga, etc., by following the eightfold path, and is engaged in *maggabhāvanā* (higher meditations). His mental

---

1. *Kun.* I. p. 422. Cf. *IHQ.*, XIII, p. 569, re. Anusaya.

2. Transl. "That the physical frame of one who is practising the eightfold path is included in that path." *Points of Controversy*, p. 244.

3. Transl. "That one who is engaged in the path is practising a double morality." *Ibid.*, p. 248. *Vism.*, p. 6: Sīlena sotāpanna-sakadāgāmibhāvassa kāraṇaṃ pakāsitaṃ hoti. Sotāpanno hi sīlesu paripūrakāri ti vutto, tathā sakadāgāmi.

states are transcendental (lokuttara). The question is whether the sīla practices[1] completed by him in the pre-sotāpanna stage and still possessed by him should be regarded as lokuttara or lokiya (belonging to the spheres of Kāma, Rūpa and Arūpa)? The M. contend that the rūpa of a maggasamaṅgī (or maggaṭṭha) remain lokiya while his mental state (citta) become lokuttara, hence his sīlas which belong to the category of rūpa as shown above remains lokiya. Of the eight factors of the aṭṭhaṅgika-magga, three, *viz.*, sammā vācā, kammanta and ājīva of a sotāpanna are sīlas and as such they are lokiya but the remaining five which are mental (arūpa) may be lokuttara. A sotāpanna therefore is in possession of lokiya sīlas but if he practises sammāsati, sammāvāyama, etc. he may be said to have lokuttara-sīlas. The Th. do not make any such distinction, for, all the eight sīlas, according to them, emanate from mind;[2] so the silas of a sotāpanna, who has lokuttara-citta, are lokuttara.

(viii) Acts if intimation are virtues (viññatti sīlan ti). *Kun.* X. 10.

(ix) Acts not intimating a moral purpose is immoral[3] (aviññatti dussilyan ti). *Kun.* X. 11.

Sīla, according to the M., must be positive action and not mere restraint (saṃvarar), so any *viññatti* (intimation) by means of body or speech is sīla. Salutation, rising to welcome, folding hands, etc., are sīlas. The M., in view of their opinion that there may be accumulation of demerits without "the association of mind (*cittavippayuttaṃ apuññupacayaṃ*), contend "that acts not intimating a moral purpose are immoral."

(x) Insight is dissociated from mind (ñāṇam cittavippayuttaṃ). *Kun.* XI 3.

(xi) One should not be called 'ñāṇī' (possessed of insight) though his *aññāṇa* (spiritual ignorance) is gone when his mind is dissociated from perception. (Aññāṇe vigate ñāṇavippayutte citte vattamāne na vattabbaṃ 'ñāṇī' ti). *Kun.* XI. 2.

In this controversy ñāṇa means maggañāṇa (insight belonging to the adepts who are in one of the four maggas). The M. contend that at the moment when an adept has cakkhuviññāṇa, etc., he can not have maggañāṇa. In other words they mean to say that it is only when an adept develops maggañāṇa and stops his sense perceptions (viññāṇas), he may be described as 'ñāṇī', hence ñāṇa is not associated with mind (citta=viññāṇa).

---

1. See *Dhammasaṅganī*, p. 60.
2. Cf. *Vism.*, p. 6: Kiṃ sīlan ti? Cetanā sīlaṃ, cetasikaṃ sīlaṃ, saṃvaro sīlaṃ, avītikkamo sīlan ti (quoted from *Paṭisambhidāmagga*, I, p. 44).
3. See *P. of C.*, p. 252. For definition of Viññatti, see *Atthas.*, pp. 83 ff.

(xii) *Akusalmūlaṃ paṭisandahati kusalamūlan ti.*[1] *Kun.* XIV. 1.

The M. contend that as the same object may be the cause of both *rāga* (attachment) and *virāga* (detachment) and as one may follow the other immediately, it may be stated that kusala is the *anantarapaccaya* (contiguous cause) of akusal and *vice versa.* The Th. point out that cultivation of kusalamūla must be made deliberately (yoniso manasikaroto) while that of akusalmūla does not require any such thinking (ayoniso manasikaroto), and also that *nekkhammasaññā* (renunciating thought) does not always follow *kāmasaññā* (worldly thought) and *vice versa*, and so kusalamūla can not be regarded generally as the contiguous cause of akusalamūla and *vice versa.*[2]

(xiii) *Paccayatā vavatthitā ti.* ("One phenomenon can be related to another in one way only"). Kun. XV. 1.

The M. now enter into the problem of *paccayas*. There are twenty-four kinds of paccayas, viz., hetu, ārammaṇa, adhipati, sahajata, anantara etc.[3] They raise the question whether one object can be placed under two or more kinds of paccayas of another object, or a clear line of distinction should be drawn between any two paccays, in other words, one can be related to another by one relation only. The Th. hold that one object may be two kinds of paccayas, e.g., *viriya* may be both *adhipati* and *sahajāta*; *viraṃsā* may be both *hetu* and *adhipati*. The M. do not subscribe to this view.

(xiv)Avijjā paccayā pi saṃkhārā, na vattbbaṃ "saṃkhārā paccayā pi avijjā ti.[4] *Kun.* XV. 2

This view of the M. is only a corollary to the previous one. The M. hold that avijjā is the *hetu* (cause) of saṃkhārā and as such there cannot be any other relation between the two. The Th., however, argue the avijjā and saṃkhārā are related to each other both as hetu sahajāta (co-existent) or aññamañña (reciprocal), hence it may be stated the saṃkhārā are sahajātapaccayā of avijjā, and *vice versa.*[5] In the *Vibhaṅga* (pp. 156 ff.) the sampayutta (associated) and aññamañña (reciprocal) relations between any two consecutive links of the chain

---

1. "That a basis of bad thought is consecutive to a basis that is good and conversely." *P.* of *C.*, p.282.
2. Cf. Tikapaṭṭhāna, pp. 168 ff.
3. See *Atthas.*, p. 9; *Dukapaṭṭhāna*, p. 3; P. of C., App., pp. 390-2; *Buddhist Psychology*, pp. 194 ff.
4. "That whereas actions are conditioned by ignorance, we may not say that ignorance is conditioned by actions."*P. of C.*, p. 294.
5. Cf. *Majjhima Nikāya*, I, p. 54-55: avijjā samudayā āsavā āsvasamudayā avijjā; also *Digha Nikāya*, II, p. 56-57: viññāṇapaccayā nāmarūpam, nāmarūpapaccayā viññāṇan ti.

of causation are exhaustively dealt with, showing clearly the attitude of the Theravādins to the problem.

This concludes all the opinions attributed to the Mahāsaṅghikas in the *Kathāvatthu* but not referred to by Vasumitra. In the *Kathāvatthu* there are several other opinions attributed to the Andhakas and the Uttarāpathakas, the later sub-sects of the Mahāsaṅghikas, but as many of these coincide with those of the Sarvāstivādins and the Sammitīyas, we propose to deal with them after the exposition of the doctrines of these two school in a subsequent issue of this journal.

Chapter - 4

Doctrines of the Sarvāstivāda School of Buddhism

Nalinaksha Dutt

In the history of the secession of schools, Sarvāstivādins are found to be a branch of the orthodox group, the Theravādins, hence there are many points of agreement between the Theravāda and Sarvāstivāda doctrines. The latter had its sphere of activity in Northern India extending from Kashmir to Mathura and was responsible for the propagation of Hīnayāna Buddhism in Central Asia whence it was carried to China. The Tripiṭaka of this school was written in mixed Sanskrit. Its Abhidharma works are quite different from those of the Theravādins, while its Vinaya text contains many matters not to be found in the Pāli Vinaya, but there is a commonness in the topics of the Abhidharma and the rules of the Vinaya. So far as the doctrines of the two schools are concerned; the principal point of difference is that the Sarvāstivādins maintain the existence of the khandhas in their abstract forms at all times, whether in the past, present or future, while the Theravādins deny any such existence. The former accept the fundamental creeds of Buddhism, *viz.*, *anatta* and *anicca* of things of the world, but their contention is that the things constituted out of the khandhas at a particular time are subject to disintegration but not the khandhas themselves, which always exist in their abstract state. Vedanā, for instance, may be kusala, akusala or avyākaya at a particular time and place but the *vedanākhandha* exists at all time.[1]

I. Do all exist?

The *Kathāvatthu* (I. 6) presents the arguments and counter arguments of the Sarvāstivādins and the Theravādins thus: The Sarvāstivādins maintain that all *dharmas* exist but not always and everywhere and in the same form. In reply to the question whether khandhas which are all different by nature exist uncombined (*ayogam*),

1. See *Points of Controversy*, Appendix, pp. 375-7.

they answer in the negative. This however, gives an opportunity to the Theravādins to show the fallacy that if all exist then both *micchādiṭṭhi* and *sammādiṭṭhi* exist together. Then again by equating past and future to present, the Theravādins show that if past and future exist then their existence should be predicated in the same way as of the present,[1] which the S. deny, saying that past and future exist but not exactly in the same way as one should speak of the present.

The Th. take recourse to the second argument saying that let the 'present material aggregate' (*paccuppanna-rūpa*) be treated as one unseparable object; now, after some time has elapsed, this material aggregate becomes past, i.e., gives up its presentness (*paccuppannabhāva*) to which the S. agree; then in the same way can it be said that the material aggregate also gives up its materiality (*rūpa-bhāva*)? The S. deny the latter inference, reasoning thus,—let a piece of 'white cloth' be regarded as one unseparable object; now, when this cloth is coloured, it gives up its whiteness (like '*paccuppannabhāva*' in the former case), but does it give up its clothness (like 'rūpabhāva' in the former case)? This disarms the opponents. The Th. however follows up this argument of the S. by the *suddhikanaya* saying that if the material aggregate (*rūpa*) does not give up its materiality (*rūpabhāva*),[2] then *rūpa* becomes permanent, eternally existing like nibbāna—a conclusion not accepted by the S., as according to the latter *rūpabhāva* is different from *nibbānabhāva*.

The next question put by the Th. is whether past (*atīta*) gives up it pastness (*atītabhāva*)? The S. answer in the negative, but takes care to note that when they say that *atītabhāva* exists they mean that *anāgatabhāva* (futurity) and *paccuppannabhāva* (presentness) do not exist like the *atītabhāva*, and similarly when they predicate existence of *anāgatabhāva*, they mean *atītabhāva* and *paccuppannabhāva* do not exist like *anāgatabhāva*. This general statement is then applied to each of the khandas. The Th. round up the discussion by their usual *suddhikanaya* saying that *atīta* or *atītabhāva* then would be the same as *nibbāna* or *nibbānabhāva* a conclusion rejected by the S. The Th. then take to the *vacanasodhana* saying that (i) if the existence of past (*atīta*) and non-past (*nvātīta*) as also future (*anāgata*) and non-future (*nvānāgata*) is denied then the S. should not say that past and future exist; so also (ii) if they do not accept the identity of *atīta*, *paccuppanna* and *anāgata*,[3] they cannot say that *atīta* and *anāgata* exist.

1. This is repeated with each of the khandhas.
2. Cy. rūpakkhandhena saṃgahitattā.
3. By taking recourse to the discussion whether hutvā hoti hutvā hoti and na hutvā na hoti, na hutvā na hoti, the Th. show logically the untenability of the assertion of the S.

The next argument of the Th. is that if the S. admit that *paccuppannabhāṇa* (present cognition) exists and it has the function of knowing things (paccuppannaṃ ñāṇaṃ atthi, tena ñāṇena ñāṇakaraṇīyaṃ karoti) and then why not the atītañāṇa and anāgatañāṇa, the existence of which is affirmed by the S., should not have the function of knowing things in analogy to that of *paccuppannabhāṇa*? This the Th. consider as illogical and rejects the contention of the S.[1] that '*atītaṃ ñāṇaṃ atthī*'.

The Th. now takes up the cases of the Arhats, Anāgāmis, etc., and show that according to the S. who state *atīta rāga* exist in an Arhat, that *atīta bhāpāda* exist in an Anāgāmi and so forth, an Arhat should be *sarāgo*, an Anāgāmī should be *byāpannacitto* and so on, but this inference is not accepted by the S.

The last argument resorted to the Th. is that if the existence of *atīta*, *paccuppanna* and *anāgata khandhas*, *dhātus*, *āyatanas* be admitted, then the S. should say that there are (3 x 5) or 15 khandhas, (3 x 18) or 54 dhātus, (3 x 12) or 36 āyatanas which the S. reject saying that they may accept the position that atīta or anāgata exists from one standpoint and does not exist from another standpoint (*atthi siyā atītaṃ or anāgataṃ or siyā nvātītaṃ or nvanāgatan ti*). The Th. then bring in their *suddhikanaya* by citing the instance of nibbāna and establishes the futility of the assertion of the S. that past and future exist. Both the Th. and S. then quote passages from the Sutta Piṭaka in support of their own contentions, one however remaining unconvinced by the other. From the controversies dealt with above the following may be taken as the opinion of the S.:

1. The past and future, as usually understood, do not exist, though they are perceptible in the present.[2] In the same sense, the non-past and non-future should also be taken as non-existing.

2. It is the *bhāva* of each of the five khandhas and not the khandhas persist in the past, present and future.

3. An object (*vastu*) may lose its pastness, presentness, or futurity but not its objectness (*vastutva*) but that objectness is not identical with nibbāna or nibbānabhāva.

4. An Arhat e.g., for instance, has *atīta rāga* but he is not therefore to be regarded as "sarāgo".[3]

---

1. In the text, this argument is elaborated by the application of this general statement to each of the sense-organs, (paras 23-28) as also to hattha, pabba, kāya, āpo, tejo and vāyu (paras 47-49).

2. E.g. anāgataṃ hutvā paccuppannaṃ hoti but *anāgata* is not identical with *paccuppanna* in the ordinary sense, though in *paccuppanna* there is (the dharma of) *anāgata* so in that sense *paccuppanna* is *anāgata*.

3. Cf. the Mahāsaṅghika view re. *anusaya*.

The S. admit impermanency (*anityatā*) of the constituted things but they contend that the "dharmas" (or bhāvas) of the past are transmitted into the present and likewise the "dharmas" of the future are latent in the present. This we may illustrate, by citing the example of a sweet mango—the past mango seed transmits into the present "mangoness" if not the "sweetness" and similarly the "future mango" receives its "mangoness" from the present: the mango seed can never produce any other fruit though there may be a change in the quality and shape and colour of the mango. The S. speak of a being in the same way. According to them a being is composed of five dharmas (not five khandhas), *viz.*, (i) *citta* (mind), (ii) *caitasika* (mental states), (iii) *rūpa* (matter), (iv) *visaṃprayuktasaṃskāra* (states independent of the mind),[1] and (v) *asaṃskṛtas* (the unconstituted).[2] The five dharmas (not elements as usually understood) persist in a being, the present being the resultant of the past, and potential of the future. An adept after becoming a *sotāpanna* remains so in his following existence proving

---

1. In Vasumitra this appears also as a separate opinion of the S.: The phenomena jāti, jarā, sthiti, anityatā are cittavisaṃprayuktas but included in saṃskāras-khandhas. One of these four items, *viz.*, jarā is discussed in the *Kun*. (VII. 8) in the topic "jarāmaranaṃ vipāko ti?" an opinion of the Andhakas, the *Kun*. supporting the opposite view that jarāmaranaṃ is not *vipāka*.

2. These five are sub-divided into seventy-five thus:-

I. Rūpa (11)—

(a) *viṣaya* (5)	(b) *indriya* (5)	(c) *avijñapti* (1)
(i) rūpa	(i) cakṣurindriya	
(ii) śabda	(ii) śrotrendriya	
(iii) gandha	(iii) ghrāṇendriya	
(iv) rasa	(iv) jihvendriya	
(v) sparśa	(v) kāyendriya	

II. Citta (1)

III. Caitasikas (46)—

(a) *Mahābbhūmika* (10)		(b) *Kuśalamahābhūmika* (10)	
(i)	vedanā	(i)	śraddhā
(ii)	saṃjñā	(ii)	vīrya
(iii)	cetanā	(iii)	upekṣā
(iv)	sparśa	(iv)	hrī
(v)	chanda	(v)	apatrāpya
(vi)	mati or prajñā	(vi)	alobha
(vii)	smṛti	(vii)	adveśa
(viii)	manaskāra	(viii)	ahiṃsā
(ix)	adhimokṣa	(ix)	praśrabdhi
(x)	samādhi	(x)	apramāda

(c) *Kleśa-mahābhūmika* (6)		(d) *Akuśala-mahābhūmika* (2)	
(i)	moha	(i)	ahrīkata
(ii)	pramāda	(ii)	anapatrāpya
(iii)	kassīdya		
(iv)	aśrāddhya		
(v)	styāna		
(vi)	auddhatya		

thereby that his past dharma continues and the three saṃyojanas[1] remain ineffective. It may be argued by the Th. that the three saṃyojanas have altogether disappeared; the Sarvāstivādins may cite the instance of the Sakadāgamin as a better illustration. A Sakadāgamin reduces rāga, dosa and moha to the minimum, and in his following births that state continues, proving thereby the continuity of past dharmas. Now we may pass on to the case of Arhats. The Arhats, it will be seen, become completely free from rāga, dosa and moha; according to the Th. they are destroyed for ever but according to the S., these rāga, dosa and moha persist though in an ineffective form and these may reappear and cause an Arhat fall from the Arhathood—a topic, discussed in the *kun*. (I. 2) and attributed by Buddhaghosa to the *S., viz., Parihāyati araha arahattā ti?*[2]

(e) *Upakleśa-bhūmika* (10)

(i) krodha
(ii) mrakṣa
(iii) mātsarya
(iv) īrṣyā
(v) pradāśa
(vi) vihiṃsā
(vii) upanāha
(viii) māyā
(ix) śāṭhya
(x) mada

(f) *Aniyata-bhumika* (8)

(i) kaukṛtya
(ii) middha
(iii) vitarka
(iv) vicāra
(v) rāga
(vi) pratigha
(vii) māna
(viii) vicikitsā

IV. Citta-viprayukta (14)

(i) prāpti
(ii) aprāpti
(iii) sabhāgatā
(iv) asaṃjñika
(v) asaṃjñi-samāpatti
(vi) nirodha-samāpatti
(vii) jīvita
(viii) jāti
(ix) sthiti
(x) jarā
(xi) anityatā
(xii) nāmakāya
(xiii) padakāya
(xiv) vyañjana-kāya

V. Asaṃskṛtas (3)

(i) ākāśa
(ii) pratisaṃkhyā-nirodha
(iii) apratisaṃkhyā-nirodha

See Rosenberg, *Die probleme der buddhistischen philosophie*, pp. 128-9. Rāhula Sāṅkṛtyāyana, *Abhidharma-kośa*, Table III.

1. *Viz., sakkāyadiṭṭhi, sīlabbataparāmāsa, vicikicchā.*
2. For its exposition, see the Doctrines of the Mahāsaṅghikas, *IHQ.*, XIII, p. 565.

Chapter - 5

Doctrines of the Sammitīya School of Buddhism

Nalinaksha Dutt

The Sammitīyas or better known as the Vātsiputrīyas branched off from the Theravādins some time in the pre-Aśokan days. We do not hear much about this school in the early history of Buddhism except a few criticisms of its radical doctrine of the temporary existence of a self—a dogma which appears on the face of it as un-Buddhistic. This school, according to the reports of the Chinese pilgrims, attained sufficient importance during the days of king Harṣa and specially in the areas corresponding to modern Sind and Bengal. Its main doctrine that there exists a self has put into shade its all other minor views and elicited vehement criticisms from two distinguished exponents of the Abhidhamma, *viz.*, Vasubandhu and Moggaliputta Tissa. The former devoted the last chapter of his monumental work *Abhidharmakośa* to the discussion of this topic while the latter took it up for discussion as the very first problem in his work the *Kathāvatthu*. As Prof. Stcherbatsky and Louis de la Vallée Poussin have exhaustively dealt with Vasubandhu's criticisms, we shall confine ourselves here only to the arguments of the *Kathāvatthu*, and state just the essential points of the long controversy relating to *Puggalo upalabbhati* (or *n'upalabbhati*) *saccikaṭṭhaparamaṭṭhenā ti* (I. 1).

The question of the Theravādins is: Whether the *puggala* is known in the same way as *that* which is real and ultimate, e.g. *Nibbāna* (or *Rūpa*) is known? (Para 1). In other words, the Theravādins want to ascertain whether the Sammitīyas admit the existence of the *puggala* either as the unchangeable, ever-existing reality like *Nibbāna*, or as a constituted (*sappaccaya-saṃkhata*) object like *rūpa* or regard it as false as a mirage (*māyāmarīcī viya*) or look upon it is simply as a hearsay. The Sam. deny practically all the four possibilities though they assert that the *puggala* is known as a real and ultimate face (*saccikaṭṭhaparamaṭṭhena*).

The Sam. now assail the Th. with the counter-question whether the latter would admit that the *puggala* is *not* known in the same way as *that* which is real and ultimate. The Th. answered in the affirmative as according to them *puggala* is not even an object like *rūpa*; it is a mere *paññatti* (conventional term), a *sammutisacca* (so-called truth).

But when the same question is repeated by the Sam. (as in paras 2 and 6)[1] the Th. reply in the negative by saying "na h' evam",[2] because the answer is to be given to a question which included both *sammutisacca* (conventional truth) and *paramatthasacca* (the highest truth). The questions and answers which follow next have a mixture of both *sammuti* and *paramattha* truths, and so they appear contradictory to a superficial reader.

Now the Th. give up the logical tricks and put the question straight (para 11) thus: whether *puggala* is a *paramattha-sacca*,[3] or not, *i.e.* whether or not the puggala is known in the same way as the real and ultimate *everywhere* (*sabbattha*) in and outside *rūpa* (material parts of the body), *always* (*sabbadā*) in this and the following existences, and in *everything* (*sabbesu*) i.e., in all khandhas, āyatanas, dhātus etc. The answer of the Sam. is also definitely in the negative, i.e., they do not consider "*puggala*" as real in the highest sense, and as existing *everywhere*, *always* and in *everything* as pointed out by the Th.

The next attempt of the Th. is to find out whether the Sam. regard puggala as something existing like any of the 57 elements, rūpa, vedanā, saññā, etc. The Sam. deny it saying they do not admit *puggala* as an element apart from the 57 elements,[4] and in support of their contention they quote from the Nikāyas (*Digha*, iii, 232; *Majjhima*, i. 341; *Aṅguttara*, ii. 95) the passage "atthi puggalo attahitāya paṭipanno", which indicates that *puggala* exists but not apart from the elements. The Th. also do not clearly state that *puggala* (as a paññatti) is different from the elements, the reason assigned by Buddhaghosa[5] being that the questions of the opponents have a mixture of *sammuti* and *paramattha* truths and as such the Th. have no other alternative but to leave them unanswered (*ṭhapanīya*)[6].

1. The remaining paras 3-5 and 7-10 are mere logical rounding up of the questions and answers put in paras, 1 & 2.
2. The question is,—Yo saccikaṭṭho paramaṭṭho tato so puggalo n'upalabbhati saccikaṭṭha-parameṭṭhaṇātī ti?
3. Perhaps like the *jīvātman* of the Vedānta
4. Samayasuttavirodhaṃ disvā paṭikkhepo paravādissa, *Aṭṭhakathā*, p. 16.
5. See his *Aṭṭhakathā*, p.16
6. Paras 130-137 dilate on the above question, comparing it with each of the 57 elements.

The next attempt of the Th. is to show that the Sam. should advocate either *Ucchedavāda* or *Sassatavāda*. With this end in view the Th. put the questions whether *puggala* is identical with *rūpa*, or different from *rūpa*, or *puggala* is in *rūpa* (like the container and the contained) or *rūpa* is in *puggala*. The Sam. reject all the four propositions as otherwise they would become either an Ucchedavādin or a Sassatavādin. Though, according to the Sam., *puggala* is of the same nature (*ekadhammo*) as *rūpa* and other elements,[1] they would not treat it as an element separate from, and independent of, the 57 elements.

The Th. now assail their opponents by questioning on *lakkhaṇas* of the *puggala*, and ask whether the *puggala* is *sappaccaya* (caused) and *saṃkhata* (constituted) like *rūpa*, or is *appaccaya* (uncaused) and *asaṃkhata* (unconstituted) like *Nibbāna*. The Sam. deny both and ask how the Ṭh. would explain the 'puggala' in the statement of Buddha: "Atthi puggalo attahitāya paṭipanno ti." Is the puggala referred to in this passage *sappaccaya*, *saṃkhata* or *appaccaya*, *asaṃkhata*? The Th. deny both, as in their opinion the term *puggala* is only a *sammutisacca*, and as such it is non-existing.

The next argument put forward by the Th. is whether the statement "*puggala* perceives" is the same as the statement. "that which perceives is *puggala*"[2] i.e. whether the two statements are identical as *citta* is with *mano* or different as *rūpa* is from *vedanā*. Buddhaghosa interprets the position of the opponents thus: the Sam. hold that *puggala* perceives but not everything that perceives is *puggala*, e.g., *rūpa*, *vedanā*, etc. are not *puggala* but that *puggala* perceives and that which perceives referred only to the percepient (*puggala*), and not to *rūpādi*.[3] The opponents, however, rely on the statement "atthi puggalo attahitāya paṭipanno ti" which, again is counteracted by the Th. by saying that the Sam. should equally rely on the statement: suññto lokaṃ avekkhassu, etc. and admit that there is no *puggala*.

The Th. now proceed to examine the *paññatti* (description) of *puggala*. In answer to the question whether the *puggala* of the *Rūpadhātu* is *rūpi* and likewise of the *Kāmadhātu* is *kāmi* and of the *Arūpadhātu*, *arūpi*, the Sam. affirm the first and the third but not the

1. *Aṭṭhakathā*, p. 18.
2. Puggalo upalabbhati (yo yo) upalabbhati (so so) puggalo ti? *Kun.*, p. 24.
3. *Aṭṭhakathā*, p. 20: The opponents say: Mana puggalo atthi puggalo 'ti satthu vacanato upalabbhati. Yo pana upalabbhati, na so sabbo puggalo. Atha kho ke hi ci puggalo ke hi ci na puggalo 'ti. Tattha kokāratthe kekāro kikāro hikāro co nipātamatto. Koci puggalo koci na puggalo 'ti ayaṃ pan' ettha attho. Idaṃ vuttaṃ hoti puggalo pi hi rūpādisi pi yo koci dhammo upalabbhyati yeva. Tattha puggala 'va puggalo rupādusy pana koci pi na puggalo 'ti.

second. The Sam. argue that *puggala=satta=jīva* and *kāya=sarīra*. Though they do not admit either the identity of, or difference between, *jīva* and *sarīra*, they hold, though not logically tenable, that *kāya* must be different from *puggala* as there are such statements as 'so kāya kāyānupassī viharati and so forth', in which "so" cannot but refer to *puggala*.

The next discussion relating to *upādāpaññatti* (rebirth) of *puggala* raises the question of transmigration. The Sam. affirm that *puggala* passes from this world to the next but it is neither the self same puggala nor a different puggala—a statement similar to what the Th. would say about the passing of the *khandhas*—avoiding the two heretical opinions of *sassatavāda* and *ucchedavāda* as also the *ekaccasassatikavāda* and *amarāvikkhepadiṭṭhi*.[1] In support of their contention the Sam. quoted the passages in which a "puggala" is said to pass from one world to another "sandhāvati saṃsarati."

Accepting the opinion of the opponents that the self-same, or a different, *puggala* does not pass from one existence to another, the Th. point out that they admit that some form of *puggala* referred to in the above-mentioned passages does pass from one existence to another. Now this *puggala* can then have no death, it once becomes a man and then a god and so forth, which is absurd.[2] In reply the Sam. point out that a sotāpanna-deva and question how can this sotāpana-hood pass from one existence to another unless there is some form of *puggala* to carry the qualities. The Th. now in order to show the unsoundness of the statement asks whether the passing puggalo is identical in every respect[3] and has not lost any of its qualities.[4] The opponents first negative it on the ground that a man does not continue to be a man in the devaloka. But on second thought they affirm it in view of the fact that the carrier of certain qualities from one existence to another is a puggala, an *antarābhavapuggala*.[5] The Sam. take care to keep clear of the two extreme views: *taṃ jīvam taṃ sarīraṃ* and *aññaṃ jīvam aññaṃ sarīraṃ*. They affirm that the identical *khandhas* and *puggala* do not pass from one existence to another but the transformed *khandhas* and *puggala* pass from one existence to another. The khandhas are, however, impermanent, constituted etc. while the *puggala* is not also permanent and unconstituted. Without khandhas, āyatana, dhātu, indriya and citta, *puggala* cannot remain alone but for that reason,

1. See my paper on Brahmajāla-sutta in the *IHQ.*, vol VIII.
2. Cf. Nāgārjuna, *Mādhyamikavṛtti*.
3. Anañño=sabbākārena ekasadiso.
4. Avigato=-ekena pi ākāreṇa, avigato.
5. The self which exists between death and rebirth.

the colour and other qualities of the khandha, āyatana, etc. do not affect the *puggala*. Again the *puggala* is not a shadow (chāyā) of the khandhas.

In reply to the question whether *puggala* is perceivable in every momentary thought, the Sam. answer in the affirmative but they would not accept the inference drawn by the Th. that the *puggala* in that case would have momentary existence (khaṇika-bhāvaṃ) i.e., die and be reborn every moment like *citta* (thoughts).

The Sam. now ask the Th. whether they would admit that one (yo) who sees something (*yaṃ*) by means of an organ of sense (*yena*) is the *puggala* or not. The Th. after assenting to it as a conventional truth (*sammutisacca*), put the same question in the negative form thus: One (*yo*) who[1] does see anything (*yaṃ*) by means of an organ of sense (*yena*) is not a *puggala*. The Sam., however, without arguing further quote a few passages in which Buddha said: I (i.e. the *puggala*) see by means of my divine eyes (*dibbena cakkhuṇā*) beings appearing and disappearing and so fourth, and infer therefrom that the seer is the *puggala*.

Their next discussions related to *purusakāra*. The Th. do not admit any doer, so they asked the Sam. whether the latter would subscribe to the same opinion. On their denial, the Th. ask whether the Sam. would admit the existence of the doer, and a creator of the doer, which is negated by the Sam. on account of the heretical doctrine is *issaranimmāṇa* (god the creator of the world) but on second thought affirmed it in view of the fact that the parents, teachers etc. are also in a sense the makers (*kattā kāretā*) of a person. The Th., without going into the implied sense of the replies, say that such a state of things, i.e., a doer having a doer and a deed implies not just a deed but also a doer, would lead to the conclusion that so long there is deed (*kamma*), there is doer (*kārako puggalo*) and hence there can be no end to *puggalaparamparā* and that would falsify the fact that by the stoppage of the wheel of actions, *dukkha* can be brought to an end. Then again nibbāna, mahāpaṭhavi, etc. must also have the Sam. In conclusion the Sam. deny that the deed and the doer can be distinct, just to avoid admitting that the *puggala* has mental properties.

In the above, the doer of a deed is enquired into, while in the following discussion, identity of the doer of a deed with the enjoyer of its fruit is enquired into.

The Th. deny the existence of a feeler or enjoyer apart from *vipākāpavatti*, (that which is realised, the fructification of an effect).

---

1. E.g., a blind man, an asaññasatta.

The Sam. hold that *paṭisaṃveditabba* is *vipāka* (result) but the *puggala* is not *vipāka*.[1] They further state that Nibbāna or Mahāpaṭhvi, etc. is not *vipāka* like *divine happiness* (dibbasukha) or *human happiness* (manussasukha) so none of them is an object of enjoyment of the *puggala* but again the Sam. do not admit that *sukha* is distinct from the *sukha-enjoyer*. The Th. logically wanted to make their opponent admit that there must be not only an enjoyer of a fruit but also an enjoyer of the enjoyer of the fruit and so on an endless chain, in other words according to them, as shown above, dukkha can have no end.

The Th. now put the crucial question thus: whether the doer of a deed is identical with, or different from, the enjoyer of its fruit. The opponents first deny both to avoid contradiction of Buddha's saying: *sayaṃ kataṃ paraṃ kataṃ sukhadukkhaṃ*, etc. but on second thought in view of their theory that there is a common element keeping the link between the present and the future life, they admit it. In short, the Sam. affirm that there is a *kāraka* (doer) and *vedaka* (feeler or enjoyer) of a deed, but the two are neither identical nor different, neither both identical and different, nor not both identical and different.

The Sam. next apply the test of abhiññā (supernormal powers), *ñāti* (relatives) and *phala* (attainments) and put the propositions thus:

(i) How can a person perform certain miracles keeping his organs of sense etc. inert and inactive, unless there is something else as *puggala*.

(ii) How can one recognise the existence of parents, castes, etc. without positing that there is a *puggala*, and

(iii) How can a *phalastha* continue to be the same in his more than one birth, unless the existence of a *puggala* is admitted.

The Th. avoid the issues by putting the counter-arguments that one who cannot perform miracles is not a *puggala*, and in this way they refute the other two propositions.

The next question of the Th. is whether *puggala* is constituted (*saṃkhata*) or unconstituted or neither constituted nor unconstituted (*n'eva saṃkhato nāsaṃkhato*). The Sam. affirm the last alternative but would not treat *puggala* as something apart (*añño*) from the *saṃkhata-khandhas*. They state that the *puggala* has certain aspects of *saṃkhata*, e.g., it is subject to sukha, dukkha, and so forth; again

1. But it may happen that puggala who is in the enjoyment of his fruits, say, merits, may be again an object of enjoyment of another *puggala*, e.g. a son enjoying the fruits of his actions may be the object of affection of his mother and so forth. This explanation of Buddhaghosa should be compared with the above like the *kāretā* of *kattā*.

it has certain aspects of *asaṃkhata*, e.g., it is subject to birth, old age and death (*jāti*, *jara*, and *maraṇa*).

In reply to the Th.'s question whether a *parinibbuto puggalo* exists in Nibbāna or not, the Sam. negative both as the affirmation of either would make them either a Sassatavādin or an Ucchedavādin.

Now the Sam. put the counter question: does not a person say that he is feeling happy or unhappy and so forth, how can a person say so unless he is a *puggala* and not a mere conglomeration of separate khandhas. In refuting this contention, the Th. put the same question in a negative form thus: well, if a person does not feel happiness or unhappiness, then there is no *puggala*. The Th. further ask whether Sam. would treat *sukha* and *puggala* as something separate and distinct. The Sam. evade a direct answer and ask, well, when a *puggala* (*koci* or *so*) is said to be *kāye kāyānupassī viharati*, does it not affirm the existence of a *puggala*?

The controversy is then closed by citations of passages from the Nikāyas, the Th. quoting only those which clearly express *anattā* of all things while the Sam. quote those in which the word *puggala* or *atthahita* or *so* appeared.

Through these controversies it is apparent that the Sam. are seeking to establish that the five khandhas which are distinct from one another cannot give rise to the consciousness of I-ness, a unity. The facts that a person acts or thinks as one and not as five separate things, and that in many passages Buddha does actually use the words *so*, *attā* and *puggala*, and that a person's attainments like *sotāpannā-hood* continue to be the same in different births, that one speaks of his past births and so forth, do lead to the conclusion that besides the five khandhas there exists some mental property which forms the seat of I-ness, and maintains the continuity of *karma* from one existence to another. That mental property, however is changing with the changing khandhas but in view of the fact that one can think of his past, even of the events of his past births, the changing khandhas alone cannot be made responsible for the memory. The Sam. therefore affirm the existence of a sixth mental property and call it *puggala* which can remain only along with khandhas and so must disappear when the khandhas disappear in Nibbāna. As this mental property or *puggala* is not khaṇika like the khandhas, it has not all the properties of a *saṃkhata* (constituted object) and again as it is not also unchanging and ever existing like Nibbāna so it is not *asaṃkhata*. Therefore the *puggala* must be said as neither *saṃkhata* nor *asaṃkhata*.[1]

1. For the arguments of Vasubandhu La Vallée Poussin's *Abhidharmakośa*, Appendix and Stcherbatsky's *Theory of the Soul*, Petersburg, 1918. See also Masuda's note in the *Asia Major*, II, pp. 53-4.

This doctrine of the Sammitiyas or the Vātsiputrīyas is presented in these words by Vasumitra: 1. The *pudgala* is neither the same as the *skandhas* nor different from the *skandhas*. The name *pudgala* is provisionally given to an aggregate of *skandhas*, *ayatanas* and *dhātus*. 2. Dharmas cannot transmigrate from one world to another apart from the *pudgala*. They can be said to transmigrate along with the *pudgala*.[1]

Vasumitra attributes to the Vātsiputriyas a few other views which have already been discussed. These are

(i) The five vikñānas conduce neither to *sarāga* (desire) nor to *virāga* (removal of desires):[2]

(ii) To become free from desire (*virāga*) one must relinquish the saṃyojans which can be destroyed by an adept when he reaches *bhāvanāmārga* and not while he ramains in *darśanamārga*;[3]

(iii) When one has entered the *samyaktvanyāma* he is called *pratipannaka* in the first twelve moments of the *darśanamārga* and when he is in the thirteenth he is called *phalastha*.[4]

Besides the above, the Sammitīyas held a few other opinions, some of which are:

(iv) Parihāyati arahā arahattā ti (*Kun*. I. 2).

(v) N'atthi devesu brahmacariyavāso ti. (*Kun*. I. 3).[5]

(vi) Odhisodhiso kilese jahatīti (*Kun*. I. 4).

(vii) Jahati puthujjano kāmarāga-byāpādan ti? (*Kun*. I. 5).[6]

---

1. Cf. Obermiller's *Analysis of the Abhisamayālaṃkāra*, III, p. 380, referring to *Tarkavāta* and Schayer, *Kamalaśīla's Kritik des Pudgalavāda*. He writes that "the Vātsiputrīyas, Bhadrayānikas, Sāmmitīyas, Dharmaguptas and Samkrāntivadins are those that admit the reality of the 'individual'. They say that the 'individual' is something inexpressible, being neither identical with the five groups of elements nor differing from them. It is to be cognised by the six forms of *vijñānas*, and is subject to saṃsāra (phenomenal existence).
2. See *IHQ*., XIV, pp. 574-6.
3. See *IHQ*., XIV, p.
4. See Masuda's notes in the *Asia Major*, II. p. 56. In short, the Sammitīyas count in all fourteen moments instead of Sarvāstivādin's sixteen; so the 13th moment of the Sammitīyas corresponds to the 15th of the Sarvāstivādins; see *IHQ*., XIV, p. 803.
5. *IHQ*., XIV, pp. 804-5.
6. *IHQ*., XIV. p. 808.

Chapter - 6

The Second Buddhist Council

N. Dutt

(A review of the recent studies)

It has been a long time past that distinguished scholars of Buddhism like Minayeff, Oldenberg, Rockhill, Kern, Otto Franke, Geiger and La Vallée Poussin[1] presented us with the account of the Second Buddhist Council as preserved in Pali, Chinese and Tibetan traditions. Some of them made a critical study of the traditions and accepted the authenticity of the Council. Recently Mons. Hofinger has performed a formidable task of making a critical and analytical study of all the traditions preserved in Chinese relating to the Second Council[2] on the lines similar to the magnificent work done by Przyluski relating to the first Council.[3]

Mons. Hofinger, supporting the view of Prof La Vallée Poussin, suggests that the traditions relating to the Second Council combines accounts of two Councils; one held at Vaiśālī and the other at Pāṭaliputra, not long after the former. In the Vaiśālī Council, he says, the orthodox monks asserted themselves and the proceedings of the Council were conducted in the traditional manner. The members of the Council accepted the views of the elders and there was no schism. In the Pāṭaliputra Council, however, the monks supporting the unorthodox views predominated and preferred to form a new group which became known as the Mahāsaṅghikas as distinguished from the orthodox group known as the Theravādins. Mons. Hofinger's findings may be summed up as follow: "The council of Vaiśālī is not a fiction. The available sources

---

1. Minayeff, *Recherches sur le Buddhisme,* Paris, 1884; Oldenberg, *Introduction to the Vinaya Piṭaka* (1879); Rockhill, *The Life of the Buddha* (1884); Kern, *Manual of Indian Buddhism* (1901); R.O. Franke, *The Buddhist Council of Rājagṛha and Vesāli,* JPTS, 1908 pp. 1-80; Geiger, *Introduction to the Mahāvaṃsa* (1912); Louis de la Vallée Poussin, *Indian Antiquary* 1908.
2. Hofinger, *Etude sur le concile de Vaisali* (Louvain, 1946).
3. Przyluski, *Le concile de Rājagṛha* (1926).

have utilised and amplified an old tradition which may be placed a century after Buddha's *parinirvāṇa*. There was a pre-canonical account of the conflict between Vaisalian monks and others of the community and the available account has been amplified in two independent currents. Of these two, the earlier is represented by the *Mahāsaṅghika-Vinaya*, which developed in the east and the later by all the other *Vinayas*, which manifest a common feature. But all these indicate the separation of the Mahāsaṅghikas from the rest of the community—a cleavage between the east and the west.

Diverse later sources have introduced new elements in the traditions of Sthavira-Sarvāstivāda, and these may be grouped as Sthavira-Mahiśāsaka, Dharma-gupta-Haimavata-Sarvāstivāda, and Mūla-Sarvāstivāda, which strangely enough has little affinity with Sarvāstivāda and appears to be older than the other canonical accounts.

There is a chronological difficulty about the time of the session of the Council. Some traditions place it at Pāṭaliputra during the reign of Aśoka the Maurya. Tāranātha (17th century) also locates it at Pāṭ aliputra, which he included in the dominion of the Licchavis. It is safer to accept the canonical tradition that the Second Council was held at Vaiśālī at the beginning of the 2nd century after Buddha's *Parinirvāṇa*."

His other findings are as follows:—"In the first hundred years of its existence, the religion of Śākyamuni reached Mathurā and converted a large portion of the Gangetic Basin. There is no doubt that the community of the western region interfered with the Vaisalian affairs. But the spiritual unity between the eastern Buddhists and the new community was not broken, i.e., there was no conflict between the east and the west. The Vṛjiputraka bhikṣus formed a well-defined group and did not represent the whole community of the eastern region. In the older accounts of the Council, there are no traces of the conflict between the east and the west as is found in the later accounts. This leads to the conclusion that sufficient time lapsed between the earlier council of Vaiśālī and the one held later at Pāṭaliputra, giving rise to the schism."

"The western community, Sthavira-Sarvāstivāda, became later divided into many sects. The geographical information available in the accounts of the different sects corresponds to the geographical dispersal of Buddhism and so the schism was a natural consequence of the territorial expansion of the religion. It brought about also differences in language, extent of influence, manner of life and also thoughts. The region of Mathurā became the cradle of Sarvāstivāda while in the south-western countries settled the Sthaviras and Mahiśāsakas. In between these two regions the Dharmaguptas had their centre.

During this period of expansion the Buddhists hierarchy maintained its continuity. For their erudition, age and sanctity some monks were placed at the head of the assemblies. The regime was democratic; questions were solved by general votes. It is not quite correct that the above-mentioned qualities were the only criteria to determine the superiority or seniority of a monk. Excepting the Mahāsaṅghikas Vinaya, all other sources refer to eight or four dignitaries, four being given the highest status and one of the four is recognised as the President of the Council. The list of patriarchs of the Mūlasarvāstivādins and the Mahāsaṅghikas appears to be more recent while contrary is the case in the account of the Sthaviravādins.

Discussing the antiquity of the Vinaya accounts, Mons. Hofinger arrived at the conclusion that the oldest was that of the Mahāsaṅghikas and Mūla-Sarvāstivāda followed by that of the Dharmagupta. Then came the Mahiśāsaka and Sthavira and lastly that of the Sarvāstivada and Haimavata."

Prof. Demiéville has closely examined the views and remarks of Mons. Hofinger and dealt with them in detail in his paper "A propos du concile de Vaisali."[1] In course of his examination he expressed grave doubts about the historical value of the Indian traditions in general and particularly about the Second Council appearing in the different recensions of the Vinaya Piṭaka. He argues that the accounts of the first two Councils are inserted in the Vinaya of the Theravādins, Dharmaguptas and Mahiśāsakas as an appendix, which bears no relation to the preceding section. It is only in the Mahāsaṅghika Vinaya only that he finds some pretext for introducing the accounts.[2] He writes appreciatively of Prof. Finot's discovery in the Mūla-Sarvāstivāda Vinaya of the account of the First Council as the concluding section of the *Mahāparinirvāṇasūtra*, adding that it does not however contain the account of the Second Council which is under discussion.

He is not prepared to agree with Mons. Hofinger's opinion that the Pali language of the ten unvinayic acts is quaint and is older than that of the main Vinaya text and that the tradition of the Second Council belongs to the pre-canonic stage.

---

1. *Toung Pao*, vol. XL.

2. In this connection he has furnished us with a very valuable information regarding the growth of the Chinese version of the Sarvāstivāda Vinaya. The Chinese translation, he writes, was begun by Kumārajīva and did not contain the account of Councils, which was to be found only in the enlarged version of Vimalākṣa.

Prof. Demiéville prefers to let alone the question of historicity of the Second Council and traces in the account a conflict between rigorism and laxism, between clearicalism and non-clericalism, between a saint and a profane, and lastly between Hīnayānism and Mahāyānism. He formed this opinion evidently on the basis of the five theses of Mahādeva. It seems that he has not examined carefully the meaning of the Pali words: *rāga, aññāṇa, kaṅkhā* and *paravitāraṇā* as elucidated in the *Kathāvatthu.*[1]

Neither the Mahāsaṅghikas nor the Mahāyānists ever deny the perfect purity attained by the Arhats, not to speak of their profaneness. All that they assert is that Hīnayānic Perfects are not omniscient as are the Mahāyānic Buddhas. Incidentally, Prof. Demiéville has discussed the identity of Yaśa and Mahādeva, the growth of the Mahāsaṅghikas in the eastern region, the distinction between an *Aśaikṣa* (=arhat) and a *Śaikṣa* (=puthujjana), and, lastly, the remarks of Hiuen Tsang about the Mahāsaṅghikas.

He has furnished us indeed with many valuable information from his study of the Chinese sources. He is however strongly of opinion that the session of the Second Council cannot be a historical fact unless and until it is corroborated by some archaeological evidence.

Recently (1955) Mons. Bareau has made a searching and exhaustive study of the materials collected by Mons. Hofinger as also of the writings on Council by other scholars particularly those of Profs. Demiéville, Przyluski and Frauwallner.

He is in agreement with Mons. Hofinger that the traditional account of the Council of Vaisali should be split up into two parts, of which the first was held about 100 E.N. to suppress the practice of the Vajjiputtaka monks to receive gold and silver, and the second was held some years later to correct the same monks about nine other unvinayic practices but the later Council failed to achieve its purpose and ended in the separation of the Mahāsaṅghikas from the Theravādins. Mons Bareau adds that the Second Council was held at Pāṭaliputra under the auspices of a king of the Nanda dynasty about 137 E.N. and the effective cause of the schism was the five theses of Mahādeva, four of which were directed against the sanctity attributed by the orthodox sects to the Arhats. He is of opinion that the nine unvinayic acts shown as the cause of the schism is a later interpolation.[2] In agreement with the Mons. Hofinger he regards the tradition of the Council of Vaiśalī as preserved in the Mahāsaṅghika and Mūla-

1. Vide my *Early Monastic Buddhism,* II, p. 85. f.
2. Bareau, *Les premiers conciles bouddhiques*, pp. 34, 78.

sarvāstivāda Vinaya texts as older than those of the other Vinayas, which are all derived from the pre-canonical version, the likely time of composition of which according to Mons. Bareau, is close to the time of the schism[1] and not anterior to it as held by Mons. Hofinger. His findings are as follows.[2] "Towards the middle of the second century after Buddha's *Nirvāṇa*, i.e. about 350 B.C. a quarrel arose between the majority of monks who advocated lax disciplinary rules and a select few who were in favour of rigorous discipline. A synod was convened for resolving the conflict but it failed to achieve its purpose and was followed by a schism. The former became known as the Mahāsaṅghikas and the latter the Sthaviravādins. The account of the synod has manifestly the aim of recounting the events which led to the schism and besides there are multiple and definite proofs about the existence of the two sects. The various old accounts are nearly in accord about the time of the schism. The convocation of a synod to settle the differences shows compliance with the Vinaya rules. In view of all these facts the common version of the Council of Vaiśālī should be regarded as authentic without going into further details. Mons. Bareau adds that there are good reasons to believe that the schism took place at Pāṭaliputra on account of the five doctrines of Mahādeva, derogatory to the status of an *Arhat*. The king of Magadha tried to arbitrate in the dispute in vain. After the schism was effected, the partisans of each group met together to revise the canon. A council was held at Pāṭaliputra for the first time at the beginning of the 2nd century after Buddha's *Nirvāṇa* and a little after the Council of Vaiśālī."

In his concluding remarks[3] Mons. Bareau writes: "In the first historical Council held about 100 E.N. at Vaiśālī at the instance of Yāśa, was condemned the quest of gold and silver by the Vṛjiputraka monks, who accepted the decision. The second council held several years later at Pāṭaliputra ended in the schism of the Mahāsaṅghikas and Sthaviras. It seems that the causes of dispute were the five theses relating to the attainments of an *Arhat*. Regarding dispersal of the sects, Mons. Bareau is definitely against the view of a geographical cleavage between the eastern and western communities of monks and noted certain preferences for the north-west of the Gangetic basin among the Mahāsaṅghikas, Theravādins and Mahiśāsakas; for Avanti and Deccan among the Sarvāstivādins and the Theravādins; for Kauśāmbī among the Mahiśāsakas and Theravādins; for Pāṭaliputra among the Sarvāstivādins, Mūlasarvāstivādins and Dharmaguptakas;

1. Bareau, *op. cit.*, p. 86.
2. *Ibid.*, p. 108-9.
3. Bareau, *op. cit.*, p. 114-5.

for Vaśālī among the Sarvāstivādins and Mūlasarvāstivādins. It is wrong, he writes, to think of the Indian territory as divided into vast fiefs occupied by the various sects separately. The assessment should be made by parish and not by regions. The different communities co-existed in the land of pilgrimages in the Gangetic basin. In the same town like Pāṭaliputra or Vaiśālī there were monasteries belonging to the different sects.

He observed further that there developed a conflict between a largely democratic and an aristocratic spirit as also an opposition to the supreme authority exercised by the members of the well-developed community. It became a source of perpetual threats of recession to the Saṅgha and occasioned appeals to the royal authority for settling the differences."

The conclusions of Mons. Hofinger and Bareau regarding the Second Council are in general agreement with certain differences in details. More than a decade ago it was pointed out by me that the five theses of Mahādeva were more responsible for the cleavage between the Mahāsaṅghikas and Sthaviras than the ten un-vinayic acts of the former, as the ten points of dispute were more or less ecclesiastical irregularities and not moral offences and could well be included in *khuddakānukhuddakāni sippāni*, which were permitted by the founder of the religion to be abrogated, if necessary, and which, in fact, formed also one of the charges against Ānanda in the session of the first Council.

The main reason for the compilers of the Vinaya texts to exclude the five theses of Mahādeva and concentrate on the unvinayic acts is that the latter loomed large in their eyes, rigid, as they had become, in the course of a century, attaching more importance to the externals than to the internal spirit. The antiquity of the five theses is established by the fact that these are discussed in the *Kathāvatthu* which should be regarded as anterior to the non-canonical or canonical accounts of the Council. The spirit underlying the theses has been rightly interpreted by Mons. Bareau as representing the conflict between a democratic and an aristocratic church organisation and an opposition to the unjustifiable claims made by some monks to the status of an *Arhat* or an *Anāgāmī* or a *Sakṛdāgāmī* or a *Srota-āpanna*. The Vajjiputtaka monks who inherited a democratic tradition and who attached a little value to the ecclesiastical formalities were naturally the first group to stage a revolt to the century old traditional practices. The democratic spirit was carried to the extreme by the Mahāsaṅghikas as stated in their Vinaya.[1] It runs thus "The Saṅgha comprised of those

1. Bareau, *op. cit.*, p. 249.

monks who knew one or two sections of the Vinaya, those who received the laws directly from the mouth of Bhagavān or Śrāvakas; there were also disciples under training (*Śaikṣa, pṛthagjana*) and the perfects (*Āśaikṣa*) including those who were proficient in *trividyā*, *ṣaḍabhijñā, balas* and *vaśīs*—a Saṅgha of seven hundred assembled at Vaiśālī" The Mahāsaṅgha was a regular medley of the perfects and the non-perfects, *arhats* and non-*arhats*, a democracy indeed.

The schism was therefore due not so much to the ten unvinayic acts as to the opposition of a section of monks to the undue claims made by the hierarchy of the well established community.[1]

Both Mons. Hofinger[2] and Mons. Bareau have attached undue importance and antiquity to the account of the Mahāsaṅghika Vinaya because of the fact that it mentions only one out of the ten un-vinayic acts and states that the Council of Vaiśālī effected suppression of same with the consent of the Vajjiputtakas. To assign antiquity to the Mahasaṅghika Vinaya just for its brief account of the Council does not appear to us to be very sound. If the *Mahāvastu* be a sample of the Vinaya of the Mahasaṅghika group, by no stretch of imagination can the Vinaya of this sect be regarded as anterior to the Pali version. Its lateness is further established by its contents, e.g., the composition of the Saṅgha, so unorthodox as stated above, and the names of partiarchs, as pointed out by Mons. Hofinger as more recent than those of the other Vinayas.[3]

Daśabala, an unknown figure, is made the direct recipient of Vinaya laws from the Master and the best interpreter of the same. His five rules of purity dealing very likely with *sīmā* regulations and his nine precepts referring to the four *Pārājikās* and five others are rather unusual.

It seems that the account of the Vaisalian Council in the Mahasaṅghika Vinaya offers a true picture of the Council of seceders, held at Vaiśālī immediately after the orthodox Council as stated in the Ceylonese chronicles.

In the *Kathāvatthu* commentary it will be observed that all the Mahasaṅghikas did not subscribe to the identical doctrines and so some of them (*ekacce mahāsaṅghikā*) were distinguished from the general Mahasaṅghikas. The question is, to which of the two groups of the Mahasaṅghikas the Vinaya is to be attributed.

---

1. For the latest exposition of the five theses of Mahādeva and valuable details regarding the life of Mahādeva, see Prof. Lamotte's paper on the "Buddhist Controversy over the Five Propositions" in the *IHQ.*, 1956 (Gautama Buddha Volume), p. 40f.
2. Hofinger, *op. cit.*, p. 146.
3. Hofinger, *op. cit.*, p. 255.

The views of Prof La Vallée Poussin, Mons. Hofinger and Mons. Bareau that the Council or Councils of Vaiśālī did not lead to the separation of the Mahasaṅghikas from the Sthaviravādins are not unreasonable. It was sometime after this event that a Council was probably held at Pāṭaliputra in which Mahādeva's five theses formed the main points of dispute.

The Mahasaṅghika Vinaya shows preference for the region round about Mathura, where also has been found an inscription referring to the existence there of the Mahasaṅghika monks. The expression "*ekacce mahāsaṅghikā*" in the *Kathāvatthu* commentary indicate that the Mahasaṅghikas did not form a single body of monks. It seems that the Mahasaṅghika Vinaya (Chinese version) studied by Mons. Hofinger may not be the recognised text of the Mahasaṅghikas of Vaiśālī or Pāṭaliputra though a copy of the same might have been found by Fahien at Pāṭaliputra.

Mons. Hofinger's view about the antiquity of the Mūlasarvāstivada Vinaya supported by Mons. Bareau is also not acceptable. The original Sanskrit of this Vinaya, which has been edited by me, is written in a good grammatical language and appears definitely to be a late text, at least later than the Pali version. In this *Vinaya*, it will be observed the question of *sīmā* has been dealt with in greater details (vide Gilgit Manuscripts, vol. iii) than in the Pali text. In the Mūlasarvāstivada list of the un-vinayic acts, stress has been laid on the question of *sīma* and it seems that the *sīmā* regulations loomed large in the eyes of the Mūlasarvāstivadins. Mūlasarvāstivada sect appeared much later than the Sarvāstivāda and its Vinaya can on no account be attributed to a date anterior to the *Daśādhyāya Vinaya* of the Sarvāstivāda.

Now let us examine the ten un-vinayic acts, as presented in the various canonical accounts, so ably translated into French by Mons. Hofinger from the Chinese sources. It is rather striking that all the accounts give most of the original Pāli or Prākṛt terms in the same form though they differ in interpretations and refer to different section of the Vinaya. This confirms the opinion of Mons. Hofinger that there was a pre-canonical version, upon which is based all the available canonical accounts. The pre-canonical terms are preserved almost in the original form in the Pali text. The terms are:

(i) *Siṅgiloṇakappa*: In Pāli it is interpreted as 'conserving salt in a horn' for use when required and not necessarily in illness. All sects agree more or less with this interpretation. The Mahāśāsākas only explain *siṅgi* as *Śṛṅgivera* (ginger).

(ii) *Dvaṅgulakappa*: In Pāli it is interpreted as "taking food when the shadow is two fingers wide", i.e., little after midday. In all other texts it means "picking up the remnants of food with two fingers", after finishing one's meal. It is not possible to decide which of the two interpretations is more reasonable but preference, I think, should be given to the Pāli interpretation.

(iii) *Gāmantarakappa*: After finishing meal in a village one can go to another village and take food there again. All the Vinayas agree on this interpretation more or less; only the Mūlasarvāstivadins are more cautions and adds the proviso that the distance between one village and another should be limited to one and a half *yojana*.

(iv) *Āvāsakappa*: To perform ecclesiastical acts separately within the same parish (*sīmā*). This is mentioned by the Sthaviras, Dharmaguptas and Sarvāstivādins but not by the Mahiśāsakas. The Mūlasarvāstivadins explain it differently thus. "To perform an eccelesiastical act in an incomplete assembly."

(v) *Ānumatikappa*: To perform an ecclesiastical act in an incomplete assembly and in order to legalise it to have afterwards the act confirmed by the member monks not present in the assembly. All the sects agree on this point.

(vi) *Āciṇṇakappa*: To do an act improperly saying that such an act was being done habitually by the older monks or from time immemorial. In Pali Vinaya, the precedents shown are the irregular acts performed by an Upajjhāya or an Ācariya with the proviso that such acts in certain cases are permissible but not in all cases. The Sarvāstivādins, it seems, have put this in a slightly different manner. They state that ecclesiastical act performed separately and then approaching the assembly requesting the members to confirm them by precedents. The Mūlasarvāstivadins have, it seems, misread the word "āciṇṇa" as "āchinna" and interpreted it as "digging earth by a monk by his own hand or by engaging men."

(vii) *Amathitakappa*: To drink unchurned milk which is neither milk nor curds after finishing one's meal. The Sarvāstivādins state "to drink a mixture of milk, curds and cheese, which is not a part of the meal, after a monk has finished eating and risen from his seat." This Mahiśāsakas and Dharmaguptas amplify it further "to drink a mixture of coagulated milk, oil, honey, fresh cheese, sugar and cream by a monk who has finished his meal and already changed his eating posture.

(viii) *Jalogim*: To drink unfermented juice which is no yet wine (Sthaviravādin, Mahiśāsaka and Dharmagupta). The Sarvāstivādins put it in a poor abode" which is amplified by the statement that the Vaisalian monks on the plea of "a poor abode" claim to distil wine and drink it. The Mūlasarvāstivadins put it in a milder form "To drink wine mixed with water as medicine."

(ix) *Adasakaṃ nisīdanam*: To use a mat without border (Sthaviravāda and Sarvāstivāda). To use an uncut mat (Dharmagupta). To use a mat large and small according to one's will (Mahiśāsaka).

(x) *Jātarūparajatam*: To accept gold and silver. All sects including the Mahāsaṅghikas agree on this point.

Scrutinising the ten un-vinayic acts it appears that all the canonical traditions were dealing with the same terms which were in a Prākṛt as suggested by Mons. Hofinger. The minor differences in interpretation are due to the lapse of time between the actual event and the time of compilation of the canonical accounts. Only in one item *dvaṅgulakappa* there is a fundamental difference between *Cullavagga* (Pali) and all other Vinaya texts. To judge by the interpretations of all the rules, it may be concluded that the Mūlasarvāstivada version appears to be the latest and more comprehensive while the Mahāsaṅghika account is purely sectarian.

Chapter - 7

MISCELANY

A New Buddhist Sect in Kanheri

Moreshwar G. Dikshit

In *ASWI.*, vol. V, p. 85, Bühler published an inscription from Kanheri cave No.76, which reads as follows:—
Lüders' List No. 1020, *ASI.*, No. 28, (*West's* No. 39).

1. Sidha(ṃ) upāsakasa Dheṇukākat(i)yasa (Kulapiyasa)
2. (Dha)ṃaṇakasa dh(u)tuya pavaïtik(ā)ya Sā(pāya the)
3. r(ā)ṇa bhadata Bōdhikāṇa Pāṇakāṇa[1] atevāsini(ya)
4. leṇa deyadhama p(ā)ṇiyapoḍhi cha saha bhagi (niya)
5. Ratinikāya saha cha saveṇa nātisabadhi (vage)
6. ṇa ch(ā)tudis(e) bhikhusagh(e) aṭhasu Puris (esu)
7. lesu? patiṭhāpita mātāpitu . . . etc.

"Success! By the female ascetic Sāpā (Sarpā) the daughter of the lay worshipper and inhabitant of Dhenukakāṭa, Kulapiya (Kulapriya) Dhamaṇaka[2] (Dharma) (and) the pupil of Thera the Rev. Bodhika, (she being associated) with her sister Ratinikā and with the whole number of her relatives and connections, a cave and a water cistern have been excavated (as) meritorious gift for the community of ascetics from the four quarters of the horizon (viz.) for eight persons and....for the benefit of her parents... etc."

From the question-mark that has been put in line 7 of his reading and the translation cited above, it appears that Bühler could not interpret satisfactorily the meaning of the terms "*aṭhasu puris*(*esu*)*lesu*" as read by him.

---

1. The word "*Pāṇakāṇa*" is missing in Dr. Bühler's transliteration and is supplied here from Dr. West's eye copy of the inscription and from the accompanying ink impressions prepared by me.
2. Pandit Bhagawanlal read "Rāmaṇaka" in place of "Dhamaṇaka" (see *Bombay Gazetteer*, XV, p. 188) but Bühler's reading is more probable.

Unfortunately Bühler did not publish any facsimile of this inscription. Recently when I examined it *in situ*, I found that the passage in question read "*Atha Aparīselesu*" and not "*aṭhasu puris(esu)lesu*" as read by Bühler.

In the previously published eye-copies, the word *Atha* (showing the dot in the circle for *tha*) is clear in Dr. Bird's facsimile,[1] while the word *Apuria* can be well made out from the transcript of Dr. E. West,[2] the forms, of the letters *a* and *su*, being almost identical in the early Brāhmī characters. The accompanying photograph of the inscription would make this reading quite clear.

The inscription would then be translated as follows:—

"A cave and a water cistern have been excavated (as) meritorious gift for the community of ascetics from the four quarters, as a special property of the Aparaśaila (sect), residing here,.......for the benefit of her parents.......etc."

It is evident from this reading, therefore, that the inscription purports to record a grant to the Aparaśaila sect of the Buddhists residing in the monastery at Kanheri.

The Purvaśaila (Pali=Pubbaseliyā) and Aparaśaila (Pali=Aparaseliyā) are known to us as the heterodoxical sects that arose in the second century after Buddha's death.[3]

They are referred to in the *Mahāvaṃśa*,[4] *Dīpavaṃśa*[5] and *Mahābodhi-vaṃśa*.[6] According to the *Kathāvatthu* commentary,[7] they belonged to the Andhaka school. Their views were similar to the Cetiyavādins.[8]

We have an interesting account of the probable origin of these sects by Hiuen Thsang, the famous Chinese traveller. He writes,[9] "In the country *T'o-na-kie-tse-kia* (Dheṇukākaṭa) there are numerous convents, mostly deserted and ruined. There are in those preserved

---

1. *Historical Researches*, (1853) Plate XLV, No. 18.
2. *JBBRAS.*, VI, No. 39.
3. Malalasekera, *Dictionary of Pali Proper Names,* vol. I, p. 118; vol. II, p. 236.
4. Geiger, *Mahāvaṁsa*, Vv. 12.
5. Geiger, *Dīpavaṁsa*, Vv. 55.
6. *Mahābodhivaṁśa*, (P.T.S.) p. 97.
7. Rhys Davids, *Points of Controversy*, xli, xliii, p. 104, 108, 115.
8. Louis de la Vallée Pousin, *JRAS.*, April, 1910, p. 413ff.
9. *Si-yu-ki*, trans. by Beal, II, p. 221; Beal, *Life of Hiuen Thsang*, p. 136, Watters, *On Yuan Chwang's Travels*, II, p. 217.

about 10,000 or so priests. They all study the Law of the Great Vehicle. To the east of the capital[1] bordering on a mountain, is a convent called Purvaśaila and to the west of the city, leaning against a mountain is a convent called Avaraśaila."

This tradition is further supported by other Tibetan accounts.[2]

Purvaśaila sect is also mentioned in the Alluru[3] inscription from the Kṛṣṇā district and in the recently discovered Dharmacakra pillar inscription[4] found at Dharaṇikoṭa. Under the name *Apara-mahā-vina-seliyā*, the Aparaśaila sect is mentioned in several Nāgārjunikoṇḍa inscription.[5] The word Purvaśaila also appears there once.[6] The records of the Cetika school, to which the Puravaśaila and Aparaśaila sects corresponded, have been found at Amarāvati,[7] in the neighbourhood of Dharaṇikoṭa.

These inscriptions indicate that the Purvaśaila and Aparaśaila sects were much favoured by the monks residing in the Kṛṣṇā district round about Dheṇukākaṭa, the place of their origin. Most of them belong to the Śātavāhana period.

---

1. Different opinions seem to prevail among scholars about the identity of the capital of the Dhenukākaṭa country. Dr. Vogel, (*Epi. Ind.*, XX. p. 8) is inclined to identify it tentatively with the remains at Nāgārjunikoṇḍa, as the name of Śri-Parvata occurs in one of the inscriptions (F) found there. According to a Tibetan tradition (Wassiljew, *Der Buddhismus*, I, p. 220) Nāgārjuna, the founder of the Mahāyāna school, is stated to have spent his last days on this mountain. *Mañju-śri-mūla-kalpa*, also refers to this mountain in the following way;—

   श्रीपर्वते महाशैले दक्षिणापथसंज्ञिके।

   श्रीधान्यकटके चैत्ये जिनधातुवरे भुवि॥ *M.M.K.* (Trivondrum Edn.) p. 8.

   Cf. also Dutt. *Ind. His. Quarterly*, V, pp. 794-96.

   The late Dr. C. Minakshi, following Sewell, *JRAS.*, (1880), p. 95ff., takes the Bezwada hills as the site for the monasteries referred to by Huen Thsang. (See his *Administration and Social Life under the Pallavas*, p. 221). Recently an attempt has been made to locate the place Dhenukākaṭa, in the island of Salsette, near Bombay, and to identify it with Dounga, a sea-port, mentioned by Ptolemy in his "Geography of India." See Dr. E.H. Johnston, *Two notes on Ptolemy's Geography of India; JRAS.*, (1941), p. 208ff.

2. Bhavya's *Nikāyabheda-vibhaṅga*, cited by Rockhill, *Life of Buddha*, p. 184.
3. *Annual Report, South Indian Epigraphy*, 1923-24 p. 97. *Annual Report, Arch. Survey of India*, 1923-24, p. 93.
4. *Epigraphia Indica*, XXIV, p. 256.
5. Vogel, *Nāgārjunikoṇḍa Inscriptions, Epi, Ind.*, XX-XXI, Inscriptions Cr. C_2, E, M_2, M_3.
6. Vogel, *Ibid.*, *Inscription* F. This, however, refers to some locality.
7. Lüders' No. 1248, *Archæological Survey of South India*, I, p. 100.

Dhenukākaṭa, as we know from history, was an early capital of the Śātavāhana kings. With the shifting of their capital from Dhenukākaṭa (modern Dharaṇikoṭa) to Pratiṣṭhāna it is probable that many of the Buddhist monks from the former place migrated to Western India. This is why perhaps we find the names of the donors from this place inscribed in the Western Indian caves.

As many as twelve pillars of the great Caitya cave at Kārle[1] were gifts from the inhabitant of Dhenukākaṭa. This place also figures in a Śelārwādi cave inscription.[2]

As the donor of the present inscription[3] hailed from Dhenukākaṭa, it would not be far wrong to state that she wanted to record her gift for the particular sect which originated in her country, or perhaps she was a devotee of.

That the Cetika school (to which Purvaśaila and Aparaśaila sects corresponded) was also followed in other places in Western India, gains some support from the fact that inscriptions referring to that sect have been found in the Junnar,[4] Nasik,[5] and Ajantā[6] caves.

---

1. *Lüders' List.* (Karle) Nos. 1090, 1092, 1093, 1096, 1097. Madho Sarup Vats, *Unpublished votive Inscriptions in the Caitya cave at Karle, Epigraphia Indica* XVIII, Inscriptions, Nos. 3, 4, 6, 7, 8, 9.

Nilakantha Sastri and Gopalachari, *Epigraphic Notes, A Karle Caitya pillar Inscription, Epi. Ind.* XXIV, p. 281.

2. *Lüders' List.* (Śelāwāḍi) No. 1121.
3. *Lüders' List.* (Kanheri) No. 1020.
4. *Lüders' List.* (Junnar) No. 1171.
5. *Lüders' List.* (Nasik) No. 1130.
6. Burgess and Bhagwanlal, *Cave Temple Inscriptions,* (*ASWI.*, vol. X) p. 85. Ajantā *painted* inscription No. 17.

Chapter - 8

The Northern Buddhism

Haraprasad Sastri

The Southern Buddhism was long known in Europe. In the beginning of the 16th century, when the Portuguese established their supremacy over the Indian Ocean and came in contact with Ceylon and Burma, the Indian Archipelago and Southern China, the Southern Buddhism with its pompous possessions, huge stūpas, big vihāras, and strict monastic system became known to them. It was after the establishment of the Asiatic Society of Bengal in 1784 that a study of the Southern Buddhist literature was earnestly undertaken. The traditional history of Buddhism speaks of a schism in the second century of the Nirvāṇa Era. In this schism two parties of Buddhist separated never to meet again. The Southern Buddhism called in Sanskrit Sthavira-vāda, in Pāli Theravāda, has a history of its own but the Northern Buddhism is entirely ignored in its religious and traditional works.

So in Europe and India, Southern Buddhism was well-known in the 19th century while the Northern was not. Even the majority of the educated people in India think that Buddhism is only to be found in the southern countries of Asia, that its literature is all written in Pāli, that it is a huge monastic system, very strict in discipline, both moral and physical, and so on. They cannot even imagine that there could be a Buddhism where monasticism is absolutely loose, where the literature is written in a language other than Pāli, where worship of images prevails and where all food regulations are completely set aside. Even in works written by eminent European scholars, Southern Buddhism looms large and Northern Buddhism is summarily disposed of. Yet the votaries of Northern Buddhism are much larger in number, its philosophy is much deeper, the paraphernalia of worship are more imposing, and its history exceedingly interesting.

The discovery of Northern Buddhism is very recent. It became known in the early 19th century and its study began late in that century. Its study has made great strides and its modern literature has grown up to a considerable extent within the last forty years. The social, intellectual and literary history of Northern India has been greatly benefited by these studies, and it is therefore desirable at this stage to write a history of its discovery and the progress of its study.

The Segauli treaty in 1816 brought to an end the most difficult war in which the East India Company was engaged in India. With extreme reluctance the Nepalese people agreed to have a British Resident in their capital. Shortly after the establishment of the Residency at Katamundu, Brian Hodgson came there as the Residency assistant. He was a learned man and well-informed in all matters relating to India. As an assistant he had not much work and his thirst after knowledge was very great. In a new country so little known to the outside world, he began to collect information on all subjects, scientific, literary, historical, and social. He found a strange religion professed by nearly half the people of the Valley, called Buddhism but differing *in toto* from the Buddhism known from books. He began to make his enquiries about this religion. Fortunately for him there was a very learned Buddhist at that time employed as the Munshi of the Residency. This was Amṛtānanda. He too had very little work and Brian Hodgson began to take his assistance. He induced the old Buddhist paṇḍit to write a book for him giving all information about the Buddhism prevailing in Nepal. The name of the book is *Dharma-koṣa-saṃgraha*. In the 78th leaf of the book, the author says:—

Ṛtūdadhinidhau varṣe śrāvaṇe kṛṣṇa āruṇe,
Śrīsāhevājñayā lekhat Amṛtaḥ Śākyaśāsanaḥ.

[The Buddhist Amṛta wrote this in N. S. 946 (1826 A.D.) under the orders of a European gentleman i.e. Brian Hodgson].

Amṛtānanda was the head of the Mahābodhivihāra in Lalitapattan, the second city in Nepal and chiefly inhabited by Buddhists. This vihāra contains a replica of the Mahābodhicaitya of Bodh-gayā. One of the Amṛtānanda's ancestors came on pilgrimage to Bodh-gayā in the middle of the 17th century and lived there for three years though in the midst of jungles, and took the plan, elevation and picture of the Bodh-gayā temple. On his return home he built a caitya exactly like that in Bodh-gayā; the caitya in still in existence. Hence the name of the vihāra is Mahābodhivihāra. Amṛtānanda was a profoundly learned man. He had already written many books in Sanskrit, and his new book is a noble performance and it gave Brian

Hodgson an insight into the Buddhism of Nepal— the last remnant of Northern Buddhism in the soil of India, with a considerable literature in Sanskrit. With the help of Amṛtānanda, Brian Hodgson began to collect Buddhist manuscripts. Some of these manuscripts are on palm-leaf and very old, dating from the 11th and 12th centuries of Christian era. Some are on daphne paper called in Nepal Vaṃśapatra kāgaja. Some are copied for Mr. Hodgson in modern Nepal paper. How these manuscripts were collected is an interesting story. The copy of the Buddhacarita then found in Nepal was incomplete at the beginning and it came up to the middle of the 14th canto. Amṛtānanda got it copied but he completed the work himself adding more than two scores of verses in the beginning, completing the 14th canto and adding four cantos more himself, to bring the account of Buddha's life to a close.

Brian Hodgson distributed the manuscripts to the Asiatic Society of Bengal, to the Bibliothéque Nationale of Paris and to the Royal Asiatic Society of Great Britain and Ireland, and to the India Office Library. On the strength of the materials thus supplied and by dint of personal observations Brian Hodgson wrote a large number of papers in the early volumes of the journal of the Asiatic Society of Bengal. The illustrious Brunouf exploited the Mss. in Paris and wrote his history of Buddhism and translated the Saddharma Puṇḍarīka. But for a long time the Mss. lay idle in all these places.

In the meanwhile, Jung Bahadur, the Prime Minister of Nepal, took the possession of one of the Nepalese Buddhist monasteries and threw away the Mss. on the street. Dr. Wright, the Residency Surgeon, coming to learn all these facts, went to Jung Bahadur and asked permission to take the Mss. away as they were of no use to him. Jung Bahadur readily gave his permission and Mr. Wright sent them to Cambridge where they remained idle for sometime. It became apparent within a short time that the Mss. were of great age. The Palaeographical Society having declared some of them to have been as old as the 9th, 10th, or 11th centuries, both Mr. Hodgson and Mr. Wright became anxious to know the contents of the Mss. Hodgson was constantly writing to the Asiatic Society to employ some scholars to make a descriptive catalogue of these Mss. and the Society after a long delay requested Raja R. L. Mitra to undertake the work. He appointed two paṇḍits to read the Mss. and to give their abstracts in Sanskrit, from which abstracts the Raja undertook to make a descriptive catalogue in English. But he fell ill and needed help, and so asked me in 1878 to look into these abstracts and render them into English. For five years the Raja, the Paṇḍits, and myself were engaged in this work and our work entitled Nepalese Buddhist Literature appeared in 1882 in the name of Raja R. L. Mitra. He spoke very kindly of my services to him and gave me an introduction in the preface of the work to the learned world which was very useful to me.

The Cambridge manuscripts were put in charge of Prof. C. C. Bendall and his catalogue of Cambridge Mss. was published in 1883. Prof. Bendall's catalogue did not go into the contents of the work beyond giving the full colophons or so to say the chapter headings, but he very accurately gave the post-colophon statements in which there were much historical information about the copying of the work, its date, the king in whose reign the copy was made and other information of the highest importance to the history of Nepal. He discovered in these Mss. oldest Bengali writings, some of them going to times before the Musalman conquest of Bengal, one in transitional Gupta character going so far back as 859 A.D. He gave an historical introduction and a palaeographical introduction to his catalogue and illustrated the description of some of the Mss. with plates. But as I have said before, he did not go into the contents of the works. That difficult task was performed by Raja R. L. Mitra. He gave the contents of every big work whether philosophical, ritualistic or religious. The shortcomings of these catalogues were many. The old writing was difficult to decipher. Many technical terms were but imperfectly understood, and the history and doctrines of Northern Buddhism were almost unknown. Yet these two works roused the interest of the savants of Europe and the students in India. The Archaeological Department of India though in its infancy had discovered in Sanchi, Barhut, Mathura and other places sculptures giving not only incidents of the life of Buddha but pictures illustrating the story of his former births and the good work done by his disciples and other great men who helped in the propagation of Buddhism. Many of these sculptures were explained by the Jātaka-avadāna stories from Rajendra Lal's Nepalese Buddhist Literature. I distinctly remember the Raja's interest in comparing these stories with those sculptures and his rapturous delight when he could identify one of the stories with one of these sculptures. The Archaeological Department also busied itself with the sculptures. The sculptures mostly went to the 1st, 2nd and 3rd century B.C. and it was wonderful that these sculptures simply reflected the stories of Buddhist literature.

The labours of that intrepid Hungarian scholar Cosma de Koros preceded by a few decades the appearance of these catalogues which brought to light a large portion of the Tibetan translations of the Sanskrit works written in India Buddhism in two grand divisions the

Kangyur and the Tangyur containing a collection of Buddha's sayings and sermons, commentaries on them and other miscellaneous works. It now became possible to trace some of these translations to their originals. Similarly the originals of some of the Chinese translations were also traceable. It opened a great vista of research which might engage generations of scholars for many centuries to come.

The publications of these two catalogues containing descriptions of old original works written in India in Sanskrit is of the highest moment in understanding the history and the doctrines of the form of Buddhism prevailing in Northern India from the 2nd century of the Nirvāṇa era to the present day. It also gave the public a good deal of information of all the stages of Buddhism in India from the 8th century A.D. when the Chinese ceased to come to the time when Buddhism became only a name in N. India. A good deal of the history of Buddhism from the 4th to the 7th centuries in India was known from the translations in European languages or the travels of the great Chinese travellers like Fa-hian, Hiuen Tsang, and I-tsing. But of the later centuries nobody knew anything. Indian people thought that Buddhism disappeared from the face of India after the advent of Śaṅkarācāryya about 800 A.D. But here was found undoubted evidence of Buddhism still flourishing in full vigour for four or five centuries more.

Soon after publishing his English catalogue of Cambridge Buddhist Mss., Prof. Bendall came to India and travelled to Nepal and Rajputana. He discovered a few Mss. and took immense materials for working out a history of Nepal and of Buddhism. The story of his meeting with me could read like a novel. He used to come to the Sanskrit College. I was also not remiss in visiting my *Alma Mater*. We often met without knowing each other. One day he wanted to see the Sanskrit College at Mulajore and Mm. Mahesh Ch. Nyāyaratna took him there. I was also requested by the Mm. to be present at Mulajore. We three examined the College and Prof. Bendall was shown all those things in which a European Sanskrit scholar was likely to be interested. The Mm. was then suffering from gout and Prof. Bendall was very anxious to see the indigenous tôls at Bhatpara. The Mm. therefore asked me to take Prof. Bendall with me and show him the tôls. We entered into a carriage and began to talk. Prof. Bendall complained that there was in India a very large number of Sanskrit scholars, but there were none who took interest in Buddhism. I asked him if he had any doubts and difficulties about Sanskrit Buddhism in which he was so much interested. He asked me a few general questions which I readily answered. Then he asked me if I could introduce him to Haraprasad Śāstrī who had been so well-spoken of by Raja R.L. Mitra.

I told him that I could easily do it, but with a significant smile. In a few minutes I had to reveal myself to him and since then we were friends. He asked me where all that Buddhism has gone. I could give him no reply. But he would not leave me. For several years we were regular correspondents and the burden of every one of his letters was 'where was all that Buddhism gone'? I was already looking for traces of Buddhism all round me without success. I picked up every bit of information that I could of the former existence of Buddhism in Bengal. But I could not find where that Buddhism had gone till at last after nearly 13 years I found Buddhism still remaining as a living religion in western Bengal. This discovery was of very great moment for the social, intellectual, moral, and even the caste history of Bengal but that is another story. I am at present concerned only with Northern Buddhism and not the cryptic Buddhism which I have discovered in Western Bengal.

The publication of the catalogues by Raja R.L. Mitra and Prof. Bendall gave an impetus to Buddhist scholars both in India and Europe[4] to publish Buddhist Sanskrit works. Raja R.L. Mitra published the *Lalitavistara* and the *Aṣṭasāhasrikā-prajñā pāramitā* in the Bibliotheca Indica Series. The first is on the life of Buddha and the second on the doctrines of the Mahāyāna Buddhism. Prof. Bendall published the *Śikṣasamuccaya* a wonderful book. It is a summary of Buddhist doctrines with a vast number of authorities quoted in Sanskrit and various Sanskritic languages. M. Senart published the *Mahāvastu-avadāna* the earliest work yet known of the Northern Buddhism, written in a language which may be termed either Sanskritised vernacular or vernacularised Sanskrit, and which M. Senart called mixed Sanskrit. I contributed my mite in publishing the Svayambū Purāṇa the only Purāṇa of the Buddhists, giving the topography of one of the most important places of pilgrimage in Nepal, with all its shrines and monasteries and stūpas. Profs. Cowell and Neil published the Divyāvadāna a collection of a vadāna-stories written at various times and various places. There was also Kāraṇḍavyūha giving the marvellous achievements in emancipating people by Avalokiteśvara. It was published not as a Buddhist work but as a Jaina work in a series of Jaina canonical works published by Paṇḍit Satyavrata Sāmaśramī under the patronage of Raja-Dhanapāl Sinha of the District of Murshidabad.

When the Svayambhū Purāṇa was printed off, I was anxious to identify the places and shrines, mentioned in that unique work, and therefore went to Nepal in 1897. I saw all the spots mentioned in the Purāṇa and all the rivers and cities in the valley of Nepal and made notes on them. But I found that Mr. Oldfield in his sketches of Nepal had already done much that I wanted to do. I might have given some more information and collated them with that given in the Purāṇa edited by me. But my interest was absorbed by the Durbar Library. There was a Durbar Library, perhaps more Durbar Libraries than one, as there were more than one independent kingdom in the small valley of Nepal. But the Libraries were dissipated on the Gorkha conquest of the Valley in 1768 and nobody knew where the Mss. of these Libraries were gone. In 1868 when I was still a school in the Sanskrit College, my attention was arrested by a small pamphlet published by Mr. R. Lawrence, Resident of Nepal, under the title "Lists of Sanskrit Works supposed by the Nepalese Paṇḍits to be rare in the Nepalese Libraries at Khatmandu". That showed that there was at that time no Durbar Library. Prof. Bendall went there in 1884, shortly after we met at Mulajore and he did not see the Library. So the Durbar Library in 1897 appeared to me to be a discovery of the highest moment. I, at once, asked permission to visit the Library and work there. The permission was readily accorded by Sir Bir Samser Jung Rana the Prime Minister who took a great interest in the Mss, and in the Library. In fact, as I subsequently learnt, it was His Highness who put all the Mss. in the palaces and started the Library in the college premises and was doing everything to bring all Mss. in the Valley to the Library. He subsequently built a spacious hall with a clock tower where the Library is now kept.

After this discovery I spent all my time in the Ms. Library examining old palm-leaf manuscripts. The Library was then kept in the college premises to the south of Rani Pokra. I discovered some unique Mss. of very great age. My notes on these Mss. were embodied in a paper in the Journal of the Asiatic Society of Bengal of that year under the title 'Notes on Mss. in the Durbar Library, Nepal,' When that paper was published, Prof. Sylvain Lévi of Paris came to Calcutta with a view to visit the Library himself. He remained at Katamundu for a month, and collected some Mss. and inscriptions. With these materials he published a history of Nepal and edited with a French translation the Mahāyāna Sūtrālaṅkāra attributed to Asaṅga, which for the first time gave the world some definite idea of the Mahāyāna system of Buddhism of the Yogācāra school. Within six months of Prof. Sylvain Lévi's departure from Nepal, Prof. Bendall was anxious to visit the same Library and arranged with the Secretary of State for India that I should accompany him and stop in Nepal for two months during the winter of 1898 and 1899. We remained in adjoining houses in the Residency and went every alternate day to the Library. His object was to write a history and chronology of Nepal and adjoining states and my object was to write a descriptive catalogue of the palm-leaf Mss. which are very old. Our joint work was issued in my name under the title of 'Catalogue of Palm-leaf and Selected Paper-Mss. in the Durbar Library of Nepal,' to which Prof. Bendall appended a history of Nepal and the surrounding countries. The catalogue was issued in 1905 before which time however Prof. Bendall had breathed his last. This catalogue brought to light the literature of many Śaiva and Buddhist sects which were all forgotten. The Tāntric works in this catalogue are unique. The opinion that the Tantras were recent, not more than five centuries old, became absolutely untenable by the discovery of a large number of Tāntric Mss. in the handwriting of the 10th century of the Christian era. The prevailing opinion in Europe was that the Purāṇas could not go back beyond 800 A.D. For this opinion Horace Hayman Wilson, I believe, is responsible. It was also believed that the Skanda Purāṇa was a myth and that it existed only in Khaṇḍas and Māhātmyas. But the discovery of a palm-leaf Ms. of that Purāṇa in later Gupta character at once made both these opinions untenable. Prof. Bendall was very unwilling to admit that the Ms. was so old, and we often talked on the subject and I maintained that the Ms. belonged to the 6th century and that the writing resembled that of the Horiuzi Ms. kept in the Horiuzi Monastery in Japan where it has been lying since 609 A.D. But Prof. Bendall could not admit that it was so old and stoutly maintained that it was written in the 9th century. Finding that we were quarrelling on these facts for several days Mrs. Bendall one day told us both to bring all the materials on which we held our opinions and to decide the questions once for all. She very kindly consented to be our umpire. So one day we three sat on the verandah of the College Library and brought all the Mss., charts, and drawings and began to show them to Mrs. Bendall. Prof. Bendall had a theory that a Ms. is old in the inverse ratio of the mātrās or the top lines of letters. I readily acceded to this theory. It was however found that Bendall's Ms. of the Pārameśvara-mata-tantra copied in 859 contained many more mātrās or top lines than the Skanda Purāṇa was at least two hundred years older than the Pārameśvara-mata-tantra i.e., the Skanda Purāṇa was written in 659 at the latest. The umpire gave her verdict in my favour. We worked from 11 to 3 o'clock in the afternoon and the verdict was passed and we all came well satisfied with our work. The antiquity of my Purāṇas was set back by several centuries and the discovery of the unique Ms. of the Skanda Purāṇa was regarded as a great event in the history of the Paurāṇic literature.

The 'Catalogue of Palm-leaf and Selected Paper Mss. in the Durbar library of Nepal' has been pronounced by Mr. Jayswal in one of his letters to me as a wonderland. The publication of these catalogues and the editions of some very interesting works found in Nepal during our joint expedition took nearly ten years and in 1907 I went once more to Nepal to examine the rest of the Library. In the year 1906, the Nepal government sent to the Asiatic Society a list of Mss. recently acquired. In this list was a Ms. entitled Nyāya-vārttika which the Society thought must be a work by the great Buddhist logician Diṅnāga. This excited my curiosity and I obtained permission to proceed to Nepal from the Govt. of Bengal and the Govt. of Nepal. But to my utter disappointment I found the Ms. to contain a portion of the Nyāya-vārttika by Udyotakara. But I took this opportunity to examine the rest of the palm-leaf Mss. and published on my return the second volume of the 'Palm-leaf and Selected Paper Mss. of the Durbar Library, Nepal,' in 1915. This contains a very large number of Buddhist works on Tantra mostly written and copied before the Muhammadan conquest in Bengal. The Nepal Government having absolutely prohibited the export of palm-leaf Mss. from the country since the re-establishment of the Durbar Library, I had to collect only paper Mss., either by purchase or by copying. During the expeditions of 1897-98 and 1907, a considerable number of Mss. was collected in the Asiatic Society's rooms, and the Society pressed me to publish a catalogue of these manuscripts. So in 1916, I published a volume of Catalogue of Buddhist manuscripts being the first volume of a large number of volumes, containing descriptions from all the Mss. collected there. It contained descriptions of 119 Mss. Like Prof. Bendall I was very careful in giving the post-colophon statements and the chapter headings. Like Rajendra Lal Mitra also I wanted to give some idea of the contents of the work, but this I did not by translating abstracts but by giving profuse abstracts which appeared to me to throw light on the doctrines of Buddhism and its history. There are works in the collection which are either not to be found among the Chinese or the Tibetan translations, or though found there, were considered to have been absolutely lost in Sanskrit.

I undertook a fourth journey to Nepal in the year 1922 and found Prof. Sylvain Lévi there. I confined myself to the examination of the Sanskrit Library and took extracts from rare Mss. already described in my catalogues. My son Benoytosh Bhattacharyya who was with me busied himself in taking photographs of Buddhist images in different vihāras for his forthcoming volume on Buddhist iconography. Thus it will be seen that in the matter of the collection of Northern Buddhist Mss. Brian Hodgson began it and I have carried it on up to now. The Ms. materials have not yet been exhausted and the report has it that the Sanskrit Buddhist Mss. may be had in large numbers in Tibet and Eastern China. These are the best materials for the study of Northern Buddhism. The Tibetan and the Chinese translations come next after them, but the value of the Sanskrit materials is much greater than that of these translations. Sanskrit materials are coming out also from other parts of India; for instance, the Kathiwar Jaina Library has already furnished the texts and commentaries of the Nyāya Vindu by Dharmottara. The Nyāyapraveśa of Dinnāga has also been found there and the Gaikwar Sanskrit Series has undertaken to publish it. Mm. Ganapati Śāstrī is also publishing a Buddhist Tantrik work entitled Ārya Mañjuśrī Sūtra Kalpa and I know other collections in Bengal and Benares containing Mss. of works on Northern Buddhism. In the 'Catalogue of the Tanjore collection of Tibetan translations' published by Beckh and the two volumes of the catalogues of the Tangyur collection published by my late lamented friend Dr. P. Cordier, as well as in the Catalogue of Chinese Tripiṭaka by Nanjio, we hear of thousands of Sanskrit Buddhist works belonging to the Northern schools of Buddhism. Of these only a very small number has been found in Sanskrit. But the Sanskrit Mss. are much more valuable than the translation. For the Chinese is a free translation, often wide from the text and the Tibetan is so absolutely literal that it is difficult to understand for one who is not a master of both the ancient Tibetan and Sanskrit. That being the case it is very difficult to write a history of Northern Buddhism from Sanskrit materials alone. But I have had the good fortune of receiving much of my information from Indrānanda the great grandson of Amṛtānanda, Hodgson's friend, philosopher, and guide. He often gave me light on the history of Buddhism which I found nowhere in printed books and Mss. But he is no more, and Buddhist scholars are becoming more and more rare in Nepal. With this preamble I now begin to give a connected history of Northern Buddhism from the second century of the Nirvāṇa era to the present day. I am fully conscious of my shortcomings and know that there are many gaps which I cannot fill up. Still I think a connected history with all its shortcomings is likely to be useful to the readers.

Chapter - 9

The Northern Buddhism

Haraprasad Sastri

Before I give a connected history of Northern Buddhism it is necessary to speak something about the Sanskrit manuscripts from Nepal on which that is to be based. The mss. brought by Hodgson were thus distributed: "85 bundles comprising 144 separate works were presented to the Asiatic Society of Bengal; 85 to the Royal Asiatic Society of London; 30 to the India Office Library; 7 to the Bodleian Library, Oxford; 174 to the Société Asiatique and M. Burnouf. The last two collections have since been deposited in the Bibliotheque Nationale of France".

Raja Rajendra Lal Mitra says that Hodgson was not only the discoverer of these most ancient and authentic records, but also the first intelligent exponent of their nature and value both in their ritualistic and in their philosophical aspects, "and his notices served more to excite than to allay curiosity in regard to them". Very few of them, almost a negligible quantity, are non-Buddhistic. Prof. Bendall's Catalogue of the Wright collection in Cambridge contains about 172 separate works. My collection in the Asiatic Society of Bengal contains 125 separate Buddhist works. In all, there would be about 700 mss. There are about 250 Buddhist works available to work upon, making allowance for all duplicates, triplicates and multiplicates of works and fragments.

The most important and earliest of them is the *Mahāvastu-avadāna*, the Vinaya or disciplinary work of the Mahāsaṅghikas, the schismatics of the second Buddhist council in the second century of the Nirvāṇa era or in the fourth century B.C. This is the only work of the Mahāsaṅghikas that has come down to us or has yet been discovered. Its importance cannot therefore be over-rated. M. Senart has published an edition of the work with notes in French. The amazing piece of information given at the outset is that the Mahāsaṅghikas were all

Lokottaravādins that, is they considered Buddha to be supermundane. Reading through the book, I find that everything in the life of Buddha is supermundane. His descent from heaven, his entrance into the womb of Māyā, his birth from her right side, his seven steps at birth, his movements, his eating, lying, sitting were all supermundane. He received no education, yet when challenged, he wrestled, he threw arrow, he fought, he jumped, with supermundane power and throughout the book the author or the compiler has maintained the supermundane character of Buddha. The opponents consider Buddha as a gifted human being but the schismatics thought he was not earthly.

Every one who reads the Pāli works knows that the schism arose form a difference on ten points, all minor points of discipline, and he wonders how such trivial things can produce such an abiding separation. The supermundane character given to Buddha by the schismatics invests the separation with greater importance. The difference of opinion was radical and far-reaching as the subsequent developments will show. Later on Buddha loses his human character altogether and becomes *Upāya*, means of salvation, and later still, there arise many hypothetical Buddhas or Dhyāni Buddhas identified with the universe both in its physical and spiritual aspects. The southern Buddhists are concerned with Śākyamuni, the Sarvārathasiddha, the son of Śuddhodana and Māyā, belonging to the solar race and to the Gotama-gotra; but the Northern Buddhists speak of him as Savajña, omniscient. The lexicographer Amarasiṃha in the fifth century A.D. speaks of two Buddhas, one Supreme Intelligence, and the other a human being. The Supreme Intelligence is placed first and has more names than the other. In the supplement to the *Amarakoṣa* written in the latest period of Buddhism in India, the supermundane Buddha has many more names than the human Buddha.

This is one aspect of N. Buddhism; the other aspects are also patent at the first reading of the *Mahāvastu*, which speaks of hundreds of Buddhas previous to this Buddha. The S. Buddhism knows only three, then eight, and last of all, 24 Tīrthaṅkaras including Mahāvīra, a contemporary of Śākyamuni. The S. Buddhism has 550 Jātaka stories. But the Northern has only a few and those few gradually dwindled into nothing. The Jātakas were substituted by Avadānas or glorious achievements not only of Buddha but of all great personages of the Buddhist faith. The Northern seems to have an aversion to the Jātakas.

In the matter of doctrine, too, there was a great difference between the two sections. The highest aim of the Southern was arahatship to be free from the bondage of birth, death and old age. The arahats cannot save others. They, however, can save themselves. It is Buddha only who can save others. The arahats can, however, prepare others for salvation but the latter will have to wait till a Buddha appears in the world after an uncertain and indefinitely long period. But the *Mahāvastu* preaches that any one who has attained salvation can save others "tīrṇo tarayeyam, mukto mocayeyam". The ideas of time and space of the N. and S. Buddhists are very different. The Southern is more circumscribed while the Northern attempts to grasp infinity as far as human limitation will allow. The S. deals with the lift of Śākyamuni only, but the N. with many of the past Buddhas who foretold that Śākyamuni would attain Buddhahood at Kapilavāstu and in one place the N. have gone so far as to speak of hundreds of Śākyamunis of Kapilavāstu. No emphasis is laid on the Śikṣāpadas or disciplinary vows in the N. but these are not altogether suppressed as in later times. But the S. is full of these vows even now. So the difference was not on 10 minor points of discipline but on fundamental conceptions and what are these ten points? To us they appear to be absolutely trivial. Some monks wanted to store a bit of salt in a horn and objection was taken to such storage. The monks were allowed to take only liquids in the afternoon. Some people wanted to mix water with curd and drink it before churning. That was objected to and so on to the number of ten. This appears to be more trivial when it is considered that Buddha on his deathbed advised monks to attach smaller importance to minor points of discipline after his death.

The Licchavis of Vaiśālī and their relations the Vajjis were a spirited race who had recently given up their nomadic habits and were impatient of control. They wanted to widen the outlook of Buddhism and they succeeded.

When I am speaking of the earliest work of the schism, the *Mahāvastu*, I cannot leave it without saying a word about its chronology and its language. The prevailing opinion is that it is written in a mixed language into which Sanskrit and Prākṛt idioms equally enter and that it is an artificial language. But I think this was the spoken language of N. India which purged by the rules of Pāṇini, Kātyāyana and Patañjali became the standard language of the brāhmaṇas of N. India. The *Bharata Nāṭya Śāstra* distinctly says that when that work was written about the second century B.C., there were in India seven language, and that each had two forms the Saṃskṛta and the Prākṛta, i.e., pure or grammatical and the ordinary, and the seven languages were all geographical. The *Mahāvastu* is written in the ungrammatical form of the language prevailing in Kośala and Vajji countries. It is neither an artificial language nor Vernacularized Sanskrit nor Sanskrit used Vernacular. The work is written in prose but every prose piece is supported by a versified piece which looks like the authority on which the prose narration is based. There is a slight variation in their language, as there must be, between prose and verse. The prose is homely and the verse is a little dignified. There are other books also written in this language. The *Lalitavistara*, I suppose, was at one time written entirely in this language but at present the prose has become Sanskrit of a sort and the poetry has retained the old language. The *Saddharama Puṇḍarīka*, as we have it, is written in the style of prose in Sanskrit and poetry in this identical language. But the palm-leaves that have been dug out from the Taklamakan desert contain an old version of the work in which both the prose and the verse are in this language. There is another work of which I have recently got a copy which is all in verse in this language but which appears to be more modern. The short dedicatory inscriptions in Sāñci, Barhaut, Mathura and other places are also in this language. It seems to have been the prevailing language of the N. Buddhists in the centuries following the schism.

So far for the language of the *Mahāvastu*; and the time for its composition or compilation is, I think, the second and third centuries of the Nirvāṇa era, namely, the third and second centuries B.C. Some scholars think that it was composed or complied in the 3rd century A.D. because it contain the word Yogācāra and the Yogācāra sect was founded in that century. The word Yogācāra in the *Mahāvastu* is not used in the sense of a sect; there it has the ordinary meaning of *Yoga* and *ācāra* and it is not in the nature of things that the vigorous sect which defied the majority of the elders should wait six centuries to write their sacred books. I think the work was written or the works were compiled in the course of the very first or second century of its existence. There would be no meaning in their composition or compilation six hundred years after, when it is well-known again that the Mahāsaṅghikas within one, or one and half a century was split up into six different sects.

So the *Mahāvastu* is a great discovery as the earliest work of N. Buddhism and as being written in the vernacular of the time when Sanskrit grammarians were trying to purify the language by strict rules, Pāṇini in the late fifth, Kātyāyana in the fourth, Vyāḍi in the third and Patañjali in the second century B.C.

The third century of the Nirvāṇa era and the early part of the fourth were the most flourishing time of Buddhism. Aśoka encouraged Buddhism and some of his successors did the same. Big monasteries were founded, the places of pilgrimage visited, grants were made to

Buddhist congregations, missions were sent to surrounding countries and assemblies held to fix the canons. But all that was good for S. Buddhism of one sect only. The strict rules framed for schismatics does not speak of great favour being shown to the people of N. Buddhism. But one thing is sure: Asoka was not in favour of persecution except when his Imperialist policy required that class privileges should be cut down.

A book, non-canonical, of course, was written by the President of the Aśoka Council held in the 17th year of his reign, detailing the points in controversy among the Buddhists from the point of view of the most favoured sect, namely, the Vibhajjavādins, an offshoot of the Theravādins. That book enunciates 20 different sects among the Buddhists, 12 among the Theravadins, 6 among the Mahāsaṅghikas and two local. But it is a well-known fact that in the council of the 17th year of Aśoka the N. Buddhists were not invited and they consequently took no part and ignored its existence. But their opinions were controverted by the President Tissa Moggaliputta in their absence in the now famous work, the *Kathāvatthu* or the points of controversy. So between the Vaiśālī split and the Aśoka council there were further and further splits among the Buddhists.

In the middle of the fourth century of the Nirvāṇa era disaster fell on all Buddhists. Aśoka prohibited the killing of animals for sacrificial purposes all over his empire, took away the cherished privileges of brāhamaṇas to suit his Imperial policy, appointed the best men in his services irrespective of caste, colour and creed. This gave offence to the brāhmaṇas, and they in the middle of the fourth century of the Nirvāṇa era destroyed the Maurya Empire and raised a Sāmavedī brāhmaṇa of the Śuṅga gotra to the throne of Magadha. The Sāmavedins were the priests of the Soma sacrifice in which many animals were killed and these were incensed at the prohibition of killing animals and they now took their vengeance by performing a Horse sacrifice in the very capital, perhaps in the very palace of Aśoka from which the edict of prohibition was promulgated. This was not all. Puṣyamitra the first king of the Śuṅga dynasty was a great persecutor of the Buddhists, he massacred the monks, destroyed their vihāras, and banished the turbulent spirits. The Buddhists fled to all parts of India, the Theravādins towards the South and the N. Buddhists towards the N. West. The brāhmaṇas remained dominant in eastern and central India for three centuries and consolidated their power within the empire. They codified their law, they gave the last finish to the *Rāmāyana* and the *Mahābhārata* and to their linguistic survey and organised the caste-system and the modern system of Hindu worship. But beyond the empire their influence was on the wane, and their empire dwindled and dwindled till the whole fabric fell before the invading hoards from the North, West, and South. Beyond the brāhmaṇa empire the Buddhists had peace and shelter but after nearly two centuries of disorganisation. They, however, kept up the form of a spiritual government. Saṅghatheras were appointed in regular succession and the show of a government was kept up. The *Milinda Pañho* a dialogue between king Menander and Nāgasena shows that beyond the brāhmaṇa empire among the foreign invaders the Buddhists enjoyed more respect than in their home provinces. Now to what sect did Nāgasena belong? The book as now extant is in Pāli and found in the South. But the editor tells us that the work had a Sanskrit original and that it most probably belonged to N. Buddhism.

The Śātakarṇis were brāhamaṇas and the Śaka kings Nāhavāna and his son-in-law Usavadāta were pro-brāhamaṇas. But they, to a certain extent, encouraged the Buddhist also. There are inscriptions in which they granted lands and privileges to Buddhists also. The dedication of stūpas and sculptures of the Buddhists and Jainas continued through their sway. But we hear very little of the Buddhists in Magadha and Central India. In the sixth century of the Nirvāṇa era, however, the Northern Buddhists made a great headway in the Punjab. The coins and inscriptions of the Parthians, Greeks, Yuechi and Kuṣānas show traces of Buddhism in them and they seem to have converted the Kuṣāna emperor, Kaṇiṣka to their faith. His conversion was a great triumph to the Buddhists. For he was the supreme ruler of all the countries from Vindhya to the Altai mountains and during his reign they had access to Central Asia where they planted their faith and remained dominant for several centuries, carrying Indian civilization to the Tokharas and Turks. In Central Asia they first made their acquaintance with the Chinese and gradually converted nearly the whole of the Celestial Empire to their faith. But that is another story.

But before giving an account of Buddhism in Kaniṣka's time it is necessary to speak of Buddhism or Buddhist works supposed to have been written before his time. These are *Laṅkāvatāra, Gaṇḍavyūha* and *Śrīghana sūtra.* Of these the *Laṅkāvatāra* is well-known. Buddha Śākyamuni preached to Rāvaṇa at Laṅkā. He solved the doubts of his hearers on such questions as from what principle of human nature ratiocination had its origin? How can agreements be made pure? How to detect fallacies? What are fallacies? Where did the emancipated go? How can one in bondage be emancipated? What is Nirvāṇa? How do Arahats and Tathāgatas hold to meditation of Bodhisattva? Whether the Tathāgata is eternal and so on? The questions are on Logic and Philosophy. I take them from Rajendra Lal's *Nepalese Buddhist Literature*. The late lamented Harinath De published a pamphlet in which 20 different systems of thought were culled out form the *Laṅkāvatāra*. The Nepalese call it a Mahāyāna Sūtra but Suzuki in his notes on the *Awakening of Faith* characterises it as pre-Mahāyāna or at least pre-Nāgārjuna. So is Gaṇḍavyūha. It is called Ghanavyūha in Chinese which the Nepalese call Mahāyāna but Suzuki pre-Nāgārjuna. It has been described by Raja R.L. Mitra.

Yuan Chwang tells us that Kaniṣka held a Council in Kāśmīra in which all the N. Buddhists were invited. The S. Buddhists were *nonest* there. There were five hundred monks, they settled the canon of N. Buddhism and made a commentary entitled *Vibhāṣā* which they inscribed in copper plates and kept the inscriptions under a huge stūpa close to the place of the Assembly. I am disposed to think that the Vaibhāṣika sect took their cue from the Vibhāṣā. But no information on this subject have come from Indian sources. All information is buried in Chinese translations. So it seems that there is no information about the Council held during the reign of emperor Kaniṣka except what is given by Yuan Chwang. But we know from Chinese sources that Kaniṣka had three eminent Indians at his Court, one is Māṭhara, the well-known commentator of Sāṃkhya Kārikās, one Caraka, the redactor of an ancient medical work by Atri and Agniveṣa and the other was Aśvaghoṣa, Kaniṣka's spiritual Guru. He was born at Sāketa in Ough, his mother's name was Suvarnākṣī. He was a *bhadanta*, he was a philosopher, a poet, a musician and a great preacher. His voice was so loud that he was called Aśvaghoṣa (or neighing like a horse). Suzuki calls him a Mahāyānist and has translated his philosophical work, Māhāyana Śraddhotpāda Sūtra, or awakening of faith in Mahāyāna. But Mahāyāna was not yet. It came two generations after Aśvaghoṣa. The *Awakening* is a wonderful work. Its original has not been yet found. Suzuki translated the Chinese translation, which treats of all the great problems of Mahāyāna. But there is nothing of Mahāyāna in Aśvaghoṣa's great epics. The Buddhacarita has been edited from very inferior materials by the late E.B. Cowell who was for some years the Principal of the Calcutta Sanskrit College. Better materials are now available as I have shown in one of my papers in the *JASB*. But Cowell had done another thing. The Sanskrit Buddhacarita is only half the work, the other half is yet unavailable. But Cowell has translated the Chinese translation of Buddhacarita also which is complete in 28 cantos. His other epic the Saundarānanda was discovered by me and has been edited by me from old and good materials. Both are epics of great merit written in Classical Sanskrit in which the majority of Buddhist works are written. The Buddhacarita deals with the epic life of Buddha and the Saundarānanda with that of his step-brother Nanda. The doctrines are those of N. Buddhism and not yet of Mahāyāna. Buddha speaks to Nanda "You have done your duty, you are emancipated, now go and preach and save others", exactly what the Mahāvastu speaks of. It is not S. Buddhism for no emphasis is laid on discipline and the regulation of conduct. The poetry of both these works is of a very high order. The character are distinct and very well-drawn. The images, the descriptions and the similes are all that can be desired. Subsequent Sanskrit poets even Kālidāsa is indebted to Aśvaghoṣa for many of his most admired similes. But I need not expatiate on them here as I have done so in the preface to my edition of the Saundarānanda.

It is said that emperor Kaniṣka invested Pataliputra. The king was not prepared to defend his capital and sued for peace but Kaniṣka demanded nine crores of rupees which the king had not. It was afterwards settled that the king should send Aśvaghoṣa to Kaniṣka and the Emperor would value him at three crores of rupees. Buddha's alms-bowl was valued at three crores of rupees and some other relic at the same price. From this it will be seen how greatly Aśvaghoṣa was appreciated by his contemporaries. Aśvaghoṣa seems to have been originally a brāhmaṇa. His knowledge of the Vedas and the brāhmaṇic law is deep and profound. He distinctly lays down that Buddha's religion was an outcome of the Sāṃkhya doctrines of Kapila. Sāṃkhya's aim was to become Kevala or absolute but Buddha saw that no entity can be absolute and unconditioned, and he so modified Kapila's doctrine as to destroy the entity of the soul. But I have spoken of Aśvaghoṣa and Kaniṣka at greater length than I proposed. I must now proceed to more important developments of Northern Buddhism.

The geographical distribution of N. and S. Buddhism was not carefully kept. There were S. Buddhist in the North and N. Buddhist in the South. The *Laṅkāvatāra* is an instance to the point. The scene was placed at Laṅkā to make it very prominent. Rāvaṇa is made one of the interlocutors. Yet the work belongs to Northern Buddhism. The scenes in the *Gaṇḍavyūha* are laid in the South but it is Northern Buddhism. The Nepalese call it even Mahāyāna. But two of the greatest figures in N. Buddhism came from the South. These are Nāgārjuna and Āryadeva. One is the father of Mahāyāna and the other his disciple. Nāgārjuna is said to have been the friend of one of the Śātakarṇis, and Āryadeva hails from Kāñci. Nāgārjuna preached the Śūnyavāda which was the essence of the Mahāyāna School.

Nāgārjuna is regarded at least as the St. Paul if not as the Christ of Mahāyāna. He is said to have drawn out from the nether world a new Buddhist scripture in Sanskrit called the Prajñāpāramitā. There is a misapprehension among the learned men as regards Prajñāpāramitā. There are several recensions of this work from Svalpākṣarā or in a few words to one of 150 ślokas, one of 700 ślokas, one of 1500 ślokas, one of 8000 ślokas, one of 10000 ślokas, one of 25000 ślokas, one of 100,000 ślokas and some say one of 125,000 ślokas. Some think that the original work was of 100000 ślokas and the rest are abridgements. But my information is otherwise. The earliest recension in that of 10000 ślokas as I learn from the Chinese sources. But it is very nearly identical with the 8000 divided into 32 parivarttas. Shortly after the time of Nāgārjuna one Maitreyanātha wrote a work in mnemonic verses called *Kārikās* in Sanskrit divided in eight chapters entitled Abhisamayālaṅkāra Kārikās which laid the foundation of the Yogācāra School and the Prajñāpāramitā of the 8000 ślokas was modified and enlarged according to these Kārikās into a recension of 25000 divided in eight chapters according to the Kārikās. The Śatasāhasrikā is still later. In Chinese the 25000 was translated first of all, then the 8000 and then the 100000 which was translated by Yuan Chwang on his return from India. The 125000 appears to be a myth but not so the 1500. Of the seven hundred I have seen two copies one in the Mss. Library of the Mahārājā of Benares where it is classed under Kāvyas and the other I collected for the A.S.B. Of the Svalpākṣarā I have seen three copies which between the usual prologue and the epilogue in Prajñāpāramitā works contains one sentence to the effect that *karuṇā* is the essential feature of Buddhism. At the end of all these copies it is stated that Nāgārjuna recovered the Prajñāpāramitā from the nether regions. Raja R. Mitra has published the Prajñāpāramitā of 8000 ślokas in the Bibl. Ind. series and the study of the work shows that it is rank Śūnyavāda. Prajñāpāramitā means knowledge par excellence. What is that? Omniscience. What is omniscience? The knowledge that all the phenomenal existence is Śūnya or void. Examine any phenomenon, it has not substratum. Go on examining all the phenomena. They are all without a substratum. The subjective phenomena too have no substratum, neither matter has any substratum nor has mind. The soul has no substratum. Everything resolves into Śūnya. What is Śūnya? Is it existence? No. Is it non-existence? No. Is it a combination of the two? No. Is it a negation of the two? No. What is it then? It is that to which neither existence nor non-existence nor a combination of the two nor a negation of the two can be predicated. What is it then? It is Anirvācya that which cannot be explained, that which cannot be spoken of. That which cannot be comprehended. That which cannot be imagined. You may call it Transcendental that which transcends our faculties. It is not what the Śrāvakas or the S. Buddhist aims at. It is beyond these narrow-minded members of the Monastic order. It is beyond the narrow-minded order of Friars. Who are its votaries then? The Bodhisattvas, those who after their exertions during innumerable births and strenuous effort have resolved upon attaining the knowledge *par excellence.* They are only waiting that some Buddha may appear in the world and prophesy that they should in some future kalpa become omniscient and resolved upon emancipating all the sentient beings. In their zeal for omniscience they developed a sense of mercy, a sense of sympathy, a sense of all embracing karuṇā for all sentient beings that they can wait for eternity or any long period of time and suffer any amount of privation, undergo any amount of suffering, undergo any number of births and deaths, in order to save all sentient beings from the bondage of births and deaths, they are prepared to suffer for any length of time.

This is in short the teaching of Nāgārjuna both in the Prajñāpāramitā and in his Mādhaymika Kārikās. The Kārikās are written in terse and vigorous philosophical language but the Prajñāpāramitā are written in the form of harangues addressed to ordinary people, and as all harangues are full of repetitions, Rajendra Lal complains that all Buddhist Sanskrit works are written in a verbose style. Yes, they must be. The author is addressing illiterate people on very abstruse subjects much beyond the comprehension even of the learned.

Chapter - 10

Notes on Buddhism

Louis De La Vallée Poussin

1. The *Abhidharmakośavyākhyā* contains the following interesting note: "Philosophies while destroying the opinion of their adversaries must carefully respect the principles of logic, because these principles are useful to them; just as kings, while destroying the soldiers of their enemies respect the field-labourer who is the common help of both armies". This observation can be compared to the observation of the Greek historians who saw with surprise that peasants peacefully practised their peaceful work in the middle of combating armies.

2. Vasubandhu (ii. 50) himself does not give a very pleasant idea of the government of the kings (or rather of the small chiefs). He establishes that there is a certain sort of cause (*hetu*), which in fact does not produce any effect: its causality only consists in the fact of not prohibiting the production of the effect by other causes. The objection is at hand: how can a thing which does not produce be called a cause? Just as the villagers say, "We are happy owing to our Lord (*svāmin, bhojaka*)" not, (of course), because their Lord helps them in any way, but because, while he is powerful enough to harm them, he remains unharmful. In the same way Montaigne says: "Les princes me donnent prou s'ils ne m'ôtnet rien" (Princes give me much when they do not take).

3. My friend G.K. Nariman has made a good collection of the Buddhist references to the method of dealing with the dead, incineration, *stūpas*, exposure to birds and beasts[1]. The comparison of the Pāli and Sanskrit Mahānāmasūtras shows perhaps that eastern or central India (home of Pāli Buddhism?) had not the rules which prevailed in western India (home of Sanskrit Buddhism?). While Saṃyutta, V, 369 or Dīgha, ii, 295 refer only to the *śmaśāna* where corpses are abandoned to the

1. Quelques paralléles entre le Bouddhisme et le Parsisme, Revue de Phistoire des religions, 1912, i, 85. — Prof. Rhys Davids, Buddhist India, p. 80.

beasts of prey, the Sanskrit redaction of the Mahānāmasūtra (quoted in the Abhidharmakośa, iii, 30a) gives an exhaustive enumeration of *mytasya khalu kālagatasya jñātaya imaṃ pūtikakāyam agninā vā dahanti udake vā plāvavanti bhūmau vā nikhananti vātātapābhyāṃ vā pariśoṣaṃ parikṣayaṃ gacchati;*—there is "incineration, immersion, sepulchre ("enterrement") and exposure of the body in a place where by the wind and the sun it becomes dry and finally disappears". No more mention of the beasts of prey. The end of the sūtra is worth quoting: *vat punar idam ucyate cittam iti vā mana iti vijñānam iti vā śraddhāparibhāvitaṃ śīlatyāgaśruta-prajñāparibhāvitaṃ tad ūrdhvagām bhavati viśeṣagāmy āyatyāṃ svargopagam*: But what is called thought, mind or consciousness, when it is perfumed by faith, morality, gift, sacred instruction, sacred wisdom, that goes above, goes to a good state, goes in the future to the paradise."

Chapter - 11

Place of Buddhism in Indian Thought

N. Dutt

It is rather striking that the early Pali texts even later Buddhist Sanskrit texts do not breathe a word about the Upaniṣads and the Upaniṣadic philosophers, although there are repeated references to the teachings of the six teachers, Pūraṇa Kassapa, Ajita Kesakambalin, Pakudha Kaccāyana, Sañjaya Belaṭṭhiputta, Maṅkhali Gosāla and Nigaṇṭha Nāṭaputta. Incidentally in the Pali texts there is also mention of the Vedic *śākhās*, viz., Addhariya, Bahvrija, Chandoka, and Tittiriya and Vedic seers, Aṭṭhaka, Vāmaka, Vāmadeva, and other who are said to have taught mainly *Brahma-sahavyatā* or the attainment of Brahmaloka, supposed to be the highest form of existence. In the sixty two views envisaged in the *Brahmajālasutta*, there are criticisms of the belief in the existence of a self and of its transmigration from one existence to another. This criticism is elaborated in later Mahāyāna texts particularly in that of Nāgārjuna.[1] In the Pāli Nikāyas there are several discourses of a stereotyped nature discussing the problem whether the soul is identical with the body or not, and the conclusion drawn is that there cannot arise any question of the existence or no-existence of soul, as from the Buddhist point of view it has no more existence than that of the son of a barren woman or that of a flower in the sky.[2] Hence it is an indeterminable problem (*avyākata*) to be left aside (*ṭhapanīya*). The fundamental query of almost all the *Upaniṣads* is the nature of soul and its transmigration from one existence to another. It seems that Buddha deliberately ignored the *Upaniṣads* as

---

1. See *Early Monastic Buddhism*, vol. I.
2. Cf. *Abhidharmakośa*, IX, 4-5:

अससत्त्वाद्भगवान् जीवं तत्त्वान्यत्वेन नावदत्।
नास्तीत्यपि च नावोचन् माभूत् प्राज्ञप्तिकोप्यसन्॥
यत्न हि स्कन्धसन्ताने शुभाशुभफलास्तिता।
जीवाख्या तत्न सा न स्याज्जीव नास्तित्वदेशनात्॥
प्रज्ञसिमात्नं स्कन्धेषु जीव इत्यपि नावदत्।
अभव्यः शून्यतां बोद्धं तदानीं तादृशो जनः॥

in them the existence of soul is taken for granted while his main thesis was the total denial of the existence of this soul (*anatta*) and through all his philosophical discourses he tried to establish that there could not exist any permanent self unalloyed by worldly impurities. Hence, it is idle to say that Buddhism issued out of the *Upaniṣads* and was a phase in the evolution of Upaniṣadic thought.[1] On the other hand, it may be stated that Buddhism was a revolt against the Upaniṣadic thought and it was this denial of soul, which undermined the belief in the efficacy of the sacrificial rituals and ceremonies. The three primary conditions which make one a true Buddhist is the elimination of the belief in the existence of a self (*sakkāyadiṭṭhi*) and in the efficacy of rituals (*sīlabbataparāmāsa*), to which is to be added the implicit faith in the *Triratna* by discarding all doubts (*vicikicchā*) about their excellence. This revolutionary teaching of Buddha instead of frightening away some of the Brāhmanic teachers and students, opened up a new vista before their eyes and made them not only staunch supporters but the best exponents of the new teaching.

Buddha subscribed to the theories of *karman* and rebirth but in a way completely different from those of the Upaniṣadas. The Upaniṣadic view of *karman* is linked up with the permanent and unchangeable self while Buddha's view was that changing *karman* could never be associated with an unchanging substance like the self. He was a strong advocate of *karman* and its effects and he laid the utmost emphasis on it throughout his teachings (see *infra*). He criticised those teachers who denied or minimised the efficacy of *karman* and it is with this purpose that he discussed the doctrines of the six teachers mentioned above and condemned them in no uncertain terms. The upholders of *Akiriyavāda* were destined to hell—this was his repeated assertion. He elaborated his cosmological ideas of heaven and hell mainly with a view to educate his large number of disciples who were not spiritually advanced and to infuse into them the spirit of doing good deeds and avoiding evils in order to assure a better and happier after-life. Of the six teachers he made an exception of only one, viz., Nigaṇṭha Nāṭ aputta, whom he regarded as a *kiriyavādin* and passed over the views of the Agnostic teacher Sañjaya Belaṭṭhiiputta.

The doctrinal views of these six teachers are presented in the Pali texts thus:

---

1. T.R.V. Murti writes in his *Central Philosophy of Buddhism*, p. 20 "The Upaniṣads and Buddhism belong ot the same spiritual genus, they differ as species, and the differentia are the acceptance or rejection of the *ātman* (permanent substance). Cf. V.Bhattacharya, *Basic Conception of Buddhism*, pp. 70-75.

(i) Pūraṇa Kassapa seems to be the oldest teacher and held views wavering between antinomianism and fatalism. His doctrine is that soul remains inactive as in Sāṅkhya and it is the body which acts, hence soul remains unaffected by the results of good and bad deeds of the body. A person earns neither merit by pious acts such as gifts, sacrifices, or by abstinence from evil acts nor demerit by killing, stealing, adultery or speaking falsehood. It is rather difficult to find out exactly what was Pūraṇa's views from such cryptic statements. It may mean that the body enjoys or suffers according to its deeds but not the soul, a doctrine which cannot reasonably, be refuted by a Sāṅkhya or a Vedānta schoolman. In Buddhism however soul and body are not admitted as two separate entities, not also as identical. Pūraṇa's doctrine is grouped in the Pāli texts as an "*Akiriyavāda*" i.e. non-existence of *karmaic* effects.

(ii) Makkhali Gosāla, the founder of the Ājīvika sect, was at first a follower of Pārśvanatha, the traditional founder of Jainism. One day he observed a sprout growing up again after it was trampled down. This changed his outlook and he came to the conclusion that beings were subject to re-animation and not death and destruction. He added to it the doctrine that all beings were subject to a fixed series of existence from the lowliest to the highest and this series was unchangeable (*niyati saṅgatibhāva*) and every existence had its own unalterable characteristic as heat is of fire or coldness of ice. He denied the effects of deeds (*karma*) and energy (*vīrya*). He upheld fatalism of the extreme type. A being when nearing the end of the several spans of its lives becomes a human being. Its existence as such is divided into six categories, viz., (i) black (*kaṇha*) as bird catchers, hunters, fishermen etc., (ii) blue (*nīla*) as ascetics observing rigorous practices, including the Buddhists (Śākyaputtiya Samaṇas), (iii) red (*lohita*) as monks of the Jaina order, (iv) yellow (*halidda*) as lay-devotees of Acelakas and Ājīvikas, (v) white (*sukha*) as Ājīvika monks like Nanda, Vaccha and Saṅkicca, and lastly (vi) very white (*paramasukka*) as Ājīvika saints. Buddhaghosa[1] has made an attempt to explain in detail the various states of existence envisaged in Maṅkhali Gosala's doctrine. In the Jaina literature[2] as also in Tamil works like the *Maṇimekhalai* of the 4th century A.D. and *Civañāṇa Cittiyar* of the 14th century, the various states of existence distinguished by colour as black, dark, blue, green, red, golden and white have been dealt with in connection with the doctrines of the Ājīvikas[3]. The distinctions made by colour,

1. *Sumaṅgalavilāsinī*, pp. 161-4.
2. *Bhagavatisūtra*, XV, 550: *Uttarādhyayana*, xxiv.
3. Basham, *History & Doctrines of the Ājīvikas*, pp. 243 ff.

though not now intelligible, must have been a prominent feature of Ājīvikism. It is not unlikely that the term '*niyati*' was introduced into Indian thought by the Ājīvikas and it cast a definite influence on the Epics particularly the *Mahābhārata*. Manu and compiler or *Hitopadeśa* tried to disabuse the minds of the people of this faith in fatalism though Bhartṛhari extolled it in his *Nītiśataka*. The Ājīvikas, it seems, attained great popularity in post-Aśokan age. There is a tradition that king Bindusāra consulted Piṅgalavatsa (Janāsana in Pali chronicles) an Ājīvika monk for ascertaining which of his two sons, Aśoka and Vītaśoka would succeed him to the throne. Aśoka's mother was very likely a follower of the Ājīvikas. After Aśoka's demise his grandson Daśaratha dedicated a few caves to the Ājīvika saints specially, showing thereby that the successors of Aśoka preferred the Ājīvikas to the Buddhists. Dr. Basham has collected reliable evidences to show that this sect became popular in South India and was in existence up to the mediaeval period.

(iii) Nigaṇṭha Nāṭaputta (fetterless son of the Nāya clan) or Mahāvīra happened to be an older contemporary of Buddha. Like Buddha he came of a noble family, perhaps the chief of the clan. He led for some time a married life and then renounced the world. He revived the teachings of Pārśvanātha, and formed an order of monks who however led a much more austere life than that of a Buddhist monk. His philosophical views are as follows: There are nine substances (*navatattva*) viz., (i) soul (*jīva*) present in all that is conscious including a tree or a fruit; (ii) non-soul (*ajīva*) which serves as the basis for the functioning of soul (*jīva*) as body is of the soul; (iii) merits and demerits (*puṇya, pāpa*) which are also substances produced by actions (*karman*) of *jīva* through mind, speech and body; (v) impurities (*āsrava*) which flow into the body due to *karmaic* effects; (vi) self-control (*saṃvara*) which arrests the flow of *karmaic* effects, and also neutralises them; (vii) bondage (*bandha*) of the soul caused by *karmaic* effects transformed into *āsrava* and leading to repeated existence (*saṁsāra*), (viii) elimination (*nirjarā*) of *karmaic* effects or *āsravas* through *saṃvara* as prescribed for the Jaina monks; and lastly (ix) liberation (*mokṣa*) attained by a monk who has perfected himself in the disciplinary practices and realised the truth as inculcated in Jaina philosophy.

In Jaina philosophy no definite statement (*syādvāda*) can be made about any object, not even about the highest truth. Every object is subject to three momentary states, viz., origin (*utpāda*), continuity (*sthiti*) and decay (*vināśa*). The object in its state of continuity may be regarded as the substance (*dravya*) while in the other two states it is subject to change (*paryāya*). According to *anekāntavāda* an object is permanent from the standpoint of continuity (*nitya*), but it is impermanent (*anitya*) from the other two standpoint. Every object had to be determined from different standpoints, as it has several aspects and so there can be no absolute statement regarding the nature of an object. This is known as the Jaina doctrine of *Anekāntavāda*. In order to have a true knowledge of an object, its examination is necessary from various aspects and it is by this means alone that the perfect knowledge can be attained. For the sake of practical application, the *Anekāntavāda* has been condensed into seven members (*saptabhaṅgī*) thus:—From seven different standpoints a being is (i) permanent; (ii) impermanent; (iii) both permanent and impermanent; (iv) indescribable; (v) permanent and indescribable; (vi) impermanent and indescribable; (vii) both permanent and impermanent as also indescribable.

This religion with its great emphasis on asceticism and rigorism imposed on monks and nuns has maintained its existence in India up to the present day. Its lay followers however are limited and still observe many hard and fast rules of self-discipline.

(iv) Sañjaya Belaṭṭhiputta did not give out any definite views about the ultimates. He is generally described as a sceptic unwilling to give any definite answer to the ultimate problems, which were, according to him, were indeterminable, a view not incompatible with Buddha's declaration that the problems: whether the soul is identical with body or nor, whether an emancipated being exists after death or not, and so forth are also indeterminable (*avyākata*) and should be left aside. Sañjaya happened to be the teacher of Sāriputra and Moggallāna who joined the Buddhist order along with the other disciples of the teacher and who were much impressed by Buddha's theory of causation, which explained that the beings of the world were in a ceaseless state of flux governed by certain causes and conditions.

(v) Ajita Kesakambalin was a materialist. He denies an after-life and so according to him there is no need of earning merits by good deeds, sacrifices or service to parents. There is no spiritual advancement or perfection in knowledge likewise. There is no demerit if one commits evil deeds. A being is composed of five elements: earth, water, air, fire and space (*ākāsa*). After death each of these returns to the corresponding mass of great elements while the senses (*indriyas*) pass into space. A person's earthly existence ends in the funeral pyre. Nothing survives after death (*bhaṣmībhūtasya dehasya punarāgamanaṃ kutaḥ*).

This doctrine of Ajita is clearly a restatement of the Lokāyata or Bārhaspatya school of thought. Dhīṣaṇa, to whom is attributed this type of doctrine in the *Padma Purāṇa*, asserts that there is no God. The variegated world exists by itself. He admits only four elements and not the fifth *ākāśa*. The combination of the four elements produces consciousness (*caitanya*) as liquor is produced by the fermentation of rice and molasses. When everything ends in death, there is no sense in performing sacrifices or in seeking heaven. It was an anti-Vedic movement and established that a being should seek his own happiness by whatever means he can devise, and not perform acts which are supposed to bring fruits in the next life. It identifies soul with body, a doctrine which has been bitterly criticised by Buddha and classed as annihilationism (*ucchedavāda*); i.e., the doctrine that a being disappears for ever with the dissolution of the body.

(vi) Pakudha Kaccāyana was a pluralist and a semi-materialist. Like Ajita he holds that a being is composed of seven elements: earth, water, air, fire, pleasure (*sukha*), pain (*dukkha*) and soul (*jīva*). These seven elements are neither created nor moulded. They are barren and fixed as a rock or a stone-pillar and do not produce anything. They neither move nor hinder one another so as to cause pain or pleasure or indifference. Hence, there is no killer nor instigator of killing, no hearer nor preacher, no learner nor teacher. If a sword passes through the body of a being, it does not destroy it but only slips through the interspaces of the elements forming the body. It is a form of atomism without any parallel. It has been criticised by Buddha as a kind of eternalism (*sassatavāda*) and grouped with Ajita's teaching of annihilationism (*ucchedavāda*), i.e., everything ends with death.

Besides these six renowned teachers there was another class of religious men known as the Paribbājakas or Wanderers. These moved about all over the country either singly or in groups. There were provisions for their residence called *Paribbājakārāma* in important villages and towns. This shows that the Paribbājaka form of life was in vogue in ancient India in the 5th century B.C. or even earlier. The Paribbājakas could be either Brāhmanic or non-Brāhmanic. From their nature of discussions with Buddha it seems that they had no confirmed doctrinal views but not without predilections for either a Brāhmanic or a particular non-Brāhmanic system. The problems broached by them with Buddha related to soul, *karman*, efficacy of ascetic practices, elimination of mental impurities, attainment of perfect knowledge, soundness of views of Nigaṇṭha Nāṭaputta and so forth. A number of Paribbājakas were impressed by Buddha's teachings and became lay-devotees and a few became full-fledged monks. The Paribbājakas were generally in quest of the Truth and tried to find out what was the best teaching which of course they did not necessarily accept. They may be regarded as students of religion and philosophy with a receptive mind, and some of them ultimately joined a particular religious order or reverted to a householder's life. From the discourses specially delivered to them, as embodied in the *Nikāyas*, it appears that they formed an important part of the religious and philosophical movement of ancient India. It is also evident that in those days change of doctrinal views was the rule of the day and there was no slur on a person even if he changed his religious affiliation. Had it not been so, Buddha could not have formed his band of disciples, whom he recruited largely from the Brāhmanic and Śreṣṭhī families and *paribbājakas*.

The Paribbājakas or the Saṅghas or Gaṇas of the six heretical teachers formed a very small section of the religieux of ancient India. In spite of Buddha's silence about the *Upaniṣads* it cannot but be taken for granted that the Upaniṣadic thinkers held the torch of religion, philosophy and culture in pre-Buddha days. There are at least ten Upaniṣads, viz., *Bṛhadāraṇyaka* and *Chāndogya, Aitareya* and *Taittirīya Īśa, Kena* and *Kaṭha, Praśna, Muṇḍaka* and *Māṇḍukya,* which are attributed to a date much earlier than Buddha's time. These are mostly compilations of dialogues and monologues of Brāhmanic seers and not systematic expositions of a particular school of thought. In some of them there are traces of *Sāṃkhya*, *Yoga* and *Mīmāṃsā* school of thought but the central theme of most of them is the exposition of the monistic philosophy, well known as *Vedānta*, developed with great subtlety in the two principal Upaniṣads, *Bṛhadāraṇyaka and Chāndogya.* The oneness of Brahman or the Reality, and the world as a diversified superimposition on the Reality are the keynotes of this philosophy.

The Sāṅkhya school of philosophy, the origin of which is traced in the *Kaṭha* and *Śvetāśvatara* Upaniṣads[1] took modified Vedāntic view. It explains that the appearance of worldly objects is due to ignorance (*avidyā*) of the separateness of the two reals, *Puruṣa* and *Prakṛti*. It however held that the appearance of phenomenal world is not wholly baseless or a delusion as the primeval cause (*prakṛti*) does undergo a change (*pariṇāmī*) and the changed object is substantially the *prakṛti*, the change being confined to characteristics (*nimitta*) only of the basic cause (*upādāna*). For this reason it is called '*satkāryavāda*' or the view that cause exists in its effect. The untenability of the

1. *Kaṭha*, I, 3. 10-11; *Śvetāśvatara*, V, 7.8.12; IV, 5.1.3.

Sāṅkhya view, as argued by the Buddhists, lies in the fact that it admits two reals with different characteristics, which are not logical, viz., one, *Puruṣa*, as unchangeable and the other *Prakṛti* as changeable (*pariṇāmī*). The later being real and eternally existing (*nitya*) it is further led to the fallacy that an eternal entity undergoes change. According to the Sāṅkhya view, the evolution of the *Prakṛti* takes place thus: Out of *Prakṛti* issues *Mahān* or its cosmic aspect or *Buddhi* or physical aspect. It is the unindividuated cosmic intellect which gives rise to *Ahaṃkāra* (egoism) or individuated intellect, which is also a substance, an active agent. In its *sāttvika* (pure) aspect it leads to the origin of *Manas* (mind), the function of which is determinate perception; *Ahaṃkāra* also gives rise to five subtle essences *Tanmātra*, which in their turn evolve into five gross elements: earth, water, fire, air and ether. Out of these originate the five sense-organs: eyes, ears, nose, tongue and body as also the five physical organs: voice, feet, hands anus and generating organ. The process of evolution as shown in the *Buddhacarita*[1] is a little different. It is as follows: The primal or ultimate cause (*Prakṛti*) and its evolutes (*vikāra*) constitute a being (*sattva*) with the concomitants: birth , old age, disease and death. The primal cause manifests itself in five great elements (*pañcabhūta*) in their minutest states (*tanmātra*), egoism (*ahaṃkāra*) and unindividuated (*avyakta*) cosmic intellect (*buddhi* or *mahān*). Their evolutes are in the sense-organs and their objects, the hands and feet, the voice, the organs of generation and excrertion and also the mind. There is the soul (*ātman*) which is conscious of the body. This consciousness or awareness is intellection, which was possessed by saints like Kapila. It is the absence of intellection that produced the world of beings. Those who develop individuation (*vyakta*) and are unable to go beyond the notion of I-ness get entangled in worldly joys and sufferings while those who discard the notion of I-ness and maintain an unindividuated mind go beyond the world of pain and pleasures. This type of Sāṅkhya teachings, according to the testimony of Aśvaghoṣa's *Buddhacarita*, was imparted to Prince Siddhārtha by his spiritual teachers, Ārāḍa Kālāma and Rudraka Rāmaputra and might have some influence on his mind in his formulation of the law of causation (*paṭiccasamuppāda*).

The Yoga philosophy is similar to that of Sāṅkhya. It has only added the existence of the God. It developed the meditational practices which perhaps were well known to the Upaniṣadic seers. There is much in common between the Yoga and the Buddhist systems of meditation including the meditational terms.

---

1. *Buddhacarita*, Ch. XII.

The Mīmāṃsakas also admit the reality of the world. According to them the souls are eternal, permanent as also the material elements composing the universe. Their universe consists (a) of living bodies, in which the soul reaps the *karmaic* effects (*bhogāyatana*), (b) of sense-organs (*indriya-bhoga-sādhana*) and (c) of sense-objects (*bhoga-viṣaya*).

The Nyāya-Vaiśeṣikas go a step further and in place of two reals of the Sāṅkhya admit six categories of reality, viz., substance (*dravya*), quality (*guṇa*), motion (*karman*), universality (*sāmānya*), particularity (*viśeṣa*) and inherence (*samavāya*). Their *dravya* consists of the four eternal constituents: space (*ākāsā*), time (*kāla*), mind (*manas*) and soul (*ātman*). Their viewpoints can also be traced in the Upaniṣads. They are opposed to mere subjectivity of the Vedāntists.

Prince Siddhārtha, educated as he was and engaged in search of the truth, must have been acquainted with most of the non-Buddhistic doctrines stated above. He no doubt denied the existence of a permanent soul but he accepted the theory of *karman* and rebirth, which, of course, he had to interpret in a way suited to his non-soul doctrine.

The doctrine of impermanence (*anityatā*) of the phenomenal world must have appealed to him most and led him to give up his princely life and luxuries. He recognised at the same time that the only means to get out of the clutches of *anityatā* was spiritual exercises as a recluse. The principle of retirement from worldly joys and pleasures is denoted as pessimism though strictly speaking the underlying force for retirement is not so much disgust with the world as the attainment of *nityatā* (eternality)—an ineffable state surpassing the highest conceivable form of worldly existence, which is unalterably associated with birth, old age, disease and death, the four factors, which according to the Buddhist traditions filled the mind of Prince Siddhārtha with consternation not so much for himself as for the humanity in general. The impetus to the Prince's retirement came from human misery and so the Prince directed his mind to evolve a path that might put an end to that misery and not so much for the unfolding of the eternal Truth, on which was concentrated the attention of the Upaniṣadic seers. But there can be no enunciation of the path unless the Truth is known and so the Prince went through a long course of spiritual exercises and succeeded ultimately in visualizing the Truth—the truth of oneness which of course was different from the oneness of *Jīvātman* and *Paramātman*. It is not known if the Upaniṣadic teachers had formulated any code of duties or chalked out a course for the guidance of their followers; perhaps it was kept secret and handed down esoterically from teacher to disciple. Buddha made no secret of the path of achieving the goal and so he laid bare his scheme of life before one and all who approached him with the sincere desire of exerting to overcome the worldly sufferings. His ethical teachings and his monastic discipline marked a complete departure from the old ways of attaining perfection in knowledge.

Dukkha (Duḥkha): Misery of phenomenal existence had already got hold of the minds of the Upaniṣadic thinkers. In the *Chāndogya* (vii. 1.3) it is stated that a wise man, the knower of self, goes beyond the sea of misery (*tarati śokam ātmavit*) while in a late text like the *Vedāntasāra* (31) appears the statement that a person oppressed by death and rebirth, and worldly fire should approach for the true knowledge a learned teacher conversant with Brahman, the Truth. The Sāṅkhya schoolmen spoke of the misery of human existence and analysed it under three heads, viz., internal (*ādhyātmika*) due to physical disorder and mental agitation, external (*ādhibhautika*) due to injuries caused by men and beasts or by any outside agency, and supernormal (*ādhidaivika*) due to supernatural factors, or the great elements (*mahābhūtas*). Thus it is evident that the pessimistic view of life was already in the air and Buddha only picked it up and made it a starting point of his teachings. Buddha told his monks to realise that the tears shed by a being in his innumerable existences if accumulated would exceed the water of a sea (*Saṃyutta Nikāya*, II, pp. 178f). In Pali texts,[1] human misery has been sub-divided in a different manner thus: mental and/or physical pain (*dukkha-dukkhatā*), pleasure turning into pain (*vipariṇāma-dukkhatā*) and pain which arises and disappears due to change (Saṅkhāra-dukkhatā). Of the four truths (*cattāri ariyasaccāni*) the first truth to be realised by the wise is "*dukkha*" pain or suffering concomitant to phenomenal existence. Its popular exposition is the non-fulfilment of one's desire causing resentment or disappointment, separation from the dear ones or association with the undesired causing mental pain. This *dukkha* is suffered by the commoners and not by the elect (*ariya*), and so, strictly speaking, such *dukkha* is not *ariyasacca*. *Dukkha* in the eyes of an advanced monk (*ariya*) is the possession of one's body of five constituents (*upādāna-khandhas*), of wealth and property, because of the fact that one's earthly possessions are evanescent and subject to decay (*vayadhammā*), to impermanence (*aniccatā*). Unless and until this nature of *dukkha* is fully comprehended by a monk, the next three truths, viz., desire as the source of *dukkha*, end of desire as the

1. *Visuddhimagga*, p. 499; *Mādhyamikavṛtti*, p. 475 n.

termination of *dukkha* and eighthfold path as leading to the end of *dukkha* remain incomprehensible to him. Realisation of *dukkha* therefore forms the first step in the Buddhist code of spiritual practices and its interpretation is more comprehensive than that of the earlier systems. In almost every school of Indian thought the woes and worries of a living being due to unfulfilled desires are spoken of and there are also suggestions about the means of avoiding the same.[1] The Buddhists however have worked out the problem of *dukkha* in as thorough a manner as possible.

Aniccatā (Anityatā): There can be no two opinions about the fact that the pessimistic view of life (*dukkha*) is based on impermanence or rather evanescence (*aniccatā*) of phenomenal objects. Buddha repeatedly reminded his disciples of this fact by saying '*aniccā vata saṅkhārā uppādavayadhammino*' (impermanent are the composites which are subject to origin and decay). Except *Nibbāna* and *Ākāsa* there is nothing unconstituted in this world. Even the infinitesmal atoms of earth, water, air and fire (i.e. *rūpa*) contain all the four elements and the four qualities: colour (*vaṇṇa*), smell (*gandha*), taste (*rasa*) and nutritive essence (*ojā*) which cannot be separated, and as such each of the material elements as distinct objects exists in thought only so are the other *khandhas*, viz., feeling (*vedanā*), perception (*saññā*), impression (*saṅkhārā*) and knowledge derived through the senses (*viññāṇa*). A being therefore is a conceptual entity and has no real existence. The Buddhist point of view differs substantially from that of the Nyāya-Vaiśeṣikas, according to whom, there are six irreducible categories of reality. The Jaina school of thought goes a step further and asserts that matter (*pudgala*) is constituted of atoms (*paramāṇu*) which are real and eternal while its action (*karma*) is also material (*paudgalika*). The Sarvāstivādins (or the Vaibhāṣikas or the Ābhidhammikas) advocated, according to some scholars, 'radical pluralism erected on the denial of substance (soul) and the acceptance of discreet momentary entities' and 'change as the replacement of one entity by another, it is the cessation of one and emergence of another. The combination (of constituents) is not real over and above the constituents. The components are real (*vastusat*), the combination is appearance (*prajñapti-sat*).' The true import of the words '*sarvam asti*' of the Sarvāstivādins is something different from what has been said above. It is a fact that the Sarvāstivādins offer a list of seventy two *dharmas* under the heads: (i) Matter (*Rūpa*)—11; (ii) Mind (*Citta*)—1; Mental states (*Caitasikas*)—46; and Non-mentals (*Citta-viprayuktas*)—

---

1. Cf. Gauḍapāda: *Āgamaśāstra*, III. 43: दुःखं सर्वमनुस्मृत्य कामभोगान् निवर्तयेत् ।

14. By "all exist" (*sarvam asti*) the Sarvāstivādins mean existence of concepts of past, present and future (*trikālasat*) and not the eternal existence of phenomenal objects or of their minutest elements, which also are impermanent but not as false as a mirage or objects seen in a dream. It is through the realisation of their impermanence and making one's mind completely free from the notion of existence of phenomenal objects that an adept can attain emancipation. Hence, the Sarvāstivādins do not really mean that all objects are real and exist eternally.

Khaṇikatta (Kṣaṇikatva): The Buddhists qualify impermanence (*anityatā*) with momentariness (*kṣaṇika*), i.e., the phenomenal objects are subject to change every moment, and within one moment take place origin (*utpatti*), duration (*sthiti*) and decay (*vināśa*). As against this contention of the Buddhists, it is argued that momentariness cannot be directly perceived and further it leads to the admission of the absence of any cause (*ahetukatva*) for the origin of the second moment, because the first momentary existence disappears then and there and cannot be effective in producing the second momentary state.[1] The counter-argument of the Buddhists is that momentariness cannot, it is true, be established by direct perception but is should be noted that momentariness is the characteristic nature (*svabhāva*) of effectiveness (*artahkriyākāritva*). By momentary cessation of an object is meant the absence of immediately preceding state (*svādhikaraṇa-samaya-prāgabhāva*). If momentariness as explained above be not admitted, then an object would remain the same for more than one moment, and the object that produces an effect in the present would also produce the same effect in the past and future and would be subject to the fallacy that there could not be an accomplished effect (*kṛta-kāritā*) of an object, in other words, the purpose of an object would not be served.[2] Hence the Buddhists rightly contend that an object is momentary and produces its effect then and there and not in the past or future. It may be argued that an object retains its potentiality which will be effective in future but this argument is also fallacious because of the fact that two opposite characteristics, viz., presentness and pastness, or presentness and futurity cannot exist together. Therefore it should be admitted that the momentariness of an object can only establish the fulfilment of a purpose and this is not possible if an

1. Cf. *Brahmasūtra*, II. 2.20: उत्तरोत्पादे च पूर्वं निरोधात्।

2. Cf. Bertrand Russell, *Mysticism and Logic*, p. 185: Cause cannot have a duration......the cause after existing placidly for some time should suddenly explode into effect......is illogical. Again, cause cannot be static, no such cause is to be found in nature.

object remains unchanged for more than one moment. The subtlety of the Buddhist interpretation of *kṣaṇika* is rather unique and may be regarded as a contribution to Indian thought. In short, it explains fully the dynamism of worldly objects or ceaseless change that takes place in worldly objects, in nature.

Paṭiccasamuppāda (Pratītyasamutpāda): The question that arises next is whether this ceaseless change is accidental or predestined or is effected by certain causes (*hetu*) and conditions (*pratyaya*). The Buddhists reject the first two views and accept the last and offer their formula of the law of causation. *Paṭiccasamuppāda*, popularly known as *Dharmacakra* or the ceaseless cycles of existences of a being. The word '*samutpāda*" created a confusion in the minds of some who took the word in its literal sense and attempted to interpret the formula as Buddha's conception of the origin of the world of beings. Buddhaghosa the great Pali commentator of the 4th century A.D. pointed out in his *Visuddhimagga* that the word *samutpāda* (origin) was used to counteract the false notion of nihilism (*asat-dṛṣṭi*) while the other word *pratītya* (dependent) as an antidote to the notion of real existence of worldly object (*satdṛṣṭi*). Buddha repeatedly asserted that his interpretation of the Truth kept clear of the two extreme views of existence (*sat / asti*) and non-existence (*asat / nāsti*) of worldly objects, of eternalism (*śāśvata*) and annihilationism (*uccheda*), of their limitedness (*antavān*) and unlimitedness (*anantavān*). This is described as the middle path (*majjhimā paṭipadā*)[1] developed later by Nāgārjuna as *Mādhyamika* or *Śūnyatā* philosophy, and by Asaṅga as Yogācāra or *Vijñaptimātratā*.

In the Abhidhamma texts like the *Paṭṭhāna* appears an exhaustive, study of the causes, (*hetu*) and conditions (*paccaya*). The formula of causation has been explained both externally in connection with material objects and internally in relation to living beings. The origin of an earthen pot depends on several causes viz., clay, water fire, potter, wheel and so forth, while that of a sprout on seed, water, gardener, etc. The origin of a being is due to non-realisation of the Truth (*avidyā*), thirst (*tṛṣṇā*), deeds (*karma*) which give a shape to its constituents, organs of sense, and mind. The *Paṭṭhāna* states that there are in all twentyfour kinds of causes, more than one of which are applicable to the origin of an object or a being. Some of these causes, again, mean invariable sequences. In fact, the complete cessation of

1. There is the other popular exposition that Buddha prescribed a middle path of spiritual culture, which described a life of ease as also a life of extreme asceticism. The life of a monk, as chalked out by his Teacher, was one approved by him as a general rule. exception however being made in the case of those who were bent upon asceticism and took up the *Dhūtaṅga* practices.

the previous momentary state cannot produce the succeeding one, and again, there is nothing to pass from the former to the latter. In that case, the law of causation really means only the Law of invariable sequence which is observed in nature. The *Laṅkāvatāra-sūtra* (p. 103) denies causal origin and speaks of sequence of objects, but it also discusses six kinds[1] of causes which are quite different from those of the *Paṭṭhāna*. Nāgārjuna in his *Mādhyamakakārikā* refers to four[2] out of the twentyfour causes mentioned in the *Paṭṭhāna*.

The Mādhyamikas and the Yogācāras like the Vedāntists do not admit the existence of the phenomenal world and so they relegate the law of causation to conventional truths (*saṃvṛtisatya*) and utilise it to establish the relative appearance of objects, e.g., long and short, red and black are mere conventional terms used relatively and have no existence whatsoever. Nāgārjuna remarks that as objects that have origination do not exist and so its existence cannot be established as uncaused, or as caused by itself, or by non-self, or by both self and non-self.[3] The *Laṅkāvatara* states that the ignorant only conceive of objects as originating out of causes and conditions, and for not knowing the true law takes repeated births in the three worlds.[4] In the *Brahmasūtra* there is the statement that there can be no origination of an ever existing substance.[5] Thus, there is complete unanimity between the Mahāyānists and the Vedāntists about the ever existent Real as causeless and conditionless.

The question then arises, why the Mahāyānists take the law of causation into their consideration. They state that this law has two-fold purpose, first to point out the relative appearance of phenomenals objects and secondly to establish by inference that the Real has nothing to do with cause and condition (*apratītyasamutpanna*). This law is needed to initiate the unliberated into the Truth of non-existence of the phenomenal world and thereby into the uncaused Truth. Both the Hīnayāna and Mahāyāna texts state that one, who comprehend the law of causation, realises the Truth and visualises the Buddha.[6] The law of

1. *Laṅkāvatāra*, p. 83: भविष्यत्हेतु; सम्बन्धहेतु; लक्षणहेतु; कारणहेतु; व्यञ्जनहेतु; उपेक्षाहेतु।
2. *Madhyamakakārikā*, I, 2.
3. *Madhyamakārikā*, I, 7; XXI. 13; XXIII. 20:
न स्वतो नापि परतो न द्वाभ्यां नाप्यहेतुतः ।
उत्पन्ना जातु विद्यन्ते भावाः क्वचन केचन ॥
cf. *Gauḍapāda*, IV. 22: खतो वा परतो वापि न किञ्चिद्वस्तु जायते।
सदसत् सदसद् वापि न किञ्चिद्वस्तु जायते ॥
4. *Laṅkāvatāra*, p. 105-6.
5. *Brahmasūtra*, II. 3.9: असम्भवस्तु सतोऽनुपपत्तेः ।
6. यः प्रतीत्यसमुत्पादं पश्यति स धर्मं पश्यति। यो धर्मं पश्यति स बुद्धं पश्यति।
See *Aspects of Mahāyāna Buddhism*, p. 51.

causation leads to the realisation of the fact that the Reality remains undisturbed by origin and decay and is beyond any description[1] and so the law is called fondly by Candrakīrti as the mother of Buddhas of ten powers.[2]

Slightly different is the line of reasoning adopted by the Hīnayānists for showing that the law of causation leads to the realisation of the Truth. They have developed a chain of illustrative terms such as ignorance (*avidyā*) of past life causing certain impressions (*saṃskāra*), which in turn produce consciousness that takes rebirth (*pratisandhi-vijñāna*). It is followed by the present life consisting of the five constituents (*nāma-rūpa*), six sense-organs and their objects (*ṣaḍāyatana*), contact (*sparśa*), feeling (*vedanā*), thirst (*tṛṣṇā*), strong attachment (*upādāna*) and lastly, clinging for rebirth (*bhava*). After this, takes place another existence (*jāti*) which ends ultimately in old age and death.[3]

Lest this formula of twelve terms creates the impression that it represents the Buddhist view of the tree of life similar to that of Sāṅkhya, Buddhaghosa pointed out in his *Visuddhimagga* (p. 525) that according to the Sāṅkhya school, the first term *Prakṛti* is uncaused and is the primeval source of the tree of life whereas *Avidyā* is not necessarily the first term in the Buddhist law of causation and also it is not uncaused and hence it cannot be the primeval source. The chain of terms may commence at any link, say thirst or even birth. *Avidyā* has for its cause thirst or wrong views, etc. The terms illustrate only some invariable sequence.

Avidyā (Ajñāna): Like the Buddhists, Śaṅkara also states that ignorance (*avidyā*) cannot be the primeval cause but he argues against the Buddhist contention that *avidyā* cannot be the cause of mental impressions (*saṃskāra*) because, logically, negation or absence of something cannot be a productive cause. In reply the Buddhists state that *avidyā* is not a mere negation but is something positive—it is the misguided knowledge due to wrong views (*mithyā-darśana*).[4] It is impure and acts as a hindrance to knowledge. It is produced by attachment, hatred and delusion (*rāga, dveṣa, moha*) and belief in a self (*satkāyadṛṣṭi*) leading to erroneous apprehensions (*viparyāsa*) e.g., evil as good, unhappiness as happiness, impurity as purity, non-soul as soul and so forth. It is due to incorrect mental application (*avoniso*

1. *Madhyamakakārikā*, VII, 16: सीत्य यद्यद्भवति तत्तत् शान्तं स्वभावतः ।
2. *Ibid*. सकलदशबलजननीं प्रतीत्यसमुत्पादमातरम् ।
3. Cf. *Laṅkāvatāra*, p. 103.
4. *Abhidharmakośa*, III, 29.

manasikāro). It means a clouded and deluded mind.[1] Śaṅkara in his comment on Brahmasūtra (I. 1) points out that *avidyā* means the apprehension of certain qualities superimposed on the attributeless Reality, the Pure Soul. The opponents argue that superimposition can take place only upon an object directly perceived and not on an imperceptible pure self. Śaṅkara in reply points out that sky (*ākāśa*) has no objective existence still the unenlightened men speak of the sky as blue or compare it with cauldron upturned and so forth. He argues further that though the pure self is attributeless still it serves as the basis of the notion of I-ness, hence it is not as no-existent as the sky. The knowledge derived through superimposition on an object and its consequent misapprehension, e.g., nacre as silver, rope as snake, is known as Nescience (*Avidyā*) in Vedānta. In his comments on *Brahmasūtra* (II. 1. 14) Śaṅkara offers another exposition of *Avidyā*. He writes that name and form (*nāma-rūpa*) are manifestations of ignorance (*avidyā*) and as such they are indescribable as existing or non-existing and are included in Īśvara or the God, the creator and are known as Cosmic Nescience (*Māya*), Energy (*Śakti*). Īśvara is different from *nāma-rūpa* but is its upholder or is circumscribed by *nāmarūpa*, i.e., *avidyā* is similar to space in an earthen jar. He is therefore the moulder of a conscious being. From the standpoint of *Avidyā*, Īśvara is supreme, omniportent and oniscient, and from the highest standpoint He is identical with Brahman, the ultimate Truth. In his subtlest form He is Īśvara, the omniscient and in His grossest form the manifested world in its infinite diversity.

The last Vedāntists have given more positive conception of nescience (*Ajñāna=Avidyā*), saying that it is composed of three qualities : purity (*sattvas*), activity (*rajas*) and impurity (*tamas*), which in turn produce the five subtle elements and so forth as found in the Sāṅkhya system. The *Ajñāna* of the Vedāntists is said to be neither existing nor non-existing because though it does not exist in reality, it has an apparent existence which is indescribable but causes delusion. The *Laṅkāvatāra* (p. 106) uses the term *Bhrānti* in place of Vedāntic '*Ajñāna*' and expatiates on it saying that the glow of a circling fire (*alātacakra*) is seen by the wise.[2] It is devoid of both existence and non-existence but at the same time it is in a sense eternal (*bhāntiḥ śāśvatā*). It continues to exist so long as one's knowledge functions but it ceases when one puts at rest all his thought constructions.[3] In other words, the *Laṅkāvatāra* supports the Vedāntic conception of *Ajñāna*.

---

1. See *Mādhyamikavṛtti*, p. 452 quoting *Pratītyasamutpādasūtra*.
2. भ्रान्तिरार्याणामपि ख्यायतेऽविपर्यासत: । Cf. *Laṅkāvatāra*, p. 298.
3. *Laṅkāvatāra*, p. 295:

   सर्वप्रपञ्चोपशमात् भ्रान्तो नाभिप्रवर्तते ।
   प्रज्ञा यावद् विकल्पन्ते भ्रान्तिस्तावत् प्रवर्तते ॥

Kamma (Karman): The Buddhists fully recognise the influence of *Karman* and its effects on a being's repeated existences. Of the twelve terms or links in the chain of causation, the second and the tenth, i.e. mental impressions (*saṃskāra*) and desire for re-existence (*bhava*) are regarded as resultants of acts of one's past life respectively.[1] The fact that a being is born with name and form, i.e., mental and material constituents, implies that in its previous existence it had mental obsessions due to lack of true knowledge (*avidyā*) and collected the so-called merits and demerits and developed certain mental dispositions (*saṃskāras*) which produced the consciousness for rebirth (*pratisandhi-vijñāna*), which in its turn brought about its re-existence and gave it a name and form. After re-existence the being in due course becomes subject to the roots of evils, viz., attachment, hatred and delusion[2] and reaches the end of its life with a desire (*bhava*) for another existence. And so it is said in the *Mahāvastu*[3] that the first and the eighth links, nescience and thirst, are the roots of *Karma* leading to rebirth. In Buddhist texts it is repeatedly stated that a being is subject to his deeds, inherits the good or bad effects, and has it origin out of his own past deeds.[4] It is on account of an individual's deeds that one becomes a cultivator, an artist or a king.[5] Deeds are divided into three categories thus: those which produce fruit (i) in this life (*diṭṭhadhammavedanīya*); (ii) in the next life (*uppajjavedanīya*); (iii) in a future life (*aparāpariyavedanīya*). Some of the *Avadānas* and *Jātakas*, particularly the *Vimā-navatthu* and *Petavatthu* and *Mahākarmavibbaṅga*[6] illustrate through stories the effects of good and evil deeds.

It is by the elimination of deeds (*kamma*) that a person attains full emancipation.[7] Self-exertion is the only means of Nirvāṇa, said Buddha and by self-exertion he meant the performance of certain deeds, spiritual or otherwise. Hence the greatest emphasis was laid on one's

---

1. *Kośa*, III, 24.
2. *Nettippakaraṇa*, 13; *Aṅguttara*, V, p. 262: कम्मनिदानानि—लोभदोसमोह।
3. III, p. 65.
4. *Suttanipāta*, 654: कम्मणा वत्तति लोको कम्मणा वत्तति पजा। *Majjhima*, III, p. 203; *Aṅguttara*, III, pp. 72, 186; V. pp. 81, 288: कमस्मका सत्ता कम्म-दायादा कम्मयोनी कम्मबन्धु... यं कम्मं करोन्ति कल्याणं वा पापकं वा तस्स दायादा भवन्ति।
5. *Suttanipāta*, 653: कस्सको कम्मणा हेति सिप्पिको होति कम्मणा—राजापि होति कम्मणा।
6. Edited by S. Lévi, Paris, 1942.
7. *Saṃyutta*, I, p. 134: सब्बकम्मक्खयं पत्तो विमुत्तो उपधिसंखये। Cf. *Aṅguttara*, V, p. 262.

acts and exertion and non-dependence on a superior power or on any ritual and ceremony. *Kamma* is inexorable and can only he counteracted by proper exertions as Aṅgulimāla got rid of his sins of indiscriminate killing by his spiritual exercises (*sādhanā*). Again, Buddha himself could not escape the effects of his past deeds as is illustrated by the event of his being wounded by a stone chip of a missile thrown by Devadatta. Śaṅkara also admits that man is the architect of his destiny and that his *karma*, past and present, must produce fruits which are to be exhausted by enjoyment or suffering. According to the Vedāntists[1] however, *karma* connotes not only meritorious and demeritorious deeds but also fulfilment of duties prescribed for a particular caste (*varṇa*) and stage of life (āśrama), as well as performance of sacrifices and expiatory ceremonies (*prāyaścitta*). Liberation is to be attained, according to Rāmānuja, not only by true knowledge (*jñāna*) but also by *karma*, by which, he meant, rituals prescribed in the *śāstras*. It is also enjoined in the Vedāntic texts that *karma* should be free from any desire for reward (*niṣkāma*) and such *karma* can destroy the accumulated effects of one's past life. *karma* is divided into three categories: (i) deed already commenced (*prārabdha*), (ii) deed already accumulated (*sañcita*), and (iii) deed that is being accumulated (*sañciyamāna*). Of these three, the first must take its own course while the second can be destroyed, and the third prevented by acquisition of true knowledge.

There is a general agreement between the Vedāntic and the Buddhist view of *karman* and its elimination, except that the former relies partially on rituals and ceremonies for neutralizing *karmaic* effects—a view wholly unacceptable to the Buddhists.

Soul and Rebirth: As the Buddhists do not admit the existence of a permanent self, they replace the word "transmigration" by "rebirth".

The conception of ātman in the Upaniṣads has given rise to two views: (i) that the self is similar to a spark issuing out of a mass of fire; and (ii) that the self is similar to space within an earthen jar. Śaṅkara gives preference to the second view and describes it as eternal, unchanging, undecaying, immaculate.[2] It is not gross, not eyes, not life-force, not mind, not doer, it is just pure intelligence.[3] It pervades the whole body though it is infinitesmally small. At death it passes out of the eyes, or skull or some other portion of the body.

The living self limited by the adjuncts of the body of an individual, his sense-organs, mind, intelligence and notion of I-ness

1. *Brahmasūtra*, III. 1. 8.
2. नित्यशुद्धबुद्धमुक्तसत्यस्वभावं प्रत्यक्चैतन्यमेवात्मतत्त्वमिति।
3. प्रत्यगस्थूलो अचक्षुरप्राणः अमना अकर्ता चैतन्यं चिन्मात्रं सत्।... नित्यचैतन्योऽयमात्मा।

becomes an empirical self, perceiving pleasant and unpleasant feelings. It is unaware of its true nature and is in the grip of nescience; its power and knowledge become limited and it becomes an agent, an enjoyer of acts, by which it accumulates merits and demerits.

The Buddhists contend that in the ultimate analysis of the constituents of a being there is no trace of a permanent soul, which according to the Vedāntists, is unconstituted (*asaṃskṛta*). They argue that the unconstituted, immaculate and permanent substance has nothing to do with the constituted (*saṃskṛta*), and logically also, two objects, having opposite characteristics, can never exist together as light and darkness. Hence they uphold the doctrine of the non-existence of a real self. They point out that the five constituents forming a being (i.e. *upādāna-skandhas*) as distinguished from the mass of elements (*skandharāśi*) give rise to the wrong notion of I-ness or *satkāyadṛṣṭi*. They do not also accept the position taken by the Sammitīya Buddhists that the five constituents on combination produce a sixth constituent called *Pudgala* which lasts as long as the *upādāna-skandhas* continue. They deny the existence of empirical self of the Vedāntists or of *Pudgala* of the Sammitīyas. Such denial leads to the question as to how the Buddhists explain the transference of *karmaic* effects of an individual from one existence to another.

The Vedāntists hold the view that the empirical self serves as the transmitter of *karmaic* effects. It continues after the death of a living being and transmigrates like a caterpillar from one existence to another. It does not give up the old body till it obtains a foothold in another body.[1] In his comments on *Brahmasūtra* (III. 1.1) Śaṅkara states that the living being at the time of his death dreams of his future existence and grows an attachment for it, and so the empirical self extends its creative effort; it is a continuation or extension (*dīrghikaraṇa*)and not exactly similar to the movement of a caterpillar. The empirical self carries with it the subtle body (*sūkṣma-śarīra=liṅga-deha*) composed of three vestures or sheaths (*koṣa*)[2] This subtle body carries with it all the merits and demerits accumulated in past existences as also nescience (*avidyā*) along with the impressions left by past experiences (*pūrvaprajñā janmāntarīya saṃskārāḥ*), leaving behind all material elements, gross or subtle. This subtle body remains along with the empirical self till the attainment of liberation.

---

1. *Bṛhadāraṇyaka*, IV, 4. 3.
2. (i) *Vijñānamaya*=consciousness as an active agent.
   (ii) *Manomaya*= will as instumental.
   (iii) *Prāṇamaya*= vital breath or physical organism as energy.

Regarding the transference of *karmaic* effects, the Buddhist view is wholly different from that of the Vedānta. The Buddhists take their stand on their doctrine of momentariness, and explain that the mental and material constituents (*nāmarūpa*) of a being undergo change, in other words, birth and death, cessation and re-appearance, decay and origination, occur at every moment, which has not even an infinitesmal duration. These are as dynamic as nature and are never static even for a moment. Hence the *karmaic* effects are transmitted every moment. At the time of death the *nāmarūpa* obtains the subtlest form modified by the impressions of past life and develops a will for re-existence (*pratisandhivijñāna*) which in turn gives rise in the next existence to the nascent mental state (*bhavaṅga-citta*) similar to the Yogācāra conception of *ālayavijñāna* or consciousness-receptacle. This *bhavaṅga-citta* comes out of the womb or the egg-shell and develops the nascent sense-organs. Hence, according to the Buddhists, there is rebirth and not transmigration and the reborn *nāmarūpa* carries with them all the *karmaic* effects of past life.

They explain the continuity of a constituted being and its *karmaic* effects as a ceaseless flux like fire passing over dry grass in a field. In the day to day life of an individual, this ceaseless change is perceptible. An individual never remains identically the same from day to day i.e., from moment to moment. In this unending flux death and rebirth are mere sequence. The flux ceases only when the individual realises the Truth and arrests the flow of *karmaic* effects or mental dispositions (*saṃskāra*).

The Mahāyānists do not admit the existence of the phenomenal world of beings and objects, which according to the Yogācāra school, is the mental creation of a being out of desires conserved in a latent form from time immemorial (*anādikālavāsanā*). It is a conceptual world (*prapañca*) of its own—a world which has no more existence than objects seen in a dream.[1] Hence the Yogācārins do not speculate about *nāmarūpa* or their momentariness. The Mādhyamikas go a step further and do not even admit that the phenomenal world is an extension of mind. They simply state that the origin, continuity and decay of the phenomenal world has no more existence than delusion, dream or city of Gandharvas[2], or the two Moons seen by jaundiced eyes.

---

1. *Laṅkāvatāra*, p. 274:
मायास्वप्ननिभाभावगन्धर्वनगरोपमाः ।
मरीच्युदकचन्द्राभाः सविकल्पां विभावयेत् ॥
cf. *Gauḍapāda*, 31:
स्वप्नमाये यथा दृष्टे गन्धर्वनगरं यथा ।
तथा विश्वं इदं सृष्टं वेदान्तेषु विचक्षणैः ॥
2. *Madhyamakakārikā*, VII, 34:
यथा माया तथा स्वप्नो गन्धर्वनगरं यथा ।
तथोत्पादस्तथा स्थानं तथा भङ्ग उदाहृतम् ॥

The Buddhists regard that the Vedāntic conception of *Jīvātman* stands in the way of the removal of the notion of I-ness (*ahaṅkāra*) which is the only means for attaining liberation.

The Reality or the Highest Truth: The conception of *Brahman* or the Absolute varies slightly in the different Upaniṣads. Śaṅkara has tried to reconcile them to propound his own *Advayavāda* or Monism. On the basis of statements mainly of the *Chāndogya Upaniṣad,* he says that Brahman is ever existent and is identical with the universe. It is both infinitely large and infinitesmally small. It is one, real, eternal, non-dual and attributeless. In the *Bṛhadāraṇyaka-upaniṣad* (II. 3.1)[1] there are references to the two aspects of Brahman, as *Parabrahma* and *Aparabrahma*. The former represents the Brahman which is pure, subtle, immortal, undefined, attributeless (*nirupadhi*), transcendent, beyond description with the limited vocabularies of the world. The latter represents Brahman as superimposed by Nescience (*Ajñāna*) when it appears as gross, limited, mortal, determinate, and possessed of certain attributes (*sopadhi*). These two aspects are expressed in the words "*tat tvam asi*" (Thou art that)[2] and compared to a snake and its coils, the snake being the Real self and the coil the individuated self. A similar simile is unlimited space limited within a jar, the former being *Parabrahma* and the later *Aparabrahma*. In the *Bṛhadāraṇyaka*, *Chāndogya* and *Taittirīya Upaniṣads,* Brahman is described as the supreme bliss (*paramānanda*) and pure intelligence (*vijñana*). In the *Māṇḍukya-kārikā* Brahman is said to be indeterminate, inexpressible, eternally refulgent and trans-empirical, while in the *Brahmasūtra* (III. 2. 22) it is stated that Brahman can only be referred to by negations of known concepts (*neti neti*). The conceptions about Brahman in the various texts may be summed up thus: (i) *Brahman* is non-dual, inexpressible, trans-empirical and can be spoken of by negative concepts only; (ii) *Brahman* exists, it is pure intelligence and supreme bliss (*sat-cit-ānanda*) and (iv) Brahman may become limited, gross and endowed with attributes from the conventional but not from the highest standpoint.

The Monistic philosophy of Vedānta finds a better exposition in the Buddhist, specially Mahāyānic texts, in which the Truth is repeatedly referred to as non-dual and non-divisible (*advayam advaidhīkāram*). In the Pāli texts Nirvāṇa is described by negatives only as not born, not diseased, not dying, not happiness, not unhappiness and so forth. It is only in popular phraseology we come

1. द्वे वाव ब्रह्मणो—रूपे मूर्तं चैवामूर्तं च, मर्त्यं चामृतं च, स्थितं च यञ्च, सञ्च तञ्च।
2. *Chāndogya*, VI, 8. 7.

across its positive account as tranquil, i.e., undisturbed by origin and decay (*śāntam*), happy (*sukham*) and deathless (*amṛtapadam*). The Mahāyānists are emphatic in their statements that the Reality is attributeless (*sūnyatā*), oneness and sameness (*tathatā*), the end of phenomenal existences (*bhūtakoṭi*), the sum-total of all existences (*dharmadhātu*). It is ever existent, unoriginated and undecaying, and as such it is unchangeable and infinite and can in no circumstances become limited. Thus, it is apparent that the Buddhists were more accurate than the Vedāntists in their exposition of the Monistic philosophy.

The first fundamental difference between Vedānta and Buddhism regarding the highest Truth is the former's attempt to offer a positive description of the Reality as existent (*sat*), pure consciousness (*cit*) and supreme bliss (*ānanda*). Excepting the attribute '*sat*' and that also used very discreetly, the other attributes are not acceptable to the Buddhists, who contend that any positive description of the transcendental implies its opposites viz., non-existence, non-consciousness and non-bliss and that any characterization of the Reality is false representation (*prapañca*). The only approach to the highest Reality, they state, is possible by negation alone. The Mādhyamikas confine themselves therefore to the description of *nirvāṇa* in pure negative terms thus: Nirvāṇa is that which is neither to be escheward nor to be obtained; which is neither eternal nor subject to extinction; which is beyond origin and decay.[1] But they do not say that Nirvāṇa or Buddha or Tathāgata is non-existent. They hold that those who attempt to characterize the inexpressible undecaying one get bewildered by characterization and do not visualise the Tathagata.[2]

The second fundamental difference between Vedānta and Buddhism lies in the Vedantic conception of the Absolute becoming limited temporarily although superficially. The Buddhists are unrelenting in their arguments that the Real must remain the Real for ever and suffer no change even superficially and temporarily because it can no longer be called Absolute. They have used the terms unreal or conventional (*saṃvṛti*) and real or absolute (*paramārtha*) but they

---

1. *Madhyamakakārikā*, XXV. 3:
अप्रहीणमसंप्राप्तमनुच्छिन्नमशाश्वतम्।
अनिरुद्धमनुत्पन्नमेतन्निर्वाणमुच्यते॥
cf. *Gauḍapāda*, 32:
न निरोधो न चात्पत्तिर्ण बद्धो न च बाधकः।
न मुमुक्षुर्णवैमुक्त इत्येषा परमार्थता॥
2. *Madhyamakakārikā*, XXII, 15:
प्रपञ्चयन्ति ये बुद्धं प्रपञ्चातीतमव्ययम्।
ते प्रपञ्चाहताः सर्वे न पश्यन्ति तथागतम्॥

regard the former as non-existent as objects seen in a dream. They hold that there is no *via media* between the two, hence, they do not accept the conception of *Aparabrahma*. Even the temporary and superficial association of two with opposite characteristics, viz., purity and impurity, unlimitedness and limitedness, they state, is as illogical as the co-existence of blackness and whiteness, of hotness and coldness.

It is noteworthy that the Vedāntic conceptions of the identity of Brahman with the universe[1] is fully endorsed by the Mādhyamikas who state that there is not the slightest difference between *Nirvāṇa* and the phenomenal world (*Saṃsāra*).[2]

The Yogācārins hold a view midway between the Mādhyamikas and the Vedāntists in that they qualify the absolute as not only existent (*sat*) but also as pure mind or consciousness (*vijñānamātra*). They have also introduced the conception of *Tathāgatagarbha* which bears comparison with the Vedāntic conception of *Jīvātman*. In the *Laṅkāvatāra* (p. 77) it is stated that the Teacher spoke of the *Tathāgatagarbha*, which is pure and refulgent by inherent nature, dwells in every living being, encased in sense-organs and other constituents forming a being. It is like an invaluable jewel wrapped in a dirty cloth. It is ever existent, unchanging, tranquil and eternal. In the text, care however has been taken to point out that their conception of *Tathāgatagarbha* is not identical with the heretical doctrine of the soul-theorists, as they do not admit the existence of the Higher Soul (*Paramātman*).

1. *Chāndogya*, III. 14. 1: सर्वं खल्विदं ब्रह्म।
2. *Madhyamakakārikā*, XXV. 19.
न संसारस्य निर्वाणात्किं चिदस्ति विशेषणाम्।
न निर्वाणास्य संसारात्किं चिदस्ति विशेषणम्॥

Chapter - 12

Zen Buddhism and Bodhidharma

W. Pachow

In the Far East, there is no Buddhist influence so profound and penetrating as that of the Ch'an (Dhyāna) School, popularly known as Zen Buddhism. It has effected a change in the cultural life as well as the general outlook towards the method of attaining the Enlightenment. Not merely that; from the beginning of the 10th century A.D. this School has gained supremacy over all other Schools in China, so much so that the monks in the monasteries throughout the country claimed in one way or the other the patriarchal lineage of celebrated Dhyāna masters. This phenomenon may be ascribed to the fact that the Dhyāna School has been the life and soul of Buddhism for over a thousand years in China. As a result of its important position, voluminous works have been produced by various writers. Some of them are compositions containing the sayings of Dhyāna masters, mystical and paradoxical in nature, and others are historical records concerning the patriarchal genealogy, especially that of the various branches of the disciples of Hui Neng, the 6th Patriarch. However, all of them unanimously claim that Bodhidharma, the sage from India, was the 28th Patriarch of the Indian tradition and the First Patriarch of the Chinese Dhyāna School. To substantiate this claim, various fabulous tales or legends have been popularized and linked with this life. We give below a few of them as an illustrations:-

1. When the Emperor Wu Ti of the Liang Dyansty (502-549 A.D.) could not understand and appreciate unusual answers given by him, he went across the Yangtse River by means of a piece of reed. He then entered the Shao Lin Monastery in Ho Nan province and practised deep meditation facing the wall for nine long years. As a sequel, it is said, he imprinted his image on the wall.

2. He is said to have attained the hoary age of 150 years, and passed away after that. However, a Chinese envoy, while returning from India,

saw Bodhidharma with one shoe dangling from his monk's staff in the Pamirs (Ts'ung Ling). When he reported this to the Emperor, his tomb was unearthed and, to their surprise, they could not find anything else in the coffin, except a broken shoe!

The stories mentioned above appear to indicate that he was a person possessing supernatural powers, or, in the derogatory sense, that he was some sort of a magician. This, indeed, is unfortunate. We shall endeavour, in the following pages, to bring out the truth about this great sage. Special attention will be paid to the conditions of this School prior to his arrival in China and after his demise.

I. Was he the founder of the Chinese Zen Buddhism?

The answer to this question may be divided into two different categories. In one case, we may say 'No,' and in the other, 'Yes, but partially.'

It is a well-known fact that when Buddhism was introduced in China, it embraced all the three aspects of that religion viz., disciplinary observance, meditation and philosophy (Śīla, Samādhi and Prajñā). As such, we find a large number of works on Dhyāna or meditation in the Chinese Tripiṭaka. The earliest ones are probably those translated by An Shih-Kao in 148-170 A. D. Take for instance:-

1. The Sūtra spoken by the Buddha on keeping thought in the manner of great Ānāpana. Nanjio No. 682;

2. The Sūtra on perception in the law of practice of meditation. Nanjio No. 683;

and the works on the same topic translated by Chih Yao in 185 A.D. (Nanjio Nos. 724, 1338), by Buddhabhadra in A.D. 398-421 (Nanjio No. 1341), and many other important texts translated by Kumārajīva in 402-412 A.D. This would show clearly that the theory and practice of Dhyāna had been known to the Chinese Buddhist quite early. Further, we find that there are 21 Dhyāna masters in the Buddhist Biographies[1] (completed in 519 A.D.) by Hui Chiao, in which the name of Bodhidharma is not included, while in the second series of the Buddhist Biographies[2] (completed in 645 A.D.) by Tao Hsuan, the names of 135 Dhyāna experts are found including a few of the immediate disciples of Bodhidharma. These facts clearly show how popular and well-known was Dhyāna Buddhism among the Buddhists at that time. They also show the Bodhidharma, who came to China round about 480 A.D., was the founder of the Dhyāna practices would not accord with truth.

1. Kao-sheng-chuan or Biographies of eminent Buddhist masters. Nanjio No. 1490.
2. Shu-kao-sheng-chuan or the second series of the Biographies of eminent Buddhist masters by Tao Hsuan. Nanjio No. 1493.

This, however, concerns only the early phase of the Dhyāna School in China which had already a firm footing before the arrival of Bodhidharma, and therefore, he is not entitled to the honour of being its founder, as is usually supposed. We must make it clear, nevertheless that the later developed Zen School has much to do with him, though the honour seemed to have been forced on him.

When we say that later developed Zen School, we mean the particular form of Zen Buddhism which flourished during the T'ang and the Sung Dynasties (618-905 and 960-1278 A.D. respectively), and was greatly popularized by Hui Neng, the 6th Patriarch who succeeded the Bodhidharma lineage. It was during the early portion of this period that the Japanese Buddhists came to China for higher studies and later took back with them the various Buddhist Schools including the Zen (Zen is the Japanese term for 'Ch'an' which in turn is derived from the Sanskrit word 'Dhyāna'). It is this form of Zen Buddhism that has been widely known to the West. It may be said of Bodhidharma that he was in some way associated with this School, though indirectly.

II. The truth of his being the 28 Patriarch.

Several Chinese records[1] of the Biographies of the Patriarchs of the Zen School claim that Bodhidharma was the 28th Patriarch of the Indian tradition starting from Mahākāśyapa. Ch'i Sung, author of two of these records, asserted that he was really the 28th Patriarch in India and refuted the authority of Fu-fa-tsang-yin-yuan-ching or 'Sūtra on the Nidāna of transmitting the Dharmapiṭaka' (Nanjio No. 1340), a Sanskrit text translated into Chinese in 427 A.D. by Chi-chia-yeh. This work gives us a list of the 'Parampara' tradition of 23 Indian patriarchs, beginning with Mahākāśyapa and ending with Siṁha Bhikṣ u. In between we have Aśvaghosa as the 11th, Nāgārjuna the 13th, Vasubandhu the 20th and so forth. In the biographical sketch of the last Patriarch, Siṁha Bhikṣu, we are told that he was killed by Mirakutsu (Mihirakula?), a king belonging to the heretic faith, known for his destruction caused to Buddhist establishments and the massacre of the Buddhist monks in Kashmir. As a sequel, the line of 'Parampara' was discontinued after his death, because he could not find a suitable person to succeed him while he was alive. On the evidence of this

1. i. Ch'i Sung: A treatise on the right School of transmitting the Law. Nanjio No. 1528.

ii. Ch'i Sung: Records of the right School of transmitting the Law. Nanjio No. 1529.

iii. Tao Yuan: Records of the transmission of the lamp upto the Ching Teh Period-1004-1007 A.D. Nanjio No. 1524.

document, it is very difficult for us to believe the claim that Bodhidharma was the 28th Patriarch of the Indian tradition. Moreover, as this claim was first made only in the 11th century A.D. by a staunch supporter of the Zen School in China, viz., Chi'i Sung, it can hardly convince us. We know that the motive behind this claim was to enhance the prestige of the said School.

III. The date of Bodhidharma's arrival in China

The popular tradition[1] recorded in the literature of the Zen School tells us that Bodhidharma reached Canton in 527 A.D. (or 520 A.D. in another version) in the reign of Emperor Wu Ti of the Liang Dynasty (502-549 A.D.). It is stated in the same source that he met the Emperor. As this Emperor chiefly devoted his attention towards the building of monasteries, giving alms to the monks and so forth, he could not understand the mystical teachings of Bodhidharma and, therefore, the latter left him without being appreciated. However, other earlier and more reliable sources present us with quite a different picture. The following cases may be cited:-

1. Tao Hsuan (595-667 A.D.), author of the second series of Buddhist Biographies gives us a life-sketch of Bodhidharma where he says: 'He first reached the territory of the Sung Dynasty (420-479 A.D.) and then proceeded towards the North'. This Sung Dynasty came to an end in 479 A.D. Moreover, he does not mention anything about his interview with the Emperor of the Liang Dynasty. If we accept this version, we may safely place the date of his arrival somewhere between 420-479 A.D.

2. One of the chief disciples fo Bodhidharma was Sheng Fu who met the Master sometime about 480 A.D. when he was about 17 years of age. Sheng Fu passed away in 524 A.D. at the age of 61 years

3. Hui Sheng,[2] another pupil of Bodhidharma learnt all the meditational methods from him and observed strictly the ascetic practices. He enjoyed the mature age of 70 years and died sometime between 502-519 A.D.

All the foregoing evidence leads us to the same conclusion, that is, that Bodhidharma reached China sometime round 480 A.D. If that is so, then the popular tradition about his arrival in 527 A.D. and about his meeting in the same year the Emperor of the Liang Dynasty, falls to the ground.

---

1. See Nanjio Nos 1528, 1529 and 1524.

2. See Nanjio No. 1493. Ch. 6.

IV. His teaching and relation with the later Zen Buddhism

According to the general belief, it is said that the way of teaching adopted by Bodhidharma differed substantially from that of all the Buddhist missionaries who found their way into China. He seemed to have been a bad linguist because he never translated any Sanskrit text into Chinese, nor did he compose any literary piece. What was worse, judging by conventional standards, was that he preached an ultra-modern doctrine which seemed to harbour a profound hatred towards the traditional Buddhism as contained in the books. We quote below an outline of the fundamental principles of Zen Buddhism:-

"A special tradition outside the Scriptures;

Not to depend on books or letters;

To point direct to the heart of man;

To see (one's own) nature and become Buddha."

These lines tell us of the Dhyāna School of the developed form. We believe they have been strictly observed by most of the Zen followers in the Far East. However, to have a glimpse of its early simple teachings and practices, we have to go back to the sayings and the mode of life of Bodhidharma and his immediate disciples.

In his short life-sketch we find that he used to instruct Hui K'e, later on known as the Second Patriarch, the following two-fold doctrine: One is 'reasoning' or the basic principle, and the other 'practice'. As regards 'reasoning' he says:-

"I firmly believe that all living things possess the same Real Nature (Svabhāva). But in most cases it has been covered by the external dust of obstruction. I now ask them to give up falsehood and return to reality by gazing at the wall and meditating. They should not try to make any distinction between the self and others, between the saintly and the profane, but to stand firmly on these foundations and not to follow any other teachings. This, indeed, will be in concordance with the 'Tao' which is silent and devoid of activities".

Among the 'practices' there are four in number:-

1. The attitude towards one's enemy—

"During the course of religious training, calamity may fall on the practitioner. Under such circumstances, he should think that in the previous Kalpas he had been led astray and had many ties of attachment and hatred. In the present life he might have been freed from them, but the suffering should be regarded as the effect of the deeds performed in one's former births. Therefore, one should willingly face all the sorrows and should not harbour any enmity towards the wrong-doer.........When this occurs in one's mind, it is in accordance with the 'Tao', because trying to understand what is the nature of enmity is to enter into the path of 'Tao'.

2. To be content with one's lot—

"There is no Ātmā (soul) in living beings. Happiness and misery should be received calmly as they came. Even if one is treated with honour, it is due to his previous deeds; when their effect is over, it would not come again. Therefore there is no occasion for rejoicing. In the case of gain or loss, there should not be any difference in the tranquillity of the mind. If the wind is calm and gentle with regard to success or failure, then, it is said to be in fitting accordance with the Dharma".

3. The avoidance of hankering—

"The ordinary folk have for a long time lost themselves in greed—that means hankering. A seeker after the Truth should be different from them. He ought to rest his mind on inactivities and let him face squarely whatever is his lot. Indeed, all the Three Worlds are full of sufferings and nobody is secure. The Sūtra says:

'Whatever you hanker after,
The sequel is suffering.
There will be happiness
When one is devoid of greed."

4. To be in accordance with the Dharma—

This is meant that the Svabhāva or Real Nature is inherently pure.

As Bodhidharma never composed anything himself, this sums up the total output of his teachings. In addition to this, we are told that he recommended to his disciples the study of the Laṅkāvatārasūtra. This is the only Mahāyāna text which had some connection with the Dhyāna School in its early stages.

Judging by the rather curt outlines of his teaching and the ascetic way of life of his immediate disciples, it appears to us that theoretically he had more or less based his philosophy on the interpretation of Buddha-nature in sentient beings as found in the Nirvāṇa Sūtra. Therefore, he regarded the saintly and the profane as on the same level, because intrinsically there would not be any difference between them. However, there is not the slightest hint of the theory of 'Sudden Enlightenment' here, though it is very prominent in the teachings of the later patriarchs and their disciples. Moreover, the apparently eccentric ways of teaching, such as giving a blow, a kick or a tweak of the nose, drawing a circle in the air, saying paradoxical things, answering questions with incoherency and all kinds of absurdities—adopted by the patriarchs after Hui Neng, the 6th Patriarch (639-713 A.D.) cannot be said to have originated with Bodhidharma, because he had nothing to do with them. On the contrary, the emphasis laid on austerity, self-contentment, self-mortification, the curb of desire, the belief in the effect of Karma, the insistence on concentration of mind by gazing at the blank wall and other ascetic trends appear more akin to the early 'Arhat' ideal than the Mahāyāna Dhyāna practices seen after the 7th century A.D. To substantiate our statement, we cite a few examples in order to show what kind of austere like Bodhidharma's disciples used to lead:-

(i) Hui K'e, his chief disciple and in later generations known as the Second Patriarch, used to practise the teachings of Bodhidharma very strictly. During the period of persecution of Buddhism started by Emperor Wu Ti of the Northern Chow Dynasty (561-578 A.D.) one of his arms was cut off by an assassin. As he took it calmly by adhering to his master's instructions, he did not feel any pain. To stop bleeding he cauterized the wound with fire and bandaged it with a piece of cloth. He went on begging his alms as if nothing had happened.

(ii) Na Ch'an-shih, or Na, the Dhyāna master, was a disciple of Hui K'e. Before his renunciation he was a renowned Confucian scholar. From the time of his becoming a monk, he gave up reading non-Buddhist literature and never touched a pen. Regarding his personal possessions, he had only a robe, and a begging bowl. He ate only one meal a day and observed the practice of 'Dhūta' very strictly.

(iii) Hui Man, a disciple of Na Ch'an-shih and a great-grand-disciple of Bodhidharma, devoted himself to the practice of non-attachment. He had only a robe and ate once a day. There was no other property belonging to him except two needles. He needed them for mending his rug in the winter, but would discard them during the summer. Once he was meditating in an open ground which was covered by snow over five feet deep. Some one saw him and offered him free board and temporary lodging. He refused that kind offer and said:

"I would accept your invitation only when no one else in the whole world is alive!"

Besides, the lives led by his other immediate disciples like Sheng Fu (who died in 524 A.D.) and Hui Sheng (who died during 502-519 A.D.) are more or less like the ones described above. If we compare their spirit of self-mortification and quiet contemplation with the boisterous daring of burning a wooden image of the Buddha (by Tan Hsia) and the killing of a cat (by Nan Chuan) and other strange acts performed by later Dhyāna masters—supposed to contain the mystery of Dhyāna ideals—we would come to the conclusion that there is hardly any common ground between them. Thus, it would appear to be an irony of Fate that Bodhidharma was placed as the First Patriarch of the Zen School.

From the foregoing evidence we are led to believe firstly, that historically speaking Bodhidharma was very sober, simple-living and comparatively less known than most of his contemporaries. The story of his meeting with the Emperor of the Liang Dynasty and other fabulous tales associated with his life cannot stand critical enquiry. Secondly, Bodhidharma's theories and practices concerning Dhyāya differed a good deal from those of the later patriarchs and their numerous disciples. If that is so, why was he regarded as the First Patriarch of the Zen School? Thirdly, the list of the six Patriarchs,

1. Bodhidharma
2. Hui K'e
3. Sheng Tsan
4. Tao Hsin
5. Hung Jen
6. Hui Neng (or Shen[1] Hsiu)

popularly known from the beginning of the 8th century A.D. and later on recorded in the Dhyāna literature written by Chi'i Sung in the 11th century A.D. was not found in early Buddhist historical records. Sheng Tsan, the Third Patriarch in our list, was not known by any author of the Buddhist Biographies (The second series completed in 645 A.D. and the third series in 988 A.D.) Tao Hsuan mentioned very briefly in his 'Biographies' the names of Tao Hsin and Hung Jen as teacher and pupil, but he did not say anything about their being the 4th and the 5th Patriarchs in the Bodhidharma line. Naturally, he could not, because he had already recorded the life-sketch of Hui Man, the great-grand-disciple of Bodhidharma.

On the face of all this, we would suggest that it is high time to correct wrong but popular traditions and beliefs concerning Bodhidharma and the patriarchs.

---

1. Shen Hsiu died in 706 A.D. The inscription on his tomb contains the above mentioned list. It is claimed that he was the 6th Patriarch.

Chapter - 13

Buddhist Studies With Special Reference to Tibetan

Vidhushekhara Bhattacharya

I

In issuing his edition of the *Kāśyapaparivarta* Baron A. von Staël-Holstin writes:

"Mahāyāna tradition is practically dead in India and in order to understand Sanskrit Buddhist texts properly we have to consult the ancient Chinese and Tibetan translations as well as the living tradition of China and Tibet. If this is not done, modern European translators, however great their knowledge of Sanskrit, are liable to make serious mistakes. Before translating Mahāyāna works from Sanskrit into European languages the texts should all be published in the three great languages of Mahāyāna Buddhism."

The following lines also occur in his preface (p. xiii) to the same work with regard to the text:

"The greatest help for understanding the defective and faulty Sanskrit texts is, no doubt, to be derived from the Tibetan translation, but the Chinese translations, being less literal, often supply information which cannot be obtained by reading the Tibetan translation."

And here is the opinion of Pūjanīya Mahāmahopādhyāya Pandit Haraprasad Śāstrī Mahāśaya in his *Presidential Address* at the fifth Oriental Conference, Lahore, 1928, p. 42:

"The Chinese translations of Buddhist Sanskrit texts are free translations, therefore not reliable. The Tibetan translations are too pedantically literal and, therefore, often unintelligible. The original Sanskrit should be always sought for, and consulted, if procurable, to cure the defects of those translations."

It is nor an established fact that for a thorough study of Mahāyāna Buddhism in all its aspects "the three great languages," Sanskrit, Chinese and Tibetan are absolutely necessary. We cannot do without any of them. Even Sanskrit alone cannot be regarded sufficient though it has a unique and the highest position. Under the present circumstances they are mutually supplementary. Therefore, under the deplorable condition of our MSS an accurate and critical edition of a Buddhist Sanskrit text is hardly possible without consulting the Chinese and Tibetan translations. This can sufficiently be proved by the facts supplied among others from a recent publication included in the Gaekwad's Oriental Series, namely the *Advayavajrasaṃgraha*, a collection of twenty-one small treatises attributed to Advayavajra, edited by Śāstri Mahāśaya himself.

Tibetan translations are "too pedantically literal," no doubt, but it is for this very fact that they have immense and incomparable importance and value. That they are so literal is indeed a boon to a student of Buddhism, specially to an Indian one, who is familiar with Sanskrit. In fact, the translators, both Indian and Tibetan, working jointly have made the impossible, possible. It is really surprising to think how they succeeded in translating the most difficult works so faithfully and accurately adopting a striking method into a language which had hardly any literature worth mentioning at that age.

Sometimes these translations may be unintelligible, but this unintelligibility must not be solely attributed to their being too literal. It may be due to various facts common to any translations of difficult texts in any language. It is not that the Tibetan translators understood *every* word correctly, or they were able to turn *every* thing properly. Nor can we say that the original texts before them were perfectly free from all sorts of defects in every case and on every point. Unintelligibility of a text sometimes depends also on the intelligence and knowledge of the subject and the language of the reader himself.

Śāstrī Mahāśaya is quite right when he says that "original Sanskrit should be always sought for and consulted, if procurable." But what is to be done when the original Sanskrit itself is unintelligible owing to its faulty and defective readings, as for instance, in the case of the *Advayavajrasaṃgraha* already referred to? He appears to suggest rightly that in such cases help is to be sought for from the Tibetan source, for he himself wanted to have the doubtful readings in the book collated with the Tibetan translation, but he could not do so as there was no Lama with him to whom he might refer (p. vi).

The special importance of Tibetan translations lies in the fact that with occasional exceptions they help us greatly in suggesting original Sanskrit readings, specially when a work is composed in verse. Let us take here a few examples. Here runs a short Tibetan sentences:

lhas. byin. tshon.po. ñin.par. zan. mi. z'o/ god *by* give fat day *in* cooked rice not eats,

Literally it means: Fat god-given one does not eat cooked rice during the day. To one who knows both the languages, Sanskrit and Tibetan, properly, it will at once suggest that *lhas.byin* is nothing but *Deva-datta*, a man. *lha=deva*, 'god'; *-s* is the sign of third case-ending, and thus *lha=devena*, 'by god'; *byin=datta, arpita* 'given'. Therefore *lhas=byin.* = *Deva-datta. tshon-po.* =*sthūla, pīna* 'fat'; *ñin. pa.* =*dina. divā,* 'day'; *-ra* is the sign of locative; thus *ñin.par=dine,* 'in the day'; *zaṇannam-odanam*, 'cooked rice'; *mi.* =*na*, 'not; *za'.* =*bhuṅkte*, 'eats'. Here a Sanskrit knowing reader will at once read the Tibetan sentence in Sanskrit *pino Devadatto divā annam na bhuṅkte*; for the expression with particular words is already known to him. Similarly reading *mchod-byin*, a name in Tibetan, a Sanskritist at once knows that in Sanskrit it is *Yajñadatta*, through the word *mchod* or *mchod.pa*, the later being the fuller form, gives the following meanings: *pūjana, arcana, yajana, ārādhanā* ('worship'), *savana, kratu, manyu, yajña* ('sacrifice'); and *byin* (prefect of *sbyin-pa* 'to give', 'to bestow') means *arpita, vitīrṇa*, etc. like *datta* 'given'. He is quite sure that in such cases the name must be *Yajñadatta* and not *Arcanādatta* or *Ārādhanārpita*, and so on. In the same way, with reference to the context he can easily understand that

de.la. chos. mthun. pa. ñid. can. ni.

is in Sanskrit nothing but *tatra sādharmyavat*, for *de=tad, la* is the sign of locative, *de.la-tatra; chos-dharma, mthun.pa-samāna, ñid* secondary suffix as in Sanskrit *-tva, 'tā, -ya* forming neuter abstract nouns; *can* secondary suffix, such as *-vat, -mat* forming possessive ajectives; and *ni* a particle of no intrinsic meaning, sometimes translated by *hi* or left untranslated, something like a *pādapūraṇa* particle in Sanskrit, or is used simply as *vākyālaṅkāra*. Thus *chos.mthun.pa.ñid=sadharmatva* which is the same as *sādharmya;* and with suffix *can=vat* it becomes *sādharmyavat.*

Sometimes, however, it is really very difficult to ascertain the original word exactly even in a verse. For instance, one reads in the Tibetan version of *Tattvasaṅgraha (De. kho. na. ñid. bsdus. pa)*, GOS, verse 15[c]: *bum. sogs. bye. brag. bshin°*. Here the word *bum (bumpa)* is for Sanskrit *ghaṭa, kumbha, kalaśa,* 'an earthen jar'; *sogs (la. sogs. pa)* means *ādi* 'beginning with,' etc.; *bye. brag* mean *viśeṣa, bheda* 'distinction', 'difference,' and *bshin* is in Sanskrit the suffix *-vat* in the sense of *iva* 'like'. Now owing to the metre one will naturally be inclined to render the above Tibetan words into Sanskrit by *ghaṭādi-bhedavat*, or *kumbhādi-bhedavat,* perfectly by the first, as in philosophical discussion in Sanskrit the world *ghaṭa* is in general use, and not *kumbha*. (For the sake of metre *kalaśa* cannot be employed). But the fact is quite different. The original Sanskrit text as in the printed edition (GOS) reads here neither *ghaṭa* nor *kumbha*, but *kuṭa* meaning the same thing, an earthern jar, the line runnin *kuṭ-ādibhedavat*. This reading is supported by the commentary of Kamalaśīla. The difference is, however, immaterial.[1]

Let us take one example more showing the strictness with which the Tibetan transltors followed Sanskrit. The Tibetan word for Sanskrit *manoratha* 'desire' or 'desired object' is *yid.kyi. śiṅ. rta. yid=manas, kyi* is the sign of genitive, *śiṅ-rta=ratha*. Thus *yid.kyi=manasaḥ*, and *śiṅ-rta-ratha*, in compound *manoratha*. Here is something very interesting to note. In translating *ratha* two words are employed in Tibetan, and what do they actually mean? *śiṅ* means both *taru* 'tree,' and '*dāru*', 'wood', 'timber'. Here it is taken in the latter sense; and *rta* means *aśva* 'horse' or 'a wooden vehicle to which a horse is yoked for drawing it.' Now the derivation of *manoratha* is given by commentators on Sanskrit *kośas* 'lexicons', and the lexicographers connect it with the word *ratha*, while in fact it has no connection whatever with it. The actual word is *mano'rtha* (manaḥ-artha) 'object of mind,' which owing to Prākṛtism or *svarabhakti* has assumed the form *manoratha* being pronounced in four syllables instead of three. But this fact was not known to a large number of Sanskrit authors and the Tibetan translators simply followed them.

Suppose that we can do without turning Chinese and Tibetan translations only with the Sanskrit works when they are procurable. But what is to be done when they are not procurable, when they are lost as in the case with hundreds of books now preserved only in Chinese or Tibetan or in both of them? Should we remain silent looking forward to the fine day when all these volumes would be brought to us being discovered from Nepal or Central Asia, or any other part of the globe? Let us not forget what important part the Indian teachers once played century after century in rendering Buddhist Sanskrit works into Chinese and Tibetan. They travelled to those countries, mastered

1. Incidentally with regard to the recent edition of the *Tattvasaṅgraha* with the *Pañjikā* it may be observed that it would have been much better if the Tibetan version could be utilized. Only one instance may be given here. The edition reads śloka 9[d]: *tulyasattve* (printed *-satve*) *paraṃ na tu*. Here *tulyasattve* is a wrong reading, it must be *tulye'sattve* and Tib. has rightly *med.par. mtshuṅs.na*. This correction could. however, be made even by consulting the commentary.

the languages of the lands, wrote standard books in them and carried on the translation work with untiring zeal. And if that was possible in those days under various unfavourable circumstances, I do not know, it should not be so at the present age when we are certainly in a position far better in every respect. If we really want to study Mahāyāna Buddhism thoroughly, we must have the lost Sanskrit works restored in *Sanskrit*. Restoration in Sanskrit is far better and far easier from every point of view than in any other language. When a work is restored in Sanskrit any Sanskritist, either here or abroad, will have easy access to it and it will not take much time to get it turned into different languages. Let the young students of Buddhism in the land of its birth take up the work in right earnest and carry it on patiently and honestly, and their labour will certainly be amply rewarded.

It is however a pity that there is growing a section, however small, of new students of Buddhism in our country that altogether ignores the importance of Chinese and Tibetan studies. They are welcome to think in accordance with their own light; but it is certain that the consequence of their aversion to these languages will lead only to their utter self-deprivation.

I have already alluded to a recent publication of a small volume (pp. xxxviii+63), *Advayavajrasaṅgrha*, in the Gœkwad's Oriental Series, and now in order to show our young students of Buddhism the value of Tibetan studies by some concrete examples, I shall examine some readings found therein. It really gives me great pains in having to criticise the eidition by Śāstrī Mahāśaya, but I feel that as a scholar, he would welcome such discussion and concede that only an honest attempt is here being made to find out, if possible, the correct readings of the texts which are so important and have been brought to light by his own diligence and painstaking efforts. It is not that he was not aware of the defective readings, for he himself says (p. vi) that they "are in many places so hopelessly corrupt that nothing can be made out of them." But it is certain that the number of corrupt readings could easily be much reduced even without consulting the Tibetan version only by taking a little more care and pain. We have nothing more to say about it when Śāstrī Mahāśaya himself writes (p. vi) "I give the book as it is, and I hope my readers will look at me with indulgence, but I venture to think that the works will throw much light on obscure points of Buddhist History and Buddhism and that is an excuse for their publications." The edition may be compared with that of the *Madhyamakavṛtti* of the Buddhist Text Society and as such should be used with much caution almost on every page.

II

For the discussion I confine myself only to the *Tattvaratnāvalī* covering only nine pages, pp. 14-22. In Tib. it is *De. kho. na. ñid. rin. po. che'i. phrin ba*, and found in Tanjur, *Rrgud. ḥgrel (Tantravṛtti),* Mi, 126ᵇ.6—13ᵇ.8 (Cordier, II, p. 215). The Xylograph used here is of the Narthang edition and belongs to our Viśvabhāratī Library. According to it the fols. are 123ᵃ.4—127ᵃ. I. On examination it is found that this edition of the Tib. version has unfortunately left out a portion of the text abruptly, and it is from *mantranayaśca*, p. 14, l. 9 to *bhāvipratyekabuddhaḥ,* p. 16, l. 6, of the Skt. edition under discussion. And though there are numerous points to be discussed in this portion, too, I would not like to do so except the kārikā "asti khalv iti°" p. 14, ll. 20-21 and the short sentence quoted without the mention of the book on p. 14, ll. 21-22. The kārikā referred to (p. 14, ll. 20-21) as edited is:

asti khalv iti nīlādi [9k] .....parā/

bhāvagrahagrahāveśagambhir[ā]pāyabhirave//

It is quoted in the *Subhāṣitasaṃgraha*, p. 14, ll. 22-20, and accordingly the *b* of the above kārikā should be *jagad iti haḍīyase*. But it is not known how *parā* in the MS. or in the edition is to be accounted for. *d* is wrongly amended, the actual reading being *gambhīranayabhīrave* as in the *Subhāṣtisaṃgraha.*

The sentence alluded to runs as follows:

asti pudgalo— "bhāravāho ṇa ṇiccaṃ bhaṇāmi ṇāṇiccaṃ bhaṇāmi" ti. As there is no Tib. version at my disposal I cannot say so definitely, but it seems to me that *bhāravāho* is to be taken with *pudgalo* and the quotation mark is to be put after it[1].Apart from the other points involved, it is very interesting to note that here is a short Prākṛt sentence and the word *bhāravāha* at once reminds one of the *Bhāravāhasūtra* which in connection with the theory of pudgala is often quoted or referred to in Buddhist or non-Buddhist works.[2]

It is in Sanskrit and there is also a Pāli version of it.[3] The Prākṛt sentence given above seems to have been quoted from the

---

1. Cf. bhārahāraḥ katamaḥ pudgala iti syād vacanīyam/— *Bhārahārasūtra*, quoted by Poussin in his *Abhidharmakośa*, x, 256, and JA, 1902, II p. 267; "bhārahāraḥ pudgalaḥ"— Tattvasṅgrahapañjikā, p. 130.

2. Besides the works named in the preceding note see *Bodhicaryāvatārapañjikā*, BI, p. 475; *Mahāyānasūtrālaṅkāra*, XVIII, 92-103 (p.159); *Nyāyavārtika*, BI, p. 342; *Muséon*, 1902, p. 2; Minayeff, *Recherches*, p. 225; *JRAS*, 1901, PP. 308, 573.

3. *Saṃyutta Nikāya*, III, p. 25. In Pāli it is simply *Bhārasutta, Visuddhimagga*, pp. 479, 512.

Bhāravāhasūtra, but it is not found in the Pāli text, nor in the fragments in Skt. quoted in different books. Should it prove to be a face it would follow that there is also a Prākṛt version of the *Bhāravāhasūtra*.

P.16

Ll. 6, 7. The text reads:

adhimātras tu catuḥkalpāsaṃkhyeyābhinirvarttyabuddha iti, prayekasya vivṛtir adhimātraśrāvaksyaiva.

Here *abhinirvarttyabuddha* has no sense. It must be *abhinirvarttyabuddhabhāvaḥ* just as in l. 25 of the same page, Tib. reading *saṅs. rgyas. ñid.*

For *Pratyekasya* Tib. *pratyekabuddhānāṃ (raṅ. saṅs. ryas, rnam kyi).*

Skt. *vivṛtiḥ* for which "The MS writes either *vivṛitiḥ* or *vivṛttiḥ* just as it pleases" (p. 66) may be supported here by Tib. (*bsad. pa*).

But in one case (p. 18, I.9) it reads *vitarkaḥ or vikalpaḥ (rnam. par. brtags. pa* being taken for *rnam. par rtog*), while in two cases (p. 17, l. 13; and p. 20, l. 2) it has simply *tarkaḥ (rtog. p'o).*

For *eva* after *śrāvakasya* read *iva* with Tib. (*bshin*).

Ll. 8-9: ayaṃ ca pratipannapudgala*śūnyācintyatālakṣaṇamācāryya*svayambhūjñānavipaśyanā*samarthaḥ*.

For *ayaṃ* Tib. *asya (ḥdi.la)*. For *śūnyācintyālakṣaṇamācāryya-* read *śūnyatā° lankṣaṇānācāryya-*as suggested by Tib. (*stoṅ.pa.ñid daṅ/ bsam. du. med. p'i mtshan. ñid. daṅ/ slop. dpon. med. pa. daṅ*); and for *samarthaḥ* Tib. *śamathaḥ* (*shi. gnas. so*).

Independently Tib. would read here: asya (ca) Pratipannapudgala-śūnyatācintyatālakṣaṇam anācāryaṃ svayambhūjñānaṃ vipaśyanāśamathaś ca.

Ll. 9-10 tatra indriyān nirodho vipaśyanā(10 k) pudgalasyānupalabdhiḥ kāyavā[kce]tasāṃ saṃya[ma] samarthaḥ

Tib. reads: tatra indriyantrodho vipaśyanā pudgalsyānupalabdhiś ca kāyavākcetasāṃ saṃyamaḥ śamathaḥ (de.la lhag.mthoṅ ni dbaṅ.po. rnams. hgag.pa.daṅ/ gaṅ shag.mi.dmigs. po/ shi. gnas. ni. lus daṅ. ṅag daṅ yid yaṅ dag sdom.po//)

But in the first part the actual reading seems to be: *indriyanirodhād* for *indriyanirodho*, and *ca* in the sentence is to be omitted.[1]

1. See *Bodhicaryāvatārapañjikā* p. 287: vipaśyanā yathābhūtatattvaparijñānasvabhāvā prajñā, śamathaḥ cittaikāgratālakṣaṇaḥ samādhiḥ.

L. 15. For *anāgatāyāṃ* Tib. lit. *āgatāyām* (ḥoṅ. bar. gyur) which for the sake of metre is to be read as *samāgatāyāṃ*, and this is the true reading.

Ll. 19-20: For

ajānānaṃ hi prajñānaṃ nidrādṛṣṭātasādhitam/
indriyoparataṃ yadvaj jñānaṃ vaiśeṣikaṃ matam//

The Tib. has:

śes.pa.med. pa'hi. ye.śes.gaṅ/
gñid.kyi.dpe.yis.[1] bsgms. pa.ni/
ḥbaṅ.po. ḥgags. pa'hi śes.pa.ste/
bye.brag.pa.yi ḥdod.pa.yin//

For *ajānānaṃ* Tib. appears to read *ajñānānāṃ* (śes.pa.med.p'i), but the Tib. phrase may be taken as present participle, *ajānānāṃ*. For *prajñānaṃ* Tib. has *yaj jñānaṃ* (*ye.śes.gaṅ*). In the second half of the kārikā tib. omits *yad vaj* altogether, but owing to the metre it seems that the original reading must have been *yat tat*, but not *yad vaj* which cannot be defended here.

Ll. 22-23. The following couplet with the introductory line 'bhagavataḥ pravacanam api' using *jetavane for vṛndāvane* as is widely known is very interesting:

varaṃ jetavane ramye śṛgālatvaṃ vrajāmy ahaṃ/
na tu vaiśeṣikaṃ mokṣaṃ gotamo gantum arthati//

The important difference in Tib. is that it reads *mantum* (ḥtshal) for *gantum*. See *Sarvasiddhāntasārasaṃgraha,* Madras, p. 28; *Saḍdarśanasamuccaya* (BI), p. 188 (with *gantum*).

I have already said that sometimes Tib. translations are wrong, and here is an instance. In the Skt. text (p. 16, l. 25) we have *śrāvakapratyekayoḥ (=°pratyekabuddhayoḥ)*, but here for *pratyeka* Tib. reads *pratyayajñāna* (*rkyen. rtogs*). And the case is the same on p. 17, l.3, where the word *pratyeka* is used again. It appears that the copy before the Tib. translator had the wrong reading, *pratyaya* for *pratyeka* and the translator rendered it into Tib. by *rkyen. rtogs* in order to mean by it *pratyeka buddha* without questioning the genuineness of the reading *pratyaya.*

P.17

L. 6 For *saṃsargāt [ca] prajāyate* Tib. clearly *nirvikalpaṃ prajāyate* (*rtog.pa.med.par.rab.tu.hbyuṅ*).

1. Xylograph *yi*.

Ll. 14-15. Tib. omits, *kalanā yat* and *sāṃkhyāṃ* reading *pratyakṣ -ato nāsti kālaḥ kriyāyāḥ (ḥdi.ni goms.par bya.baḥi. dus. yin. gyi/ mṅon.sum.du. bya.baḥi. dus.ni. ma. yin. no*).

For *paricaya* (twice) Tib. *abhyāsa (goms.pa).*

L. 16. Consistently with his edition of the *Bauddha Gān o Dohā,* Sāhitya Pariṣad Granthāvalī, Calcutta, 1323 B.S., p. 46. Śāstrī Mahāśaya corrects *cittaṃ niścintya* found in the MS. to *cittaṃ niścitya*; but Tib. reads here *cittaniścittabodhena* (*sems.kyi.sems.med.rtogs.pa.yis*) (Xylograph *yi* for *yis*), but I think the latter is the right reading.

Ll. 18. The śloka with a lacuna reads:

bhāvayed gṛhibhū........ṣilabdhākṣaṇam /
vajraparyaṅkam ādhāya nāsāgre cañcalaṃ manaḥ //

Here we have the Tib. version:

skad. cig. skad. cig. la. brtan.nas /
rdo.rje.skyil.kruṅ.bciṅs[1] nas.ni /
sna.rtser.gyo.baḥi.yid.gtad.pa /
khyim.par.gyur.kyaṅ.bsgom.par.bya //

Accordingly the following amendment may be proposed:

bhāvayed gṛhibhū[to']pi labdha[dhariyaḥ parti]kṣaṇam/
vajraparyaṅka ādhāya[2] nāsāgre° //

L. 20. Before *tritayā°* Tib adds *saṃsāra* (*ḥkhor*).[3]

Ll. 21-22. Tib. omits *prajñā° svabhāvena.* For *°pāramitācaraṇaṃ phalavaimukhye na sattvā°* one shouldread *°pāramitācaraṇaphala-vaimukhyena* as suggested by Tib. (pha.tu. phyin.pa. lṅa.la.kun.tu. spyod.ciṅ ḥbras.bu.la.re.ba.med.par). For *vaimukṅya* Tib. literally *nairāśya* (*re.bo.med.pa*).

L.22 Tib. simply *dṛṣṭiḥ (lta.baḥo)* for *taddṛṣṭeḥ*, and that is better.

Ll. 23-24. One reads in the edition:

ṣaṭkena yugapad yogācāre [para-] māṇoḥ ṣaḍaṅgatetyādinā.

Her *yogācāre* must be *yogāt* or *yoga*[4] and one should read *ṣ-aḍaṃśatā* for *ṣaḍaṇgatā,* the line reading:

---

1. Xylograph *bcas.*
2. Tib. would read *ābadhya.*
3. Here *saṃsāratritaya* may mean *lokatraya, tridhātu.*
4. In the original kārika of Vasubandhu we have *-yogāt*, while in the vṛtti there is *yoge* supported by Tib, reading *sbyor.ba.na.* In the Benares edition of the *Nyāyavārtika*, IV, 2,25, there is *yogāt* but the Calcutta edition reads *Yoge.* This is the first half of Vasubandhu's very well-known and widely quoted kārika in his *Viṃśatikārikā*, ed. Lévi, 16.

ṣaṭkena yugapad yogāt paramāṇoḥ ṣaḍaṃśatā/

L. 25. For *anupapatteḥ* Tib. *anupalabdhiḥ* (dmigs.par.mi.ḥgyur.gyi). After *idam* Tib. adds. *sarvam* (thams. cad). Tib. omits *cittākāradhāri* (for *citrākāra°* see p. 18, l. 8). For °bhāva° Tib. °ākārarūpa° (rnam.paḥi.ṅo.bo). For °*vinirmuktaṃ prakāśam* one should read read *vinirmuktaprakāśaṃ pra°* (ḥbral. ba. gsal. ba. ñid. gsal. ba. rab.tu°).

P. 18

L. 6. For *citteṣu* Tib *cittaṭah* (*sems.las*). Tib. puts the first half in slightly different words which may be translated in prose as follows: indriyārthasvarūpaṃ cittād anyan na bhavati. The Tib. text reads:

dbaṅ.poḥi.don.gyi.ṅo.bo.ñid/

sems.las.gshan.yod.ma.yin.te/

L.8 After *citrākāraṃ* Tib. adds. *sthitaṃ (bshag)*. For *paraṃ nirapekṣyaprakāśyaṃ prakāśate* one should read with Tib. *paranirapekṣ -am* (or figuratevely *nirapekṣyaprakāśaṃ*) *prakāśate* (gshan. la. ma bltos (X *ltos*) rab.tu.gasal.ba).

Ll. 12-13 *bāhye na°*. This kārikā of the *Laṅkāvatāra*, ed. N. Nanjio, Kyoto, 1923, p. 235 (X, 154) is quoted in a number of works (*Subhāṣitasaṃgraha*, p. 18; *Saḍdarśanasamuccaya* (Bl), p. 40; *Tattvasaṃgraha* (405) p. 14; and so on), but nowhere, so far as I know, is the reading *bāhye* as in the present book for *bāhyo* which is quite right.

Ll. 16-17. For *rūpakāyau tadudbhūtau* Tib. singular number, *rūpakāyas tadudbhūtaḥ (de.las.byuṅ.baḥi.gzugs.kyi.sku)*. For *eva* in *māyaiva* read *iva* with Tib.(*bshin*). The case is the same also with L.14.

L.18 For *-saccitra-* read *sacitra-* as in Tib (*sna.tshogs.daṅ.bcas.pa*)

L. 22. For *sāla* Tib. *satya (bden.pa)* and for *-citta-* it has *-jñāna. (ye.śes)*.

P. 19

Ll. 1-2. The kārikā runs:

vijñānamātram evedam ity ayam hy upalabhataḥ /

sthāpayen na sa kiñcit [tu] tanmātreṇāvatiṣṭhate //

In our Xylograph the first three words of *b* are extremely illegible and could not be read. The karikā is quoted below.

hdi. dag.-thams.cad. sems.tsam. shes /
...yaṅ.dmigs.nas.su /
ci.yaṅ ruṅ ste mdun ḥjog na /
de.ñid. tsam.la. mi.gnas.so //

In *b* of the Skt. text *ayaṃ hi* is doubtful, and could not be examined. In *c* for *na sa* there is nothing in Tib., nor is anything for the inserted [tu].

For *d* Tib. clearly reads *tanmātre nāva°*.

Ll. 3-4. In the kārikā yadā° read *ālambanaṃ (dmigs.pa)* in *a*, and *upalabhate* (*ñe.bar. dmigs.pa*) in *b* for *ālambanam* and *upalabhyate* respectively. In *c* one should read *sthitaṃ* (Tib. *gnas.pa*) for *sthitaḥ* and in *d grāhyābhāve* (*gsuṅ.ba.med.pas*) for *grāhyabhāve*.

Ll. 6-7. This śloka occurs again on p.29 with some different readings and emendations without any attempt to account for the variance. Let them be quoted below as they are edited:

yad yad yad dṛśyate kiñcit tat tat brahmeti kalpayet/
tato nānyagataṃ cittaṃ brahmaṇaivātiṣṭhate// p.19
yad yad vai dṛśyate kiñcit [tat] tad brahmeti kalpayet/
tato'nyagatacittaṃ [tu] brahmaṇaivātiṣṭhate// p. 29

And her is the Tib. version:

cuṅ.shig.gaṅ.daṅ.gaṅ.mthoṅ.ba/
de.daṅ.de.ni.tshaṅs.par.rtog/
sems.ni.de.las.gshaṅ.pa.med/
tshaṅs.pa.ñid.la.ṅes.par.gnas//

Taking all these into consideration we may have the following:

yad yad vai dṛśyate kiñcit tat tad brahmeti kalpayet/
tato'nānyagataṃ cittaṃ brahmaṇy evāvatiṣṭhate//

L.14. For *-ānanda* Tib. *-ananta- (mthaḥ-med.pa)* which seems to have been misread by the Tib. translator, or the MS. before him contained that reading.

L. 15. The first half of the kārikā runs:—

bodhāmbho(mbo)dhau mayi svacchaṃ
tucchāyaṃ viśvabuddhyaḥ/

Here are three mistakes, and Tib. gives the true readings: for *svacchaṃ* Tib. *svacche (dwaṅs.pa.la)*. for *tucchāyaṃ* it has *tuccho'yaṃ (gsob.ḥdi)*, and for *viśvabuddhayaḥ* it reads *viśvabudbudaḥ (sna.tshogs.chu.bur)*.

L.24. For *ābhāsanavaśāt* Tib. has *vāsanāvaśād asatyam ābhasate* [iti] (*bag.chags.kyi.dbaṅ.gis mis.bden.par snaṅ.baḥo*).

For *doṣād dvandvāt* Tib. *doṣa-dvandvāt* or °*dvayāt (skyon.gñis.yad.pas*). [*na*] is supported by Tib. (*ma.yin.no*).

Ll. 25-26. For *pūrvetaraparāmarśa* Tib. suggests *purvottarāparāmarśa (sṅon.daṅ.da.ltar.dpyad.pa.med.par*).

P.20

L.1. *mūrti*° *saṅgaḥ* is not clear also in Tib. in which there is nothing of *mūrti* and *vastuśakti* of the Sk. text. Tib. reads: *sna.tshogs.ji.ltar.snaṅ.ba. de.ltar. rjes.su.bden.pa. ci.shig gaṅ.du thal.bar ḥgyur.* And it my be literally translated thus: *citram yathābhāsate tathānantaraṃ kasya satyasya kutra prasaṅgaḥ.* But what does it mean?

Ll. 7-8. The kārikā runs:

na mataṃ śāśvataṃ viśvaṃ na cocchedi samīhitam/
śāśvatocchedino yugmyaṃ nānubhayaṃ vinobhayam//

The first half is all right, but apparently the second half is defective. The Tib. text is given below:—

sna.tshogs rtag.pa.ma.yin.te/
chad.par yaṅ.ni.khas.mi.len/
rtag.daṅ.chad.pa.gñis.ka.yaṅ/
gñis-ka. min.paḥaṅ. ma.yin.no//

The last two lines of it being put in prose literally mean: *śāśvatam ucchedi ca ubhayam api anubhayam api na.* It is very clear, and accordingly the second half of the Skt. text may be emended as follows:

śāśvatocchedinor yugmaṃ nānubhayaṃ na cobhayam/

Ll 9-10. For *pratiṣṭhāne [ca] read aprati-ṣṭhāne* (Tib. *mi.gnas.pas* lit. *apratiṣṭhānāt*). Cf. °*apratiṣṭhānavādināṃ* 1.6. The exact reading in *a* according to Tib. seems to be *iha sarvāpratiṣṭhānāt (ḥdi.ni.thams.cad.mi.gnas.pas*). The last half of the kārikā reading *athaiṣā kalpanā navia yac cid vetti na cittatām* differs from Tib. which suggests *īdṛśena vikalpena cittaṃ vetti na cittatāṃ (ḥdi.lta. bu.yi.rnam rtog.gis/sems.ni.sems.kyis rig.ma.yin/*). Before the second half of the kārikā Tib. separately adds *tena (des.na*).

Ll. 11-12. For *sarvasamāropaḥ* read *sarvaḥ samāropaḥ* (Tib. *sgro.btags.thams.cad.ni*). For *nirāropaḥ* Tib. preferably reads *asamāropaḥ (sgro.btags.med)*. For *tatrāropavidhī kutaḥ* Tib. *tan niṣ-edhavidhī na hi (des.na.dgag.daṅ.sgrub.pa.med*).

Ll. 13-14. For the emended reading *anābhoge* originally in the MS *anābhoga* read *anābhogaṃ* with Tib. *lhun grub. pa*. The last half of the kārikā is as follows:

sañcitya yad acintyaṃ vai tad a[ci]ntyaṃ bhaven na hi/

And the Tib. text reads:

bsams. bshin.du.ni.mi.sems.pa/

de.la.bsam.mi.khyab.mi.brjod//

Accordingly the Sanskrit reading should be:

sañcintayad acittam vai tad acintyad bhaven na hi/

Strictly with Tib. one is to read *na cakṣate* for *bhaven na hi* in *d*.

Ll. 15.16. In *yenājātaṃ jagad buddham* for *yena* read *svena* with Tib. (*bdag.gis*), and *iti* or *nāma* (*shes*) for *buddhaṃ* which may, however, be retained disagreeing with Tib; According to Tib. *jagatsatyam* is a compound (*ḥgro.baḥi. gñug.ma. bden.pa. ñid.=jagato nijaṃ satyam)*. For *anābhogena*. Tib. *anāyāsena (ḥbad.pa.med)*. The verb 'to be' ($\sqrt{}$ *bhū*) is understood here.

Ll. 18 For *-nirmukte* and *-tattve* one should read*-nirmuktaṃ* and *tattvaṃ* respectively (Tib. *ñes.hgral.ba* and *de.ñid.du*), Tib. reads *pracakṣate (brjod)* for *cakāśati* which may also be retained as an use in Buddhist Skt.

P. 21

Ll. 22-25. The śloka as printed runs:

eka hi yāna nayaś ca ekaḥ
ekā ceyaṃ deśana nāyakānām /
upāyakauśalya mamevarūpaṃ
yantrāni yānany upadarśayāmi //

As mentioned in the work itself it is quoted from the *Saddharma-puṇḍarīka*, BB, II. 69 (p. 48). Here in *d yantrāni* does not give any sense. The editor even without consulting Tib. rightly reads here *gaṅ.yaṅ.theg.pa gsum=yat trīṇi yānāni*.

The other reading in the śloka could also be emended or modified. The *Saddharmapuṇḍarīka* is edited by H.Kern and B.Nanjio from not less than eight MSS., and thus the readings adopted there cannot be ignored altogether. Compare the other readings in the *Tattvaratnāvalī* with those in the *Saddharmapuṇḍarīka*. Accordingly one should read *ekaṃ hi yānaṃ* and *eka* for *eka hi yāna* and *ekaḥ* respectively in *a*. One should also read *cityaṃ* as was in fact in the MS. for emended *ceyaṃ* in *b*; and *mamaiva rūpaṃ* for *mameva* in *c*.

P. 22

Ll. 2-3. One reads here:

dharmadhātor asaṃbhedād dhyānabhedo'sti na prabho /
yanatritayam ākhyātaṃ tvayā sattvāvatārataḥ //

The original kārikā occurs in Nāgarjuna's *Nisrupamastava* 21, and is quited also in the *Subhāṣitasaṃgraha*, p. 14. Here *dhyānabhedaḥ* ia *b* is a wrong reading, the actual one being *yāna*° (Tib.*theg.dbye*).

L. 5. We read the following:

muktis tu śūnyatādṛṣṭis tadarthāśeṣabhāvanā /

Here *dṛṣṭih* should be corrected to *dṛṣṭih* as in the *Bodhicaryāvatārapañjikā*, p. 438, and the *Subhāṣitasaṃgraha*, 22, where it is quoted. It is quoted also in the commentary by Guṇaratna on the *Saḍdarśanasamuccaya* ed. Suali, Bl, p. 47, but with a wrong reading. Instead of two *pādas* of the kārikā as quoted above in the *Tattvaratnāvalī* and the works referred to, Tib. has here three pādas:

stoṅ.pa ñid-kyis.[1] grol.bar.ḥgyur /
de.ma.śes.pas.ḥchiṅ.bar.hgyur /
bagom.pa. lhag.ma. de.don. yin /

The first line gives the Skt. equivalent: *muktiḥ* (which may be taken as *muktis tu*) *śūnyatayā*. This suggests that according to the Tib. translator who has left out the word *dṛṣṭi* untranslated, the reading is *dṛṣṭyā* and not *dṛṣṭeḥ* (=*darśanāt*). The last two lines of the Tib. text may be translated as follows:

tadjñānena bandhanam /
tadarthāśeṣabhāvanā //

We have thus three *pādas* of the karikā, first, second, and fourth, only the third is missing. The kārikā is of Nāgārjuna as mentioned in the *Bodhicaryāvatārapañjikā*, p. 437.

Ll. 6-7. This sentence with grammatical mistakes is evidently defective and as such does not give any clear sense. The Tib. version gives us some help though not quite satisfactory. It runs:

de.lta. buḥi. theg. pa. gsum. rab. tu. bstan. pa. yaṅ. rtags. pa. daṅ. bcas. pa. daṅ/ rñog.pa med. pas. stoṅ.pa. sñam. sems. paḥi. daṅ. rtogs. par. bys. baḥi. phyir. ro //

It may be rendered thus:

īdṛsaṃ ca yānatritayaprakāśanaṃ saliṅgaṃ ceti śūnyatāmanyanārtham avagantyavyam iti.

---

1. Xylograph *kyi*.

Ll. 8-9. Here is a śloka:

nodāhṛtaṃ tvayā kiñcid ekam apy akṣaraṃ vibho /
kṛtsanś ca vai māyajanodharmavarṣaṇatarṣiṭah //

Here in the original MS in *c* there was *mayajano* (p. 63) which is emended in the present edition as *māyajano*. But why? What sense does it give? Again, what is the meaning of *dharmavarṣaṇatarṣiṭa*? In fact, the second half of the kārikā must be:

kṛtsnaś ca vaineyajano dharmavarṣaṇatarpitaḥ /

And it is entirely supported by Tib:

gdul. byaḥi. ḥgrao. ba. ma. lus. la /
chos. kyi. char. gyis. tshim. paḥaṅ. mdzod||

This kārikā is taken from Nāgārjuna's *Catustava* and quoted also in the *Bodhicaryāvatarapañjikā*, p. 420.

Ll. 10-11. This śloka is quoted also in the *Kuḍṛṣṭinirghātana (Adbvayavajrasaṃgraha*, p. 1). It may be noted here that in *b* of this śloka the words *vāyu* is omitted in Tib. version of the *Tattvaratnāvalī*, while, in that of the *Kuḍṛṣṭinirghātana* it is not so.

Ll. 12-13. For *sambhāro bedhasāmarthyāt* one should read *sambhārabhedasāmarthyāt* with Tib. reading: *tohogs. khi dbye. ba. nus.pa.yis.*

Ll. 14-15. The kārikā *yānānāṃ* is from the *Laṅkāvatāra*, III 204; X 458 (pp. 135, 322).[1] The variation to be noted is that in the *Laṅkāvatāra*, *vatāra* we have *citte tu vai parāvṛtte* for *parāvṛtte tu vai eitte* in *c*. For *yaylnaḥ* in *d* supported by Tib. (*hgro. ba*), some of the MSS of the *Laṅkāvatāra* read *yāninaḥ*. For *parāvṛtte* in *c* Tib. has *paribhūte* (*yoñs. su.gyur. pa.na.*)

Ll. 16-17. The kārikā in the present edition is:

saddharmaratnaghaṭikā vāg hy atra grathitāmalā /
hṛdaye kriyatāṃ dhirās tattvaratnāvalī mudā ||

And here runs the Tib. version:

dam. chos. las. grub. rin. po. che /
dri. med. ṅag. gi. skud. pas. brgyud /
dgaḥ. ba. skyed. byed. rin. chen. phreṅ /
brtan. pas. sñin. gdags. par. bgyi ||

---

1. In the *Bauddha Gān O Dohā*, p. 45, it is quoted with a wrong reading in *c*.

A few words of the original are here figuatively translated. Yet, it helps us in correcting two wrong readings in the Skt. kārikā. For *ghaṭikā* and *vāg hy atra* in the first half read *ghaṭitā* (Tib. *grub*) and *vāksūtra* (Tib. *ṅag. gi. skud*) respectively.

Ll. 18-19. The kārikā reads:

saṃgrahaṃ tu priyatvena vistaradveṣiṇā mayā /

bhūrira[nu] ttame tasmin kṣantavayaṃ vistarapriyāḥ //

Here for *saṃgrahaṃ tu* in *a* which cannot be construed, one may read *saṃgrahasya*. But according to Tib. *saṃgrahaṃ* is t be read *sārasya (sñiṅ.pa.la)*. For *c* (*bhūrira[nu]ttame tasmin*), which is evidently a wrong reading, read *bhūri tv anuktam etasmin* with Tib. *rgyas.par.bstam pa. ma lags.pa*. Tib. omits here *etasmin* and *vistaradveṣiṇā* in *b*, but adds *vicakṣaṇāḥ (mkas.pa)* or any suitable synonym for it in *d*.

In the last śloka (l. 20) *bhavyārthanayā* is to be separated from *prayatnād*.

There is still a number of other points to be discussed in the *Tattvaratnāvalī* as edited in the Gækwad's Oriental Series, but to avoid prolixity, I refrain now from doing so. I may think, however that I have succeeded in showing by what has been said above that the importance of Tibetan studies can in no way be underrated by true students of Buddhism.

Chapter - 14

Popular Buddhism

N. Dutt

Early Buddhism though propagated in different provincial dialects could not be appreciated by the common-folk in general.[1] The insistence on retirement from worldly life was a great handicap in the way of its popularity; so during the first century of its existence, it remained confined to the recluses and monasteries, and hardly reached the home and the hearth. It was perhaps about a century after Buddha's death that the religion became dynamic, assimilating some of the ideas and thoughts current around and stepped down from its high pedestal of exclusiveness and abstruse ideals to appeal to the more intellectual and faithful among the common-folk. This move towards popularity too did not proceed far as we find that it just allowed a little scope for rituals of a sober character, a little of faith and worship, and a slight relaxation from the stringency of disciplinary rules. Aśoka as a ruler gave preference to the popular ideals, producing good citizens, and not to the spiritual, making the people unsocial. It cannot be ascertained how far Aśoka had a hand in the matter of making the religion popular but the history of the religion shows that after the days of Aśoka, it developed new aspects which became so very popular that the reoriented religion spread all over India, marking every notable spot with magnificent structures of rare artistic value, and ultimately reaching countries beyond the borders of India. There are, in fact, two stages in the course of its attainment of popularity, one of the pre-Aśokan days and other of the post-Aśokan.

I. Pre-Aśokan Period

The pre-Aśokan form of the religion provided no scope for emotion, nor for devotion or worship, not to speak of rituals. Its dry-

---

1. Cf. Grünwedel, *Buddhist Art in India*, p. 67: "Originally, Buddhism was only a philosophy, no religion; but therein consisted the weakness of the Buddha doctrines, which speedily became unpopular on that account."

as-dust ethical principles and doctrinal teachings based on so-called reason hardly attracted the attention of the common-folk. Among the householders it was only the cultured few like Anāthapiṇḍika and Visākhā, Jīvaka and Āmrapālī, Citta and Nakulapitā who took interest in the religion and worked for its success. Among the recluses and intellectuals also there were not very many who could dive deep into the truths of the religion, and it was probably this lack of appreciation of his teachings that made Buddha hesitate to preach the religion to one and all.

Ecclesiastical Rituals

In course of time, however, there was some accretion of rituals in the form of *trisaraṇa*, lower and higher ordinations, observance of *uposatha*, *vassā* and *pavāraṇā*. These rituals attracted some converts of a mediocre type and appreciably helped the enlargement of the body hitherto known as Śākyaputtiya Samaṇas. Around this body grew up a number of householders, who impressed by the saintly character of some of the monks as also by simple ethical teachings of the religion, and the rituals of *Trisaraṇa*, and other ecclesiastical functions like *Pavāraṇā* requiring the services of laymen, avowed themselves as *upāsakas* and *upāsikās*.[1] It is rather remarkable that the religion did not yield to the wishes of the mass any further, by providing objects of worship or by allowing the laymen to take any part in the ecclesiastical functions.

Trisaraṇa. There was no form of prayer except an expression of faith in the *Triratna*. The three articles of faith, compulsory for every monk and nun or layman and lay-woman was the thrice utterance of the formula,—

(i) *Buddhaṃ saraṇaṃ gacchāmi*

(ii) *Dhammaṃ saraṇaṃ gacchāmi*

and

(iii) *Saṃghaṃ saraṇaṃ gacchāmi*.

There has been a good deal of discussion among the Buddhist scholiasts about the meaning of *saraṇa* and of *Buddha*, *Dharma* and *Saṅgha*. The best and the earliest interpretation is found in a few couplets preserved in the canonical texts.[2] These are.—

1. Dutt, *Early Monastic Buddhism* (henceforth abbreviated as *EMB*.), I, chap. xii.
2. *Dhammapada*, pp. 188-192; *Udānavarga*, xxvii, 28-30; *Divyāvadāna*, p. 164; *Abhidharmakośa*, iv, 80 etc. See L. de la Vallée Poussin, *Doctrine des Réfuges*, in "Mélanges chinois et bouddhiques," i, (1931-32), p. 75.

वहवः शरणं यान्ति पर्वतांश्च वनानि च।
आरामंश्चैत्यवृक्षांश्च मनुष्या भयतर्जिताः॥
न ह्येतच्छरणं श्रेष्ठं नैतच्छरणमुत्तमम्।
नैतच्छरणमागम्य सर्वदुःखात् प्रमुञ्चते॥
यस्तु बुद्धं च धर्म संघं च शरणं गतः।
आर्यसत्यानि चत्वारि पश्यति प्रज्ञया सदा॥
दुःखं दुःस्वसमुत्पादं दुःखस्य समतिक्रमम्।
आर्यं चाष्टाङ्गिकं मार्गं क्षेमनिर्वाणगामिनम्॥
एतद्धि शरणं श्रेष्ठं एतच्छरणमुत्तमम्।
एतच्छरणमागम्य सर्वदुःखात् प्रमुच्यते॥

In these couplets, *saraṇaṃ* means 'seeking protection' from evils. In the formulae of *Triratna*, the protection that one seeks is not from the worldly evils but from the suffering to which a human being is destined.[1] Such protection can be secured by developing faith in Buddha, Dharma and Saṅgha, and by realising the four truths and the eightfold path, and not by leading solitary meditative life in the hills or forests nor by visiting temples and shrines (*caityas*).

The faith in the *Triratna* is usually expressed in these terms:

(i) *Iti pi so Bhagavā arahaṃ sammāsambuddho vijjācaraṇasampanno sugato lokavidu anuttaro purisadammasārathi satthā devamanussānaṃ.*

(Bhagavā, the enlightened, is endowed with knowledge and good conduct, he is the knower of the world, the guide in disciplining men, the incomparable, the teacher of men and gods).

(ii) *Svakkhāto Bhagavatā dhammo sandiṭṭhiko akāliko ehipassiko opanayiko paccattaṃ veditabbo viññūhi.*

(The Dhamma preached by Bhagavā produces fruit in his life, invites everybody, has no limitation of time, leads one to the goal and is realisable only by the wise within one's ownself).

(iii) *Supaṭipanno Bhagavato sāvakasaṅgho yad idam cattāri purisayugāni aṭṭhapurisapuggalā, esa Bhagavato sāvakasaṅgho āhuṇeyyo pāhuṇeyyo dakkhiṇeyyo añjalikaraṇīyo anuttaraṃ puññkkhettaṃ lokassa.*

(The Saṅgha consists of monks, who are in one of the four stages of sanctification, are righteous, exerting for knowledge,

1. *Sumaṅgala Vilāsini*, I, p. 230.

observing good conduct, who are worthy of gifts, praise and respects, and who are fit recipients of gifts from laymen).

The Buddhist scholiasts,[1] who were imbued with the principles of early Buddhism, were at a loss to justify these three articles of faith. Some of them, who looked upon Buddha's mortal body as impure, said that 'Buddha' in the formulae implied a collection of *dharmas*, while *Dharma* implied only the last two truths viz., *duḥkha-nirodha*[2] and the *aṣṭāṅgikamārga*, which are pure, the other two denoting impure *dharmas*. Saṅgha in the formulae implied *śīlas* or the moral duties which make a person an *arhat*, and not merely a member of the order. It is doubtful how far this interpretation of the scholiasts appealed to the common-folk. We know that the utterance of the *Trisaraṇa* formulae was made compulsory for both monks and laity, and that this utterance alone transformed a non-Buddhist to a Buddhist.[3] Hence, we may safely state that these three articles of faith served as a means of popularising the religion, and these were also looked upon as spells (*paritta*) for protection from evils, or evil destiny.

The utterance of the Trisaraṇa is usually followed nowadays by taking the vow of observing the first five *śīlas* and then by chanting the *Maṅgala Sutta*. In the canonical texts, however, there is no indication of this procedure.

Uposatha. It is admitted in the Vinaya[4] that the idea of holding fortnightly meetings was suggested to Buddha by Bimbisāra, whose object was that the monks should deliver religious discourses to the people at large on certain days of the month. These assemblies however soon turned into ritualistic institutions, requiring monks to be present at the meetings and confess their sins, if any committed during the preceding fortnight, after the formal recital of the Pātimokka rules.[5] This ceremony undoubtedly gave satisfaction to a class of monks who viewed the observance of Pātimokkha rules as more important than

---

1. See La Vallée Poussin, *op. cit.* In the *Jñānaprasthāna sūtra*, we find the following exposition:—
(i) The real *dharmas*, which have for name or appellation or designation the expression 'Buddha'—those who take refuge in the *Aśaikṣa-dharmas*, which make the Buddha, are said to take refuge in Buddha.
(ii) The real *dharmas*, which have for their name, appellation or designation the word 'Dharma'—those who take refuge in the removal of thirst, i.e, destruction, detachment, Nirvāṇa are said to have taken refuge in Dharma.
(iii) The real *dharmas*, which have for their name, appellation or designation the word 'Saṃgha'—those who take refuge in both the *Śaikṣa* and *Aśaikṣa-dharmas*, are said to have taken refuge in the Saṃgha.
2. *Divyāvadāna*, p. 617.
3. *EMB.*, II. Ch. XII.
4. *Vinaya*, i. p. 617.
5. For details see *EMB.*, vol. I, pp. 289f.

the inner spiritual development and attracted some men of the mediocre type.

Pabbajjā and *Upasampadā*. The ceremony of ordination was originally a very simple affair. It was done by Buddha by the mere utterance of *ehi bhikkhu*. Gradually it turned into a fairly long ceremony with two ordinations, one lower (*pabbajjā*) and the other higher (*upasampadā*).[1] This ceremony, which required shaving of head, donning of yellow robes and living in a monastery, attracted some men who could not fully comprehend the philosophical teachings. In the *Sāmaññaphala Sutta* there are also some hints about the gains and honour received by an ordained person, e.g., it is said that the immediate gain of a person, whatever his status might be before his ordination, is that he is respected by kings and nobles, and obtains robes, food, bed, medicine and other requisities.[2]

Vassāvāsa, *Pavāraṇā* and *Kaṭhina*.[3] The other ceremonical functions which gradually crept into the religion were the formal observance of the rainy season retreat. The monks were required to stay during the three months of the rainy season at a fixed abode. At the close of the retreat, the monks performed the *Pavāraṇā* ceremony, which is similar to the Uposatha, but on account of the occasion on which it is performed, special importance was attached to it, and householders were told that gifts made on his particular occasion were more meritorious than at other times. With this *Pavāraṇā* ceremony was associated another ceremony called *Kaṭhina* in which the making of robes formed the chief object. These two ceremonies Pavāraṇā and Kaṭhina served to popularise the religion not only among those who wanted to join the order but also among the householders, who patiently waited for these days for making their gifts, particularly robes, and thereby assure their happiness in this existence and rebirth in the heavens.

The ceremonies mentioned above were no doubt useful for the spiritual development of a person, but strictly speaking, were not in consonance with the principles laid down for the attainment of spiritual perfection. It has got to be admitted that these ceremonies were introduced in imitation of, or competition with, other contemporary religious systems in order to secure more converts, and it is not improbable that by these ceremonies, the religion attracted more men than it would otherwise had done.

---

1. For details, see *EMB.*, vol. 1, pp. 280-281.
2. *Dīgha.*, p. p. 61-62.
3. For details, see *EMB.*, I, p. 292-3.

Worship of Catiya and Stūpa

Neither in the *Vinaya* nor in the *Sutta-piṭaka*, except the *Mahā-parinibbānasutta*, there is any direction for making and worshipping *Catiya and Stūpas*. In the *Vinaya* there is mention of two Cetiyas[1] where Buddha stopped, while in the *Pāṭikasuttanta*[2] as also in the *Mahāparinibbānasutta*,[3] there are references to the Cetiyas situated around Vesāli, viz., Gotamaka-cetiya on the south, Sattamba-cetiya on the west, Bahuputta-cetiya on the north. The other Cetiyas mentioned in the *Mahāparinibbānasutta* are Udena, Sarandada, Cāpāla,[4] Ānanda,[5] (in Bohganagara), and Makuṭabandhana[6] of the Mallas.

From the list of cetiyas given above, it is apparent that long before Buddhism made its appearance, there was prevalence of worship of *cetiyas*, which might be a tree, a stone and a spot believed to be sanctified or haunted by a good or evil spirit.[7] The existence of Cetiyas is taken as an admitted fact by Buddha himself.

Apart from the Cetiyas, there was also the ancient custom of erecting mounds (*stūpas*) on the relics of saintly persons or distinguished kings, princes and nobles as also over the sites sanctified by a saint's presence. It was this ancient custom which we find re-iterated in the *Mahāparinibbāna-sutta*. Buddha is made to say that *stūpas* should be erected on the relics of (i) a Tathāgata, (ii) a Paccekabuddha, (iii) a Tathāgatasāvaka and (iv) a monarch (cakkavatti) evidently with a view to make the Buddhists refrain from erecting and worshipping any mound sanctified by a spirit or a non-Buddhist saint. The most suitable site recommended for the erection of a *stūpa*, is the crossing of four highways. Worship of such four kinds of *stūpa* by garlands, scents, or coloured powders was regarded as meritorious, as it gave an expression to one's deep faith in the religion. Along with these directions, there is the description of the manner in which the earthly remains of a Tathāgata should be cremated. The erection of *stūpa* over Buddha's relics has created history, and even today the sight of the relics deposited in some of the monasteries is a matter of awe and inspiration to the devotees.

---

1. *Vinaya*, i, p. 35: Supatiṭṭha cetiya near Rājagaha; ii. p. 172: Aggālavacetiya at Alavi.
2. *Dīgha*, iii, p. 9-10.
3. *Dīgha*, ii, pp. 102-3, 118.
4. *Ibid.*
5. *Ibid.*, pp. 123, 126.
6. *Ibid.*, p. 160-61.
7. See the gāthās cited above p. 246-7. Also Gisbert Combaz, *L'evolution du stūpa en Asie* in ' Mélanges chinois et bouddhiques', ii (1932-33), pp. 168ff.

The whole account of the erection and worship of *stūpa*, particularly over Buddha's relics and the merit accruing therefrom was undoubtedly incorporated into the *Mahāparinibbāna-sutta* after Buddha's demise and had nothing to do with the great Teacher, who evidently could not have thought of what would become of his relics and who would be their claimants. This idea of erection and worship of *stūpa* was undoubtedly a post-Buddha development. The interpolator, who put in the directions for worshipping *cetiyas* and *stūpas* and held out the hope that by such worship one would be reborn in the heavens, realised the inconsistency with the principles of the religion, and immediately corrected himself by adding the remark that the advanced monks were not to occupy themselves with such worship of *stūpas*, and that they must exert to attain the goal while the worship of *stūpas* should be left to the laity alone, the wise brāhmaṇas, khattiyas and gahapatis.[1] The traditions about Aśoka's zeal to collect the relics and erect *stūpas* over them also prove that the stūpa-worship became widely prevalent. It is very likely that by Aśoka's time, the stūpa-worship became a regular feature of the religion.[2]

Four Places of Pilgrimage

Like the worship of *cetiyas* and *stūpas*, it must be sometime after Buddha's *parinirvāṇa* that idea of pilgrimage came into the minds of some Buddhist monks, at whose instance, some imaginary discourses attributed to Buddha were incorporated into the *Mahāparinibbāna Sutta*. It sounds strange in the mouth of Buddha, who was all along averse to any form of worship[3] and taught *attadīpo attasaraṇo anaññasaraṇo dhammadīpo dhammasaraṇo anaññasaraṇo*[4] (depend on your own self as the light, as the refuge and not on anything else; depend on the *dhamma* as the light, as the refuge, and not on anything else) to have admonished his disciples to earn merit by paying a visit to the four places sanctified by his (i) birth, (ii) attainment of bodhi, (iii) promulgation of *dhammacakka* and (iv) *parinirvāṇa*. The inconsistency is at once apparent in the fact that one of the places recommended for visit is the site of his demise. Hence, there can be no doubt that the idea of pilgrimage was not that of Buddha but was of his disciples and of a time when Buddha had passed away. The idea, however, caught the imagination of the people, particularly, of the

---

1. *Dīgha*, ii p. 141.
2. See the account in the *Divyāvadāna*.
3. *Dīgha*, ii, p. 138; *Na kho Ānanda ettavatā Tatthāgato sakkato vā hoti garukato vā pūjito vā apacito vā etc.*
4. Cf. *Mahāvastu*, X. p. 334.

lay-disciples. The most remarkable an instance of this is that of Aśoka who paid a visit to the birth place of Buddha, evidently with the hope of earning some merit. Throughout the history of Buddhism since the days of Aśoka, the idea of pilgrimage appealed strongly to the Buddhist, both monks and laymen, and even today the Buddhist devotees from far off countries like Burma and Ceylon, China and Japan regard this pilgrimage as an act of great merit.

Nirvāṇa through Faith

In the earliest form of monastic Buddhism the only means recommended for the attainment of emancipation was perfection in the *sīlacitta-paññā* practices.[1] Occasionally perfection in the *satipaṭṭhāna* practices was recognised as another means for reaching the goal,[2] but nowhere *saddhā* and practice of *brahmavihāra* were recognised as such. It is therefore striking that we should find in the *Majjhima Nikāya* a discourse[3] in which *saddhā* is made the basic and perfection in the *brahmavihāras* as the ultimate factors for the attainment of Nirvāṇa. This new path, which attached less importance to the observance of the Pātimokkha rules, was definitely a step towards making the religion popular among a certain section of the people, who were not able to lead the life of a bhikkhu.

Saddhā (faith),[4] as expressed in the formulae *Trisarṇa*,[5] is mentioned as an essential element for spiritual progress, but that *saddhā* was looked upon only as an antidote to inclination to non-Buddhist religious faith. It was an antidote to *vicikicchā* or doubt about the greatness of Buddha, excellence of his teaching and uprightness of his disciples. In the *Vatthupamasutta*,[6] the process of attainment of *Nibbāna* through *saddhā* is detailed thus:—

(i) An adept should first get rid of the mental impurities, such as *abhijjā* (undue desire for gain), *macchariya* (miserliness), *makkha* (hypocrisy), *māyā* (deceifulness) *sāṭheyya* (double-dealing), *thambhosārambho* (pride or excitement caused by attachment to one's own acquisitions), and *pamāda* (carelessness).

---

1. See *EMB.*, vol I, pp. 199f.
2. *Majjhima*, i. p. 55: Ekāyano ayaṃ bhikkhave maggo sattānaṃ visuddhiyā yad idaṃ cattāro satipaṭṭhanā.
3. Vatthupamasutta, *Majjhima*, i. p. 36f.
4. For an exhaustive exposition of *Saddhā*, see. B.M. Barua, 'Faith in Buddhism' in *Buddhistic Studies*, p. 329.

   Cf. Saddhāya tarati ogham appamādena aṇṇavaṃ
   viriyena dukkhaṃ acceti paññāya parisujjhati *Suttanipāta*, v. 184.
5. See above, p. 246.
6. *Majjhima*, i. p. 36f.

(ii) After the removal of the above-mentioned impurities, the adept is required to develop unflinching faith (*saddhā*) in the *Triratna*.

(iii) The more the metal impurities are removed the stronger becomes his faith (*saddhā*) in Buddha, Dhamma and Saṅgha. Such faith produces in his mind the satisfaction that he has achieved something good. Such satisfaction in turn produces joy and deep pleasure (*pīti*) which makes the body calm and the mind serene, and ultimately leads to mental concentration.

(iv) After developing perfect concentration of mind, the adept is required to practise the four *brahamvihāras*, in other words, he must practise *mettā* (love), *karuṇā* (compassion), muditā (feeling of joy at others' success) and *upekkhā* (equanimity) towards all beings of all corners of the world.[1]

(v) After attaining perfection in the four *brahmavihāras*, the adept realises the four truths, removes the three impurities (*āsavas*) viz., *kāma* (desire), *bhava* (desire for rebirth) and *avijjā* (ignorance of the truth). He then feels convinced that he has completed his task, and will have no more rebirth, i.e., he attains Nibbāna. Thus we see that by *saddhā* and *brahmavihāra* one could achieve *Nibbāna* and this path could be taken by the householders as there was no question of renunciation or observance of Pātimokkha rules. This new process was really a move to make the religion popular among the householders and a product of a time midway between Buddha and Aśoka.

It may be argued that *saddhā* is not devotion (*bhakti*)[2] and hence it has no fitting place in the popular form of the religion. There is some force in this argument, but what is needed to be pointed out is that *saddhā* eliminates the long process of observance of *sīlas*, i.e., the *pātimokkha* rules, and the process dealt with above eliminates many of the arduous tasks imposed upon a monk to attain perfection in the four *jhānas*, and to comprehend the *anattā* and *anicca* theories. It brings a new element, the *brahmavihāras*, which so far had no place in early Buddhism. In short, it is a new and shorter process suited to a person who is not necessarily a monk or nun, and that it was meant so is clear from the remarks in the above mentioned *sutta* that a person taking recourse to this new process may take luxurious food as that of a householder and that it would not stand in his way of attaining the goal. This is significant of the fact that the process was intended more for the laity than for the recluses and actually we find this particular course recommended to the householder, Mahānāma,[3]

1. See *Infra* and *EMB.*, I. p. 228f.
2. Contrast Har Dayal's remarks in his *Bodhisattva Doctrine*. p. 32.
3. See *Aṅguttara*, V, pp. 320-332.

who was addressed by Buddha in these words: "O Mahānāma, when you bear in mind that you have unflinching faith in the *Triratna*, when you realise that you have observed the precepts fully, when you are convinced that you are great in charity and when you feel assured that you possess *saddhā,sīla, suta, cāga* and *paññā* as that of the gods, you would surely be reborn as a god. Again, when your mind becomes free from attachment (*rāga*), hatred (*dosa*) and delusion (*moha*) and you will feel that you have achieved something good, you will have joy and serene pleasure, which in turn will make your body calm and at ease and your mind will get concentrated". In another discourse[1] the same Mahānāma was told that an upāsaka by firm faith could become quick-witted (*hāsapaññā javanpaññā*) and attain emancipation by the realisation of *akiññcaññā* (desirelessness whether for heavenly life or Nibbāna,) *suññatā* (essencelessness of worldly objects) and *animittatā* (characteristiclessness of worldly objects). In the *Majjhima Nikāya*,[2] however, it is pointed out that some monks by saddhā attain the Anāgāmi stage only, because they regard Bhagavā as omniscient and that his teaching excellent and they exert strenuously so that their bodies become dried up into skin, bones and sinews. It seems, therefore, that *saddhā* gradually rose in the estimation of the Buddhist monks and came to be recognised as a means to the goal. The importance of *saddhā* in the life of layman has already been dealt with; it assured them rebirth in one of the heavens, and it was only a step further that *saddhā* combined with the perfection in *brahmavihāras* brought them full emancipation.

The early Buddhists were aware of the practice of *brahmavihāras,* which they classed as *appamaññas* (immeasurables). By this practice one developed a sublime mental state,—in which, he could look upon all beings of the world with the same feeling of love and compassion as one would have towards his son;—in which, he felt happy at the spiritual or material success of every person, be he a friend or foe; and—in which, he remains unmoved by weal or woe. The *brahmavihāras*, however were not included in the list of thirtyseven *bodhipakkhiya* and other dhammas which Buddha declared as his own teaching.[3] In the *Visuddhimagga*, their place is given after the four *jhānas* (meditations) and before the four *samāpattis* (higher trances),[4] but in any case, their practice was not regarded as compulsory for the attainment of Nibbāna. The trend of the remark in the Pāli texts[5] is

1. *Saṃyutta*, v, pp. 376f.
2. *Majjhima*, i. p. 480-481.
3. See *Majjhima*, ii, p. 11f.
4. See *EMB.*, I. p. 228f.
5. *Majjhima*, ii, p. 76; *Dīgha*, i, p.251; *Aṅguttara*, ii, p. 129.

that their practice led to rebirth in one of the Brahmalokas only, i.e., the highest form of existence in the constituted sphere, in other words, it did not conduce to Nibbāna. These remarks point to the fact that practice of *brahmavihāras* did not form a part of original Buddhism.

Mrs. Rhys Davids, it seems, was justified in writing that it was taught by the "unknown co-founder of Buddhism."[1] The fact that these practices appear also in the *Yogasūtra* of Patañjali leads us to infer that these originated among the non-Buddhist or pre-Buddhist thinkers. The nature of mental practices envisaged in the *brahmavihāras* also suggest that these were meant more for the householders than for the recluses.[2] In the *Saddhamapuṇḍarīka* the practice of *brahmavihāras* is given a place next to the *pāramitās*.[3] While in the *Mahāvastu*[4] it is stated that a monk can attain *nirvāṇa* by practising the four *brahmavihāras*. In the *Daśabhūmikasūtra*, the practice of *brahmavihāras* is placed next to the four *dhyānas* in the exercises prescribed for the attainment of the third *bhūmi*.[5] A bodhisattva is expected to continue this practice of four *brahmavihāras* up to the seventh *bhūmi*,[6] in which he realises the *tathatā*, and goes beyond the training stage.

Relaxation of Disciplinary Rules

There is a hint, in the path of *saddhā* and *brahmavihāra,* that for the attainment of Nirvāṇa, one need not always be a strict observer of the monastic rules of discipline (see above). Buddha no doubt laid more emphasis on the control of the mind than on the control of body and speech,[7] though it was for from his intention that his followers should show laxity in observing monastic rules. A century after Buddha's death, appeared the Mahasaṅghikas who put a new interpretation on Buddha's directions, and set on foot a movement against the rigid orthodoxy of the earlier disciples, whose over-zealousness for the observance of monastic rules led to the sacrifice of essentials. It is an indication that a group of thinkers attached more value to the purification of body and mind and the study of logic than to the punctillious observance of Vinaya rules. We have on the authority of Paramārtha, the following statement attributed to the Kaukulikas an

1. C.A.F Rhys Davids, *Gotama*, p. 180; *JRAS.*, 1928, p. 271.
2. See above.
3. p. 142.
4. iii, p. 421.
5. *Ibid.*, p. 276.
6. *Aspects of Mahāyāna Buddhism*, Ch. IV.
7. *Majjhima*, i. p. 372: Imesaṃ tiṇṇaṃ kammāaṃ evam paṭivibhattānaṃ manokammaṃ mahāsāvajjataraṃ paññāpemi.

off-shoot of the Mahāsaṅghikas that "a bhiksu may or may not have three robes for covering his body; may or may not reside in a monastery; and may or may not take his meal within the time-limit. The Vinaya rules about residence and food were abrogated by Buddha; it is clear that the real teaching of Buddha was not Vinaya; but the study of the logical principles (*nyāya*),[1] i.e., Abhidharma. According to the Dharmaguptas, the Prātimokṣa rules were lost when the *saddharma* disappeared, hence there are no more rules, *sīmabandha* and *karmānta*.[2]

It is not improbable that this new viewpoint attracted a large number of recruits and helped to increase its followers. The relaxation in the monastic rules, of course, had nothing to do with the laity, and so whatever appeal, it could have, was confined to the monks and nuns.

We may now sum up the factors that made Buddhism popular in the pre-Aśokan period thus:—

(i) *Trisaraṇa* was regarded as the three articles of faith.

(ii) The ecclesiastical ceremonies gave satisfaction to the less philosophically minded disciples.

(iii) Worship of *Caityas* and *Stūpas* allowed some scope for the expression of devotion (*bhakti*).

(iv) Visits to the four places of pilgrimage were looked upon as attractive means of earning merit.

(v) *Saddhā* and *brahmavihāra* practices were regarded by some persons as the simpler and shorter means for the attainment of Nibbāna. And lastly,

(vi) Relaxation in the stringency of the Vinaya rules appealed to a class of persons who did not approve the rigid orthodoxy of the earlier schools of disciples.

II. Post-Aśokan Period

The few deviations from the earliest principles of Buddhism dealt with above were hardly enough to make the religion popular. The persons who took to *saddhā* and *brahmavihāra* path for emancipation were few and far between; the emphasis was still on the monastic life. The cult of *cetiyas* and *stūpa*-worship made very little progress and the householders with their *Trisaraṇa* and other rituals still remained outside the Buddhist fold as mere suppliers of material needs of the monks and nuns and as faithful listeners to the moral

---

1. See Paul Demievelle *L' origine des sects bouddhiques* in *Mélanges chinois et bouddhiques,* vol. I. 1931-321 pp. 19. 46.
2. *Abbidarmakośa*, iv. 39.

discourses delivered to them by the monks on certain occasions. The Aśokan edicts reveal no change in this austere attitude of the early Buddhists—the only relieving feature being that Aśoka favoured the view that the people should not care very much for recluse-life and should perform good deeds (*kuśalakarma-pathas*) to ensure them an after-life in the heavens. Hence we may say that the real move to make the religion popular among the common-folk was taken after Aśoka. This movement consisted mainly in the following five ways:—

(i) Deification of Buddha.

(ii) Compilation of Jātaka-literature.

(iii) Sanction of Image-worship.

(iv) Introduction of Pāramitā-cult. And

(v) Promulgation of Bodhisattva Doctrine.

Deification of Buddha

In the pre-Aśokan days, Buddha had already come to be looked upon as the highest god superior to Brahmā, Viṣṇu or Śiva. This deification should be attributed first to the Mahāsaṅghikas and the Andhakas, and then to the Sarvāstivādins. It has been shown[1] while discussing the doctrines of the Mahāsaṅghikas and their offshoots that Buddha had been given all the attributes of the highest god, and that his appearance in this world was only a make-belief. He took birth as Siddhārtha Gautama, went through all the ways of a householder and ultimately renounced the world to become a saint just in order to follow the ways of the world (*lokānuvartana*).[2] Buddha was supra-mundane (*lokottara*) and was made of pure *dharmas*. Everything of the great *ṛṣi* was transcendental including his advent into the world. In the *Mahāvastu*,[3] he is described thus:—

लोकोत्तरा भगवतो चर्या लोकोत्तरं कुशलमूलम।
गमनं स्थितं निषणं शयितं लोकोत्तरं मुनिनो ॥
यत् तत् सुगतशरीरं भवते भवस्य बन्धनक्षयकरणम्।
लोकोत्तरं तदपि भो इत्यत्र न संशयः कार्यो ॥
चीवरधरणं मुनिनो लोकोत्तरं अत्र संशयो नास्ति।
आहाराहरणमथो लोकोत्तरभेव सुगतस्य ॥
देशना नरनागानां सर्वलोकोत्तरा मता।
यथातथं प्रवक्ष्यामि माहात्म्यं बरबुद्धिनाम् ॥
देशकालवशं प्राप्य परिपाकं च कर्मणः।
सत्यं वा अभिनिर्वृत्तं धर्मं देशेन्ति नायकाः ॥
लोकानुवर्तनां बुद्धा अनुवर्तन्ति लोकिकीम्।
प्रज्ञप्तिमनुवर्तन्ति यथा लोकात्तरामपि ॥ etc.

1. See *EMB.*, II. pp. 63-75f.
2. *Mahāvastu*, I. p. 167-8.
3. *Ibid.*

The above and other passages in the *Mahāvastu* leave no room for doubt that about the time of its composition (i.e., 2nd century B.C.)[1] Buddha had already become the highest god, at least, to a large section of the Buddhists.

The account of Buddha's life in the *Lalitavistara*, the accredited text of the Sarvāstivādins, does not extol Buddha so much as has been done in the *Mahāvastu*. It is more realistic though it attributes divine and super-divine qualities to the Teacher. It says that Buddha while staying in the womb of his mother was enclosed in a casket and from there he was delivering discourses to the gods who paid him visits.[2] After his birth, he appears to exist at the same moment in all the houses built for him by the faithful. He pays the customary visit to the temples but the gods therein bow down to him. In his boyhood, he was so learned that the teacher stagger in his presence. In his youth, he possessed already all the kingly powers and skill and surpassed everybody in strength. In this text[3] he is eulogized thus:—

जातस्य मह्य इय कम्पितः त्रिसहस्रः।
शकश्च ब्रह्मा सुराश्च महोरगाश्च॥
चन्द्रश्च सूर्य तथ वैश्रवणः कुमारो।
मूर्द्धा कमेषु निपतितस्य नमस्ययन्ते॥
कतमोऽन्य देव मम उत्तरियो विशिष्टो।
यस्मिन् मम प्रणयसे त्वमिहाद्य अम्ब॥
देवातिदेव अहू उत्तम सर्वदेवैः।
देवो न मेऽस्ति सदृशः कुत उत्तरा वा॥
लोकानुवर्तन प्रतीत इति अम्ब यास्ये।
दृष्टा विकुर्वित ममा जनता उदग्रा॥
अधिमात्र गौरव करिष्यति विचित्रकारो।
ज्ञास्यन्ति देवमनुजा स्वयमेव देवः॥

— — — — —

शास्त्राणि यानि प्रचरन्ति च देवलोके
संख्या लिपिश्च गणनाऽपि च धातुतन्त्रम्।
ये शिल्पयोग पृथुलौकिक अप्रमेया-
स्तेष्वेषु शिक्षितु पुरा बहुकल्पकोट्यः॥
किन्तू जनस्य अनुवर्तनतां करोति
लिपिशालामगतुं सुशिक्षित-शिक्षणार्थम्।

---

1. Winterniuz, *History of Indian Literature*, II, p. 247.
2. Cf. also *Mahavastu*, I, p. 214.
3. R.L. Mitra, *Lalitavistara*, pp. 136, 142.

परिपाचनार्थं बहुदारक अग्रयाने
अन्यांश्च सत्त्वनियुतानमृते विनेतुम्।

Though this text maintains a more sober outlook than the *Mahāvastu*, there is no doubt that Buddha was regarded by the Sarvāstivādins as a divine being though not the highest god. Though he was proficient in everything, he followed the way of the world to educate the people. The time of composition of this work, according to Winternitz, spread over a long period commencing from the early Christian eras.[1] It may therefore be safely stated that in the 2nd and 1st centuries B.C., a certain section of the Buddhist regarded Buddha as the highest god while another section as a great divine being, endowed with all possible virtues and knowledge.

We need not discuss the conception of the Sthaviravādins, who tried to maintain even at this day that Buddha was after all a human saint but with attributes surpassing those of the gods and that in purity and knowledge he was the highest of all constituted beings.[2] This school of thought maintained the realistic conception throughout its long history but it did not gain the same amount of popularity as the Mahāsaṅghikas and the Sarvāstivādins did in the southern and northern parts of India respectively. However realistic the Theravādins might have been, they had to yield to the popular demand of Buddha-worship, and in course of time they allowed the placing of images of Buddha in their temples, and in one of their late texts the *Mahāvaṃsa*, there is also an elaborate description as to how the first image of Buddha was made and how grand were the ceremonies and festivals for putting up the image.

Image-Worship

In the *Mahāvastu* and the *Lalitavistara* Buddha is deified but there are no directions for making images of Buddha. The earliest literary evidence relating to image-making is yielded by the *Divyāvadāna*, in which Aśoka is found to be consulting Piṇḍola Bharadvāja regarding the features (*mahāpuruṣa-lakṣaṇa*) of the image.[3]

1. See Winternitz, *op. cit.*, p. 255-6: "It is therefore only correct to say that the *Lalitavistara* offers us very old traditions concerning the Buddha legend as well as some which are centuries later"..........."It is, however, most informative as regards the development of the Buddha legend from its earliest beginnings when only the chief events in the life of the great founder of the religion are adorned with miracles, down to that boundless deification of the Master, in which, from the beginning to the end of his career he appears mainly as a god above all gods."

2. *Majjhima*, i, p. 171:—Sabbābhindhu sabbovidu'haṃ asmi/
sabbesu dhammesu anupalitata//
sabbaṃjaho taṇhakkhaye vimutto/
sayam abiññāya kam uddisayyam// Cf. *Mahāvastu*

3. See *Infro*.

In the *Mahāvaṃsa* too is recorded a similar attempt of Aśoka who consulted the Nāga king for an account of the image. One need not be so credulous as to take this tradition of Aśoka as authentic, but the fact is that the practice of image-worship was taken up by the Buddhist sometime before the 4th century A.D. about which time the *Divyāvadāna* and the *Mahāvaṃsa* were composed. We may now pass on to the monumental evidences. In the Sanchi and Barhut sculptures there are no images of Buddha. The most significant fact is that the seats of Buddha are shown as vacant. The earlier methods of indicating Buddha's place in a scence were by depicting his Vajrāsana, Bodhi tree or *pādukā* (wooden slippers) or stūpa. If the date of Sanchi and Barhut sculptures be placed in the 2nd and 1st century B.C. we have to admit that image-worship did not prevail at that period. The practice of image-worship therefore came into vogue about the 1st or 2nd century A.D. at the earliest. The Amarāvati sculptures, belonging to the Mahāsaṅghikas and their offshoots, are studded with numerous Buddha-images but the dates of these sculptures are placed by the archaeologists in the 2nd century A.D.[1]

Though the image of Buddha is wanting in the earlier sculptures there are ample evidences to show the wide prevalence of symbol worship. The artists probably did not make an image of the omniscient refulgent Buddha with all the signs of great men (*mahāpuruṣa*), but the feeling of adoration to Buddha was there, and this they expressed by concourse of men and gods and even animals, bowing down reverentially to the stūpas, Bodhi-tree or the Vajrāsana, or offering flowers and garlands. In the post-Christian eras, however, the Buddha images not only came into vogue, but practically the Buddhist centres were flooded with such innumerable images, some of exquisite Gandharan art while others of indigenous local developments. Merit accrued to both the artist and the donor of an image, and so it was quite natural there should be such an exuberance of Buddha-images in the post-Christian eras. Both the Hīnayānists and the Mahāyānists started making images and temples and decorated the *stūpas* with countless images.

Jātakas and Avadānas

In the *Mahāvastu* and the *Abhiniṣkramaṇasūtra* we have not only a biography of Buddha but also a number of stories dealing with Buddha's supposed previous existence as also other traditions. The underlying object of the stories of Buddha's previous births is to show that each event in this life was the result of a past deed of his. These

1. *Buddhist Remains in Andhra*, etc. by K.R. Subramanian, 1932, p. 15.

stories served not only to establish the law of *karma* which Buddhism has borrowed from the pre-Buddhistic thoughts but also to convince the common-folk that any act of theirs would similarly be fruitful, and it may be that some of them might sow the seeds of merit like Siddhārtha Gautama and ultimately attain Buddhahood. In the latter case, they would be Bodhisattvas as was Siddhārtha Gautama in his previous lives. The *Lalitavistara* refers to the meritorious deeds performed by him in his previous existences[1] but does not give the stories in detail which were to be found partly in the Vinaya piṭaka of the Sarvāstivādins, and partly in the Avadānd collections. The biographies, and particularly the Jātakas, made a strong appeal to the mass, kindled their devotion and gave them an opportunity to express the same by depicting the stories indelibly on stone. These made them feel within their innermost heart that Buddhahood for them was not an impossibility as has so long been preached by the early Buddhists. The task, of course, was arduous and the path long covering several existences and entailing extreme self-sacrifices. This literature therefore gave a new and forceful impetus to the mass, and paved the way for the glorious days which Buddhism had for a long time in the early Christian eras. Observing the effect of the Jātaka stories on the mass, the Sarvāstivādins began to multiply them and produced large collections of these, calling them Avadānas. They incorporated in it stories dealing with the previous births not only of Buddha but also of his noted disciples. The puritanic Theravādins could not help following them, and started making a collection of stories without intermingling them with the biography of Buddha. They however supplied the events of the present life by way of introduction (*paccuppannavatthu*) and ended the stories by indentifying the characters with Buddha and other persons. The object of all these collections was identical, viz., the edification of the mass and popularisation of the religion.

Strangely enough all these *Jātakas* and *Avadānas* are non-Buddhist in character. This have nothing to do with the fundamental teachings of Buddhism—there is not a word about soul, component elements of a being, law of causation, *ātman, Skandhas, paṭ-iccasamuppada* or *nirvāṇa*. These stories deal in a general way with

1. *Lalitavistara* (R. L. Mitra). p. 192:—

पुरि तुम सुपुरुष ऋषिवरु यदभूर्द्विज तव उपगतु भव मम शरणम्।
भणि ऋषि द्विजवर नररिपु उपने त्यजि स्वय स्वकि तनु न च द्विज त्यजसे॥
स्मर ऋषि उपगतु पुरि द्रुमनिचये
रुचि भणि तरुरुह कति इम गणये।
सुविदित सुगणित यथ तहि किशला
तथ तव अवितथ समगिर रचिता॥

moral virtues but not with the *sīlas*, as detailed in the Piṭakas. These speak highly of a retired life but do not discountenance the life of a householder. On the contrary, the stories are concerned mainly with the social life of the householders and not with the unsocial life of a recluse. These do no breathe a word about monks or their life in monasteries. If not for the use of the term 'Bodhisattva' in every story, the collections could not have been recognised as forming a part of the Buddhist literature. It is really a universal literature dealing with universal moral principles, and a large number of the stories belongs to the common heritage of the Indians of the pre-Aśokan period. These stories teach more altruistic moral principles man negative ethical ideals (*veramaṇis*) as was the practice with the Buddhists. The stories well-known to the common folk of the then age and were found a convenient medium for propagating the Bodhisattva conception and along with it the greatness of the Teacher.

The Pāramitā-cult

The Jātaka-stories, according to the late Buddhist traditions, had in view Bodhisattva's attainment of perfection[1] in six or ten virtues: viz.,(i) liberality (*dāna*); (ii) righteousness (*śīla*), (iii) forbearance or endurance (*kṣānti*), (iv) mental strength (*vīrya*) (v) mental concentration (*dhyāna*) and (vi) realisation of the truth (*prajñā*). The number was latterly raised to ten by the addition of (i) skilfulness in expedients (*upāyakauśalya*), (ii) vow or resolution (*praṇidhāna*), (iii) attainment of certain powers (*bala*) and (iv) knowledge (*jñāna*).[2] The above list is to be found in Buddhist-Sanskrit works while the list in the Pāli texts is slightly different. It agrees with five of the above, viz., *dāna, sīla, kṣānti, viriya* and *paññā*. The remaining five are (i) renunciation (*nekkhamma*), (ii) truthfulness (*sacca*), (iii) resolution (*adhiṭṭhāna*), (iv) love (*mettā*) and (v) equanimity (*upekkhā*). Of these five, *adhiṭṭhāna* may be taken as a synonym of *praṇidhāna* of the supplementary list. The agreement of the two lists in five items indicates their comparative antiquity than the remaining five. It seems that the list was not a pre-meditated one. The stories were originally written just to illustrate that the episodes of Buddha's life were not untoward events but the outcome of the deeds of his previous existences. In course of time these stories were multiplied without any definite plan.

The earliest mention of the six *pāramitās* is found in the *Mahāvastu* (iii. p. 226), *Lalitavistara* (p. 340), and *Aṣṭasahasrikā*

---

1. *Pāramitā*, as suggested by Har Dayal should be derived from '*parama*' (highest, excellent, extreme). A Bodhisattva makes most extreme exertion or sacrifice for acquiring the virtues of gift, etc.
2. Mr. Har Dayal rightly describes these four as supplementary *pāramitās*. See his *Bodhisattva Doctrine* etc. pp. 167, 168. See also his remarks re. five *pāramitās*.

Prajñāpāramitā (p. 194) while that of ten in the *Mahāyāna Sūtrālaṅkāra, Daśabhūmikasūtra, Bodhisattvabhūmi,* and *Samādhirājasūtra.*[1] In the *Mahāvastu* again, mention of the six pāramitās is few and far between[2] while the word *pāramitā* has been used in the ordinary sense (viz. perfection) in compounds like *garbhāvakrāntipāramitā*[3] (the last entrance of the Bodhisattva into the womb), *sarvakuśaladharmavaśi-bhāvapāramitā* (perfect attainment of domain over all good actions),[4] and *prajñāpāramitā*, (i.e. perfection in Śrāvaka's knowledge).[5] This shows that the word 'pāramitā' did not carry the meaning attributed to it in the later texts. Like *pāramiṃ gato* in Pāli, there are several uses of the phrase '*pāramiprāpta*'[6] and '*paramiṃ gato*'[7] in the *Mahāvastu*. In speaking of Bodhisattva's several attainments perfection in the six *pāramitās*[8] as a condition precedent to a Bodhisattva's progress from a lower to a higher *bhūmi*, is not insisted upon,[9] as has been done in the *Daśabhūmikasūtra.*[10] At the time of composition (2nd century B.C.) of the *Mahāvastu,*[11] the doctrine of *pāramitā*, it seems, was not well developed. Unlike the *Mahāvastu*, we have in the *Lalitavistara*, not only frequent references to the six *pāramitās*, but also eulogistic accounts of the deeds of Bodhisattva for attaining perfection in the six *pāramitās.*[12] These gāthās imply wide currency of the *Jātaka*-stories as also a great popularity of the *pāramitā*-doctrine.[13] In the *Aṣṭ-asāhasrikāprajñāpāramitā*, six *pāramitās* are systematically mentioned in the enumeration of Bodhisattva's attainments, with the rider that these perfections are not to be taken as reals[14] (*pāramārtha*). Thus, we may say that the doctrine of *pāramitā* was fully developed before the time of composition of the *Lalitavistara* and the *Aṣṭasāhasrikā*, i.e., about 1st century A.D. and after the date of the *Mahāvastu*, i.e., 2nd century B.C.

---

1. See Har Dayal, *op. cit.* p. 167.
2. *Mahāvastu*, i. p. 214; ii. p. 296; iii, p. 226.
3. *Mahāvastu,* ii, p. 17.
4. *Ibid.*, ii, p. 261.
5. *Ibid.*, iii, p. 67.
6. *Ibid.*, i, p. 152.
7. *Ibid.*, i, p. 74, etc.
8. *Ibid.*, i, p. 133-4.
9. *Ibid.*, i, pp. 89ff.
10. Cf. Dutt, *Aspects of Hinayāna and Mahāyāna Buddhism.* (henceforth abbreviated as *AHMB*), pp. 267, 270f.
11. Winternitz, *History of Literature* (Cal. Uni.) II, p. 247.
12 Cf. e.g. *Lalitavistara* (R.L. Mitra's ed.) pp. 38, 60, 185, 188, 199, 212, etc.
13. Cf. e.g. *Ibid.*, p. 60:
14. See, e.g. pp. 194.

The practice of *pāramitās* occupies an important place in the Mahāyānic code of discipline. In the *Saddharma-puṇḍarīka,*[1] one of the early Mahāyāna texts, it is repeatedly stated that the teaching for the Śrāvakas consisted of the four truths, law of causation, which put an end to suffering and led to Nirvāṇa, while the teaching for the Bodhisattvas consisted of the practice of *pāramitās*, leading to the highest knowledge or omniscience. In the *Daśabhūmika-Sūtra*, the practice of a particular *pāramitā* is enjoined for the attainment of a particular *bhūmi.*[2] Thus we see that the *pāramitās* formed one of the fundamentals of the Mahāyanic code of discipline and spiritual progress.

The doctrine of *pāramitā* is not mentioned in the early Pali texts, and was very likely unknown to the early Buddhists.[3] The words '*pāraniṃ gato* or *pāramippatto*' (attained perfection) occur in the Nikāyas[4] but nowhere in the Pāli Tripiṭaka, barring the *Khuddakanikāya*, the *pāramitās* are mentioned. The number of *pāramis*, listed in the later Pāli texts, is ten and not six. Dhammapāla, in his commentary on the *Cariyāpiṭaka*, contributes on the ten *pāramis* a long dissertation,[5] in which he tells us that there were various ways of classifying the *pāramis*. There was also the system of enumerating the *pāramis* as six viz., *dāna-sīla-khanti-viriya-jhāna-paññā*, which is exactly the list as given in the Buddhist-Sanskrit texts. He writes that according to this enumeration, 'sīla' includes *nekkhama* (renunciation) as also *sacca* (truthfulness), the latter being only an aspect (*ekadeso*) of sīla; paññā includes *ñāṇa* while *jhāna* and *paññā* together include *upekkhā*; *adhiṭṭhāna* he says, is associated with all the six *pāramis*. Though Dhammapāla was aware of this sixfold classification of *pāramis*, the Pāli texts usually mention ten and it seems that this was made out by the Theravādins some time after the currency of the six *pāramitās* among the sects other than Theravāda. The supplementary four *pāramitās* of the later Buddhist Sanskrit texts and the Pali list of ten pāramitās were very likely the products of the same period.

This doctrine of *pāramitā* is evidently a later accretion to the fundamental principles of Buddhism, and this took place about the 1st

---

1. *Saddharmapuñḍarika*, pp. 17f, 334f.
2. See *AHMB.*, ch. iv: *dāna* in 1st bhūmi (p. 259), *sīla* in the 2nd (p. 262), *kṣānti* in the 3rd (p. 267), *vīrya* in the 4th (p. 270), *dhyāna* in the 5th (p. 27) and *prajñā* in the sixth (p. 275).
3. See *AHMB.*, p. 12.
4. *Suttanipāta*, vs. 1018, 1020; *Majjhima*, iii, p. 28.
5. *Paramatthadīpani*, p. 321.

century B.C. Of the several sects that appeared after the Second Council, the Mahāsaṅghikas and their offshoot, the Andhakas, were the first to deify Buddha and introduce the conception of Bodhisattvas. Their *Mahāvastu* is the earliest text to mention the doctrine. The object of this group of sects was not only the deification of Buddha but also to find a place for the laity within the religion, to create an interest among the householders in Buddhism. This doctrine of *pāramitā* was meant primarily for householders; three of the *pāramitās* were already included in the duties prescribed for the laity, viz., *sīla, cāga* (=*dāna*) and *paññā*.[1] The remaining the *pāramitās* are *kṣānti, vīrya* and *dhyāna*. These, it will be observed, are included in the subsidiary practices prescribed for the laity. The distinction between the *pāramitā*-practices which made a Bodhisattva and the practices prescribed for the laity is that the former practices had to be carried to the extreme that one can conceive of, while the latter was meant only as a general moral training. The doctrine of pāramitā illustrated by the Jātaka stories made a strong appeal to the common-folk, and became instrumental in propagating the religion among the mass. The success of the Mahāsaṅghikas and their offshoots in increasing their followers led other schools like the Sarvāstivādins and Dharmaguptas, and later the most orthodox of the schools the Theravādins to incorporate this new doctrine into their code; though it was not consistent with their teachings and ideals. The Sarvāstivādins, however, changed their outlook in the altered circumstances of the day, and produced an extensive literature in the shape of *Avadānas* to popularise this new cult.

Bodhisattva-doctrine

As has already been mentioned, the Mahāsaṅghikas were the first to usher in the conception of Bodhisatva, viz., that a being in any form of existence can have or develop the determination to attain *bodhi* (*bodhicittotpāda*) at sometime or other, however long and arduous the process may be, no matter even if it entails self-immolation, not once but several times in different existences. This conception is not quite clearly expressed in the *Mahāvastu*, where we find the first attempt to detail the career of a Bodhisattva, which is as follows:—

(i) *Prakṛti-caryā* (duties while a common man)

(ii) *Praṇidhāna-caryā*[2] (duties when taking the vow for attaining Buddhahood)

---

1. The other two are *saddhā* and *suta*. See above.

2. After *bodhicittotpāda* and *praṇidhāna*, there must be also *vyākaraṇa* (prophesy) by a Buddha that such and such a being will become the Buddha.

(iii) Anuloma-caryā (duties for spiritual progress to Buddhahood)

(iv) *Anivartana-caryā*[1] (duties for remaining firm in a particular stage of spiritual progress)

(i) *Prakṛti-caryā*[2] has no corresponding practice in the full-fledged Mahāyānism. A Bodhisattva is a common man (*puthujjana*) while he is in *prakṛti-caryā*. This *caryā* requires a Bodhisattva to be a good, if not an ideal, householder, fulfilling the duties towards his parents, recluses and Brāhmaṇas, respecting the elders of the family, observing the ten moral rules,[3] admonishing others to be charitable and virtuous, worshipping Buddhas and Śrāvakas, but not developing the mental state to attain *bodhi*.[4] Gautama Buddha was in his *prakṛti-caryā* during the time of Aparājitadhvaja Buddha.[5]

(ii) *Praṇidhāna-caryā* corresponds to *bodhicittotpāda* of the developed Mahāyānism. While in this *caryā*, a Bodhisattva takes the vow that by the merits that have so far accrued to him, he may become omniscient, that his zeal in keeping his vow may not flag, that he may end his past evil acts by suffering pains, and that he may wander over this world like the Buddha untouched by the worldly objects as the incomparable teacher, revered by men and gods, and ultimately roll the wheel of law,[6] preach the truth, and train up beings like the Buddha, the lamp of this world.[7]

---

1. In the *Bodhisattvabhūmi*, the four *caryās* are given differently thus. *Bodhipakṣ-ya caryā, Abhijñācaryā, Pāramitā caryā. Sattvaparipāka-caryā*. Har Dayal has preferred this scheme of *Caryās*. See his *Bodhisattva Doctrine*, p. 76. See also Thomas, *History of Buddhist Thought*, p. 201: *AHMB*., pp. 286-289.

2. *Mahāvastu*, i. pp. 46-47, 815 cf. *Cariyāpiṭaka Cy*., p. 162.

3. See *Mahāvastu*,i, p. 107, II 14-16. The daśa kuśala-karmapathas are:—Refraining from (i) *prāṇātipāta* (killing), (ii) *adattādāna* (stealing), (iii) *kāma-mithyācāra* (misconduct), (iv) *anṛtavacana* (speaking falsehood), (v) *piśuṇavacana* (malignant speech), (vi) *paruṣavacana* (harsh speech), (vii) *sambhinnapradīpa* (frivolous talk), (viii) *abhidhyā* (avariciousness), (ix) *vyāpannacitta* (malevolence) and (x) *mithyādṛṣṭi* (wrong view).

4. See *Mahāvastu*, 47, 81:

 नैव ताव जनयन्तिमानसं अग्रपुद्गलगतं नरोत्तमा।
 — — — — —
 नैव ताव जनयन्ति मानसं सर्वधर्मविदुताय पण्डिताः।
 — — — — —
 नैव ताव जनयन्ति मानसं ज्ञानसागरताय नायकाः।

5. *Mahāvastu*, p. 1; but see p. 60 where it is said that he offered valuable robes to Aparājitadhvaja Buddha and prayed for attainment of *sambodhi*.

6. *Mahāvastu*, i, p. 50:—

 एव महं लोकमिमं चरेयं यथा अयं चरति असंगमानसो।
 चक्रं प्रवर्तेयं अनन्यसादृशो भवेयमहं देवमनुष्यपूजितो॥

7. *Ibid*., p. 54:—

 अर्थ चरेयं लोके देवमनुष्यानां देशिय धर्मं।
 एवं विनेय सत्त्वां यथा अयं लोकप्रद्योतो॥

Gautama Buddha first took this vow during the time of a past Śākyamuni Buddha after offering him a drink of gruel. He took the vow for the second time during the time of Samitāvi Buddha, and later as the monk Abhiya during the time of Sarvābhibhu Buddha. In this way he took this vow five times.

(iii) *Anuloma-caryā* corresponds to *Bodhiprasthāna-citta* of the *Bodhicaryāvatāra* (p. 23). A Bodhisattva immediately after taking the vow, mentioned above, commences performing the duties prescribed for his spiritual progress. The duties to be performed and the virtues to be acquired by a Bodhisattva are endless. In some texts[1] an attempt has been made to arrange the duties and virtues in a gradual order in ten stages (*bhūmis*). The keynote of the Bodhisattva practices is self-sacrifice for the good of others with a firm resolution for the attainment of *bodhi*. The practices mentioned in the *Mahāvastu* are not only much less elaborate than those found in the later texts, but also are not in a progressive order. Briefly, these are as follows:—

In the 1st *bhūmi* (*dūrārohā*)[2] the Bodhisattva cultivates charity (*tyāga*), compassion (*karuṇā*), unweariness, (aparikheda), conceit-lessness (*amāna*), love for study (*sarvaśāstrādhyāyitā*), valour (*vikrama*), knowledge of the worldly ways (*lokānujñā*) and patience (*dhṛti*).

In the 2nd *bhūmi* (*Baddhamānā*) the Bodhisattva develops twenty kinds of strong inclinations (*adhyāśaya*) viz., excellent (*kalyāṇa*), quiet (*snigdha*), sweet (*madhura*), etc. Each of these inclinations is explained in verse.[3]

In the 3rd *bhūmi* (*Puṣpamaṇḍitā*) the Bodhisattva exerts for making all beings happy without seeking happiness for his ownself, and sacrifices everything even his life for listening to wise sayings.

In the 4th *bhūmi* (*Rucirā*) the Bodhisattva refrains from commission of any of the extreme offences, viz., patricide, matricide and arhanticide, and dissension in the Saṅgha, and stūpa-desecration; he avoids heretic views, performs the ten good deeds[4] (*kuśalakarmapatha*); does not use any magical spell for injuring others, does not get depressed in danger nor becomes elated in success, remains pure in physical, mental and vocal acts, as also in his indications (*adhyāśaya*).

---

1. *Daśabhumikasutra; Bodhisattvabhūmi; Sūtrālaṅkāra* of Asaṅga.
2. See *Mahāvastu*, i, pp. 85-89.
3. A bodhisattva while in the first bhūmi remains a *pṛthagjana* (common man), but deserving gifts. See *Mahāvastu*, i. p.78.
4. See above, p. 266n.

In the 5th *bhūmi* (*Citravistarā*) the Bodhisattva realised the fact that worldly existences are ablaze with attachment (*rāga*), hatred (*dosa*), and delusion (*moha*).

In the 6th *bhūmi* (*Rūpavatī*) the Bodhisattva comprehends that existence in the world is unhappy and painful.

In the 7th *bhūmi* (*Durjayā*) the Bodhisattva attains complete self-control and wishes for the good of all beings.

In the 8th *bhūmi* (*Janmanirdeśa*) the Bodhisattva sacrifices everything including the dearest things which are very difficult to part with. From this *bhūmi* onwards the bodhisattva should be looked upon as the *Samyaksambuddha* as he has mastered the higher meditational practices, acquired full knowledge and delivers wise discourses.

In the 9th and 10th *bhūmis* (*Yauvarājya* and *Abhiṣeka*)[1] therefore the Bodhisattva has nothing more to attain. Now he can take rebirth in whatever form he likes; he can also become a universal monarch. These two *bhūmis*, evidently, were reached by Gautama Buddha in his last two existence in the Tuṣita heaven and in the mortal world.[2] He decided to take rebirth as a human being for imparting instructions to men and gods, leading them to *arhathood* or other attainments. In the later Mahāyānic texts, the Bodhisattva in the eighth *bhūmi* becomes a Buddha gotra, and guarded henceforward by the gods and Vajrapāni.[3] In the 9th *bhūmi*, according to these texts, the Bodhisattva becomes a *dharma* preacher, a guide to other beings. In the 10th *bhūmi* he obtains the resplendent body and omniscience while in meditation;[4] he is now consecrated as the *Samyaksambuddha* and so this *bhūmi* is called *Abhiṣ eka*.

(iv) *Anivartana-caryā* of the *Mahāvastu* is equated by Dr. Thomas[5] to the *Anivartana-caryā* of the later Mahāyānic texts. In the *Mahāvastu*, however, it carries a slightly different sense. In this text some lapses are pointed out as causes for retrogression of a Bodhisattva from a higher to a lower *bhūmi*, and so a Bodhisattva is warned about these lapses in connection with every *bhūmi* that may be reached by him. The word *avaivartiya* is used as an adjective of the Bodhisattva[6]

---

1. *Mahāvastu*, i, pp. 105-6.
2. Thomas, *History of Buddhist Thought*, p. 203.
3. *AHMB.*, p. 282.
4. *Ibid.*, p. 283.
5. *History of Buddhist Thought*, p. 201.
6. *Mahāvastu*, i, p. 82: यं पुनर्भो जिनपुत्र अवैवर्तियो बोधिसत्त्वो प्रथमं चित्त-मुत्पादयति etc; p. 83: ये इमे भो जिनपुत्र अवैवर्तिका बोधिसत्त्वा केवत्तकानि तै प्रथमायां भूमौं स्थितैः दुष्कराणि कृतानीति etc.

in every *bhūmi*, implying that the resolution of the Bodhisattva for attaining bodhi remains unflinching all along. Incidentally the text[1] mentions that the Bodhisattva while in one of the first seven *bhūmis* may, for any serious lapse, be reborn in one of the lower forms of existence. In the later Mahāyānic texts, the 8th bhūmi is called *Avaivartya* or *Acalā*, from which the Bodhisattva can never have any retrogresssion; he is destined to attain *bodhi* and become a *samyaksambuddha*.

The Bodhisattva conception apparently was not fully developed in the *Mahāvastu*. The conception presented in the text is half-way between Hīnayāna and Mahāyāna. The Bodhisattva, it has in view, is the previous existences of Gautama Buddha.[2] It makes no reference to the acquisition of *pāramitās* in the duties prescribed for Bodhisattvas, not to speak of the inconceivable and immeasurable virtues acquired by Bodhisattvas in the several *bhūmis*, as detailed in the *Daśabhūmikasūtra*[3] or the *Bodhisattvabhūmi*.[4] There can be no doubt therefore that in the *Mahāvastu*, we have not only the earliest speculations about the life and career of a Bodhisattva, but also the earliest Jātaka stories. It is in the *Saddharmapuṇḍarīka*[5] that we find a fairly developed conception of the Bodhisattva. The Śrāvakas in this work are not disparaged as is done in the later Mahāyāna texts, and a hope is held out to them, that by taking recourse to certain Bodhisattva practices they could still achieve Buddhahood. The new ideals preached in this text electrified the mass, made Buddhism an all-India religion, and we may say that the popular form of Buddhism reached its climax about the time of composition of this work, i.e., about the 2nd century A.D.

Gṛhī-Bodhisattvas: In the early Mahāyāna texts, there is no express mention of householder-bodhisattvas.[6] In the *Saddharma-puṇḍarīka* (p. 20), a Bodhisattva is said to have 800 disciples (*antevāsins*), but it is not known whether they were householders or recluses. In the *Daśabhūmikasūtra*,[7] it is stated that in the fourth *bhūmi*, the Bodhisattva takes ordination, which implies that he could remain

1. *Mahāvastu*, i, pp. 102-4.
2. Cf. Thomas, *History of Buddhist Thought*, p. 201: "The conception of the career in the *Mahāvastu* also shows more primitive features. It is described not as a career for any bodhisattva, but as having been the career of Sākyamuni and previous Buddhas."
3. See *AHMB*.
4. *Bodhisattvabhūmi* (ed. Wogihara), Tokyo.
5. *Saddharmapuṇḍarīka*, p. 221.
6. See *AHMB*., p. 270.
7. Cf. *Bodhisattvabhūmi* (Wogihara), p. 138:—तत्र कतमद बोधिसत्त्वस्य सर्वशीलम्। समासतो बोधिसत्त्वस्य गृहिपक्षगतं प्रव्रजितपक्षगतं च शीलं सर्वशीलमित्युच्यते।

a householder up to the forth *bhūmi*, or the practice of *vīrya-pāramitā*. The *dhyāna* and *prajñā pāramitās* are to be accomplished after a bodhisattva becomes a monk. In the later Mahāyana texts like *Ugradattaparipṛcchā* and *Śikṣāsamuccaya*, a special code has been framed for the conduct of the householder-bodhisattvas.[1] The *pāramitās*, it seems, were meant more for the householders than for the recluses. In actual practice, as is found in the *Jātaka* stories, the pāramitās were being accomplished by laymen, gods and animals, and rarely by ascetics. In the *Mahāvastu* and other early Mahāyāna texts, the duties of Gṛhi-bodhi-sattvas are not distinctly prescribed, but in course of time this desideratum of a code was removed and the career of a householder bodhisattva was clearly chalked out.[2]

Conclusion: In the pre-Aśokan days Buddhism hardly became a popular movement. It was confined to recluses, the number of which increased to a certain extent owing to the slight deviations made from the austere principles of the earliest form of Buddhism. In his edicts Aśoka did not fully approve of the emphasis laid by early Buddhism on retirement from household life. This attitude of Aśoka might have some effect on the religion. During Aśoka's reign, the *caitya* and *stūpa* worship came more and more into vogue and not long after Aśoka, worship of Buddha's images got currency. About two centuries had elapsed since Buddha's demise, and during this long period, Buddha came to be deified inspite of all the textual injunctions to the contrary. The laymen expressed their devotion by erecting *stūpas* and decorating them with Buddha images. The laity, however, still remained outside the Buddhist fold, and earned merits only by making gifts to the monks and offering worship to the Buddhist *stūpas*. They were held out the hope of rebirth in one of the heavens, but not emancipation. At this stage, about the 2nd century B.C. appeared the *Jātakas* and *Avadānas* depicting the previous lives of Buddha and his disciples. These stories caught the imagination of the generality of the people, who now hoped that they could become Bodhisattvas and earned necessary merits to become a Buddha in the long run. Their hopes were further strengthened by the doctrine of *pāramitās*, and special texts were composed to show that the perfection in the *pāramitās* assured one. Buddhahood and that the practice of *pāramitās* was open to all, recluses or householders. The laymen now felt that they could become actual followers of the religion and derive the benefits. The self-sacrifice preached in the *pāramitā* doctrine had a wide appeal and made Buddhism an all-India religion. It was through the propagation of the *pāramitā* cult that the religion reached the pinnacle of its glory.

1. *Ibid.*, pp. 295-301.
2. For further details, see *AHMB.*, pp. 295f.; and *Bodhisattva Prātimokṣa Sūtra*.

Chapter - 15

Sources of Buddhist Logic

(From the traditional point of view)

Durgacharan Chatterji

As the Brāhmaṇas are anxious to trace every doctrine to the Vedas or the Śruti, so the Buddhists try to affiliate every tenet of theirs, however late, to some *Buddha-vacana*, or *Āgama* as they usually call it. While introducing the problem of *Pramāṇas* Kamalaśīla in the *Tattvasaṃgrahapañjikā* (=TSP), the elaborate commentary on the *Tattvasaṃgraha* (=TS) of Śāntirakṣita, (cf. Barnett, *JRAS.*, 1927, P. 862) refers to some statements ascribed to Buddha, the nucleus of Buddhist Logic. In order to emphasise the rational attitude of Buddhism, he incidentally quotes a statement of Buddha in which he exhorts his followers to examine his words thoroughly before accepting them as does an expert with a piece of gold by heating, filing and testing on a touchstone.[1] Though this attempt to connect the origin of Logic or Pramāṇa-śātra with Buddha has but little chance of being accepted as historical truth, it exhibitis the philosophical ingenuity of the scholiast.

Pratyakṣa (or perception) in the Brāhmaṇical system is ordinarily divided into two: (i) *nirvikalpa* and (ii) *savikalpa*. But the Buddhists reject the second and accept the first, though with them it means something entirely different from what it does with the Brāhmaṇas. On this point we have a *Buddhavacana*[2] as quoted by Kamalaśīla, which says that one with visual cognition (*cakṣur vijñāna,*

---

1. *tāpācchedācca nikaṣāt suvarṇam iva paṇḍitaiḥ/parīkṣya bhikṣavo grākyaṃ madvaco na tu gauravāt //TSP.*, p. 12, *also TS.*, *Kārikā*, 3588.

2. *cakṣurvijñānasaṅgī nīlaṃ vijānāti na tu nīlam iti. TSP.*, P. 12.

A person in association with the visual consciousness cognizes the blue, as blue but not that it is blue. This *Buddhavacana* or *Āgama* is also quoted by Candrakīrtti in his *Prasannapadā*, the renowned commentary on the *Mūlama-dhyamakakārikā* of Nāgārjuna, Bib. Buddhica, p. 74, 11. 8-9. Prof. Poussin in footnote 6 in the same can perceive the unique character of a think (*nīlaṃ vijānāti—nirvikalpajñāna*) but not its common character (*nilam iti vijānātiṭ savikalpajñāna*), the former corresponding roughly to an acquaintance with an object while the latter to a descriptive knowledge about it.[1]

With regard to *Anumāna* (or inference) we also have, on the authority of Kamalaśīla, a statement of Buddha, that the *liṅga*, (or the mark) inseparably connected with *sādhya (probandum)*, if definitely ascertained (*viniścita*), is the cause of inferential knowledge.[2] This is illustrated in the well-known Buddhist doctrine that all the has the character of being effected (*samudayadharmaka*) has also the character of being destroyed (*nirodhadharmaka*). Here we have a statement of concomitance (*vyāpti*) between the *probans*, the character of being produced (*hetu—samudayadharmakatvam*) and the *probandum*, the character of being destroyed (*sādhya—nirodhadharmaka*). Though there is no direct mention of the thesis or the conclusion, (*pakṣa*), it is evident from the statement of *vyāpti* which is implicitly contained in it.[3]

The above example illustrates, as suggested by Kamalaśīla, the *svabhāva hetu* which is one of the three types of *hetus* of the Buddhist

---

page has doubted the correctness of the reading of the Ms. *nīlamitīti, cāgamasya.* and has emended the text as *nīlam iti cāgamasya.* But as a matter of fact Prof. Poussin's emendation is unnecessary and the reading of the Ms. is all right and has also the support of the Tibetan translation. It is to be noted that one *iti* will not convey the intended sense at all. The first *iti* is connected with *nīlam*, and the second *iti* separates the whole Āgama from the subsequent expressions, and thus the antithesis between *nīlam* and *nīlam iti* is brought out without the least ambiguity, *nīlam vijānāti* means 'cognises blue as blue'; hence the cognition is strictly in correspondence with the external or the externalised object, i.e. the cognition is *nirvikalpa*. And *nīlam iti (vijānāti)* means '(cognises) that it is blue; the cognition in this case involves as association of the object cognised with name, class, and the like, which are of a universal character (*kalpanā*) i.e. the regnition is savikalpaka.

From the above discussion it will be clear that the last inverted commas in the reading of the Āgama in the *TSP.*, P. 12. 1. 22 should be placed after *iti* and not after *nīlam*, as has been printed. Again Prof. Poussin has emended *vijñānasaṅgī* to *vijñānasaṅgī*. This is also unnecessary nor has it the support of the Tibetan translation.

The Āgama which Prof. Poussin has traced to the *Abhidharma*, and the *Nyāyabindupūrvapakṣasaṃkṣepa* is also found in the *Pramāṇasamuccayarṛtti*(Tib.) with the variant noted by him, as a quotation from the *Abhidharma. chos mṅon pa las kyan mig gi rnam par shes pa daṅ ldan pas sṅon po shes khi sṅon poḥi sñam du ni ma yin no* (Mdo. Ce 14-a 2; Narthang).

1. *Indian Philosophy* by Dr. Radhakrishanan in the *Encyclopaedia Britannica*, 14th ed. Vol. 12.

2. *sādhyārthāvinābhūtaṃ liṅgaṃ viniścitaṃ sadanumānajñānasya kāraṃam, tacca yat kiṃcit bhikṣavaḥ samudayadharmakaṃ sarraṃ tan* (printed as *sarvatra*) *nirodhadharmaka iti. TSP.*, p. 12.

3. According to Dharmakīrtti *pakṣa* need not be explicitly stated in a syllogistic argument (see *Nyāyabindu*, III, 36-37 and the Ṭīkā thereon).

logicians—(i) *svabhāva*, (ii) *kārya*, and (iii) *anupalabdhi*—these being the three principal relations in which the *probans* (*hetu*) may be connected with the *probandum* (*sādhya*).

Kārya hetu is illustrated in the following examples summed up in a verse:

(i) It is fiery because it has smoke.

(ii) There is water because there are cranes.

(iii) He is Bodhisattva because he has auspicious signs.

With reference to *anupalabdhi-hetu,*[1] Kamalaśīla attributes another statement to Buddha which object to the validity of a conclusion from mere negation. Buddha is said to be admonishing his followers thus: "O Bhikṣus, let not an individual (*pudgalaḥ*) try to prove the soul (*pudgalaṃ*), nor let him seek proofs in support of it.[2] It is I or some body like myself who can prove the soul." According to the Buddhist logicians,[3] negation of objects not entering the zone of cognition owing to impediments in respect of time, space, and nature, is a source of problematic knowledge, as it is excluded both from perception and inference. A cause (*kāraṇa*) or a fact of wider extension (*vyāpaka*) being absent will make the effect or the subordinate fact (*vyāpya*) absent. In as much as the knowledge of an object is neither the cause nor a fact of wider extent with reference to the object, the absence of the knowledge of an object does not prove the non-existence of the object. Therefore the negation of the imperceptible (*adṛśyānupalabdhi*) cannot prove anything, but gives rise to doubt.

So from mere non-apprehension of the soul (*pudgala*) no definite conclusion as to its existence or otherwise can be made. The above statement ascribed to Buddha, therefore, seeks to establish that *anupalabdhi* to be a valid source of knowledge (*pramāṇa*) should be *dṛśyānupalabdhi* (i.e. non-perception of what is capable of being

---

1. *kāryākhyam api—*

dhūmena jñāyate vahniḥ salilaṃ ca balākayā.

nimittair jñāyate gotraṃ bodhisattvasya dhḥmataḥ. TSP., p. 13.

Quoted in the *Subhāṣitasaṃgraha* ed. by Bendall 14-13 and traced in the *Gaṇḍavyūhasūtra*.

Compare:—*anukampā priyākhyānaṃ dhīratā muktahastatā.*
gambhīrasandhinirmokṣo liṅgānyetāni dhīmatām.
tetra prathamena ślokena pañca bodhisattvaliṅgāni darśayati.
Mahāyānasūtrālaṅkāra. ed. by Sylvain Lévi, p. 175.

2. *mā bhikṣavaḥ pudgalaḥ pudgalaṃ pramiṇotu pudgale vā pramāṇam udgṛhṇātu, kṣaṇyate hi bhiṣsavaḥ pudgalaḥ pudgalaṃ pramiṇvan ahaṃ vā pudjalaṃ pramiṇuyāṃ yo vā syān mādṛśaḥ. TSP.* p. 13.

3. *Nyāyabindu*, II, 48-49.

perceived) and not mere *adṛśyānupalabdhi* (non-perception of the imperceptible).

In conclusion it may be observed that genuine doubt may be expressed as to the statements or *āgamas* being gathered upon Buddha; nevertheless they may be taken as laying the foundation-stone of the edifice of the Buddhist logic, which became in subsequent times a structure of great splendour and beauty.

Chapter - 16

The Four Ways and the Four Fruits in Pāli Buddhism

I.B. Horner

In the Pāli Piṭakas are to be found various words which are manifestly important: *dhamma, magga, nibbāna, arahan* (the moral law, the way, nirvāṇa, and the person who is worthy) to mention only a very few. But these four are sufficient briefly to delineate the teaching which was at the root of early Buddhism.

Now early Buddhism falls roughly into two divisions: (1) Sākya, or the oral teaching of Gotama and his co-founders. This,because it was oral, has not come down to us intact; (2) monastic Buddhism, or the views and tenets of the monks who lived two or three centuries after Gotama's death. These are the monks who "edited" the texts as we have them to-day, collecting the material for the stringing together of the Founder's reputed discourses from "repeaters." These "repeated" to the "editors" all that they could remember of the tradition handed down to them orally.

One of the differences between these two forms of Buddhism lies in the different value that each ascribed to the terms mentioned above. For the Founder *dhamma* was much like Kant's "moral law within the breast," the inner guide and monitor; for the monk it became an externalised body of doctrine. For the Founder *magga* was very probably the Way for becoming (*bhara*), for becoming greater, nobler, better during many life-spans to come; for the monk it was merely the eightfold Way (or Path) of eight fitnesses. For the Founder *nibbāna* was a cathartic process, a cleansing from the fires of passion, hatred and illusion; for the monk it was a waning of the self of man. When we come to the term *arahan*, it is not easy to say what it meant for the Founder and his fellow workers. But as it is closely connected with the subject of this paper, I may be allowed to consider it at some length.

The term *arahan*, like these other terms, has had a long history. In the *Ṛg-Veda* it is sometimes applied to the god Agni; while in the *Satapatha Brāhmaṇa* the term appears to be an honorific title bestowed upon some high official, important on account of his worldly status. In Jaina literature the epithet is given exclusively to the revealer of the religion. Turning to Pāli literature we do not find the *arahan* emerging just as a *ṛṣi*, a recluse; nor as a person with magic powers (*iddhi*) such as the six heretical leaders (*Vin.* II. 210) and Kassapa (*Vin.* I. 25 *ff.*) are recorded to have claimed to possess; nor yet as a person addicted to the performance of physical austerities. For these interpretations of *arahan* were rejected. What we do find is that the available documentary material shows the *arahan* already emerged as a man or woman who has won perfection here and now; and arahanship as a highly desirable state to be won here and now. Arahanship so regarded is the offspring of monastic Buddhism with its dread of renewed becomings. Thus nearly every description of *arahan* is in terms of finite achievement. The notion of consummation was contracted to something that man might conceive and name in this rebirth.

So rapidly, appareatly, did the term *arahan* come to mean the finished product that we do not know what it had meant for Gotama. But a great Teacher would not have seen perfection as realisable under physical conditions: he would have thought of man growing up to perfection as he ran on and fared on, his thought, word and deed becoming finer and purer in each new rebirth. It is apparent that the notion of winning perfection here and now cuts across this larger viw. The ideal becomes one which only the few can grasp.

Under monastic Buddhism this goal of arahanship, of perfection to be won here and now, was the goal held up to every zealous bhikkhu (monk) and bhikkhunī (nun). According to the thought of the time, those who attained the end desired were able to do so because the whole trend of their lives and characters had been set in this direction during more or fewer becomings (*i.e.*, lives), according to their different destinies. There may have been some whose destiny it might not necessarily have been ever to attain arahanship: these like Devadatta, might have been incurable, *atekiccha* (*Vin.* II. 202; *A.* III. 402. etc.). Again there were many disciples who were not able to achieve arahanship in this life.

Nevertheless the majority of those who had entered the Order was reckoned to be on an upward way, sufficiently advanced to merit a designation conveying spiritual achievement. These who have progressed well are not ranked merely as non-arahans (*i.e.*, as "not saints" or as "not men perfected") but are brought under one of three headings which, with the arahans as the fourth heading, are together classified into a fourfold group. Of this the arahan is naturally the highest member. This group consists of those people who were on what is known as the "Four Ways"; and within the Buddhist interpretation of the Indian belief in a chain of rebirths (*saṃsāra*) this group has some importance.

When each of the four ways (*maggā*) had been fully mastered, it was said to yield a fruit (*phala*). The fruit of one way was not immediate attainment to the next way; but was the gaining of definite subsequent conditions (fully stated in the texts, *see below* p. 789). These conditions had to be spent before extrance to the next way, if this was destined, could take place. Strictly speaking, the last way and the last way only was the Way to arahanship.

The person who is on the first Way (*sotāpattimagga*), the Way of stream-attainment, is called *sotāpanna*, a stream-winner, a stream-attainer, or a stream-entrant. He who is in the second Way (*sakadāgāmimagga*), the Way of Once-returning, is called a *sakadāgāmin*, an once-returner. He who is on the third Way (*anāgāmimagga*), the Way of No-return, is called an *anāgāmin*, a non-returner. He who is on the fourth and highest Way (*arahattamagga*), the Way of Arahanship, is, when he has reaped the fruit of this Way, an arahan. The fruit of this Way is also the goal of the good life and the highest and sweetest fruit in the life of a recluse. But when it has been gained, then the task is done, for the arahan has nothing further to do.

At some time, we do not know exactly when, *the* Way became divided into this group of the four Ways. These represent stages of the Way, and have nothing to do with the other classification of the Way into eight component parts. But because the one Way was, or came to be, the Way to arahanship, these four Ways are also in a sense Ways to arahanship. Yet they are nowhere called by this name in the Pāli Canon. Moreover there exist, so far as I know, only a few Vibhaṅga passages (*Vbh.* 322 *ff*, 335) where the generic term "the four Ways" is used. Ordinarily each one is referred to specifically. It is most suggestive to find that in the *Saṅgīti-Suttanta*, although the four limbs of stream-attainment, the four limbs of the stream-attainer and the four fruits of samaṇahood (which are identical with the fruits of the four Ways) are named, the four Ways themselves are not catalogued. They are indeed doubly absent. In the first place there is no heading called the "Four Ways." In the second place, under the heading the "fruits of samaṇaship" the fruits are said not to be those of the Ways—the way of stream-attainment and so on—but are said to be those of stream-attainment and so on, the word *magga* not appearing. This omission of the four Ways from among the Fours of the *Saṅgīti Suttanta* is as remarkable as the omission from among its Eights of the Way (or Path) as eightfold. Here the eight "fitnesses" or "rightnesses" (*sammatta*) are catalogued. And that is all.

This suggests that at the time when this Suttanta was written down the Four Ways had not been established as a group, and the sub-division of the Way into stages (each one of which was called *magga*), or into eight component parts (*aṅga*) was not as yet very important. But since *bhava*, becoming, which as I hve suggested was originally implicit in the Way, came to be connected with recurring experience of Ill and was hence a thing to be dreaded, the teaching on the Ways appears to have been used as a tool—not for holding out the hope of a number of subsequent rebirths, but for holding out the hope of greatly reducing the number of rebirths to this world, with the possibility of not rturning to it again. Thus as time went on it is probable that the Ways came to receive more emphasis than the fruits. The *Dhammasaṅgani*, for example, has sections on each of the four Ways (277-364), but not on the fruits. I think it possible that the notion of the four fruits preceded that of the four Ways; that there were perhaps originally only three fruits corresponding to the various aspects of renewed becomings, which were thought of as going on after life here had ceased; that the fruit of arahanship was a later accretion added when the finite concept, that of man perfected with nothing more to do, ousted the concept of an infinite becoming; and that the division of the Way into four parts was also a later device made to balance the four fruits.

The term "stream-winning" especially appears to belong to an earlier date than do the other terms in this group. It represents a facet of a notion which was of the essence of Sākya, for it suggests a perpetual flowing along to join the greater, as rivers flow to join the ocean. This ocean of *vṃsāra* (rebirths) had originally been regarded as a thing full of the promise of infinite opportunities for progress. Later it came to lie regarded with dread, as a process to be stopped at the cost of life renewed and renewable. Then it will have been that *śolāpatti* was dethroned from it sovereignty over becoming and was relegated tothe lowest place in the fourfold Way; and then too, that the conception of the four Ways was probably crystallised into formulæ. Such formulæ were wanted in order to hold out to as many as possible, besides those who were arahans, the consolation of the cessation of lives. It was in order that the majority should be able to look forward to ultimate enlightenment and, more particularly, to returning here once only or not at all, in either case ultimately waning utterly, that the conception of the Four Ways was put forward.

Before going on to a discussion of other points concerning the Ways and the Fruits, it will be as well to quote the passage which perhaps occurs most frequently, and which shows how the characteristics and destinies of those on the four Ways were formulated. It clearly shows a cathartic process, arahanship, not being possible until all the moral faults and obstructions which are to be goot rid of by progressing along the lower Ways, are truly eliminated as these Ways are mastered. This quotation is taken from the *Dīgha-Nikāya* (I. 156; III. 107, 132) or Collection of Long Discourses, but it occurs also in other Nikāyas:—

"A bhikkhu by the complete destruction of the three fetters (delusions of the self, doubt, trust in the efficacy of good works) is a stream-winner, one who cannot be reborn in any state of woe, assured, bound for enlightenment. A bhikku by the complete destruction of the three fetters and by reducing to a minimum pasion, hatred and delusion is a once-returner, who by returning once to this world shall make an end of ill. A bhikkhu by the complete destruction of the five fetters (the above three with sensuality and ill-will added) which pertain to this world is onne who takes birth spontaneously[1] in the Pure Abode, there to wane utterly, thence never to return. A bhikkhu by the destruction of the āsavas (of desire for sense-pleasures, for re-birth, of ignorance and of false views) comes here and now to realise for himself that emancipation of heart and mind which is arahanship, and continues to abide therein."

It will be observed that there is no indication of what the bourn or destiny of an arahan might be.

In the *Aṅguttara* (I. 233) this process of spiritual development is made dependent on training in those rules which together are said to combine to make the threefold training: the higher morality, the higher thought and the higher insight. Again "pondering with method" is stated to be a possible means of rising not only from stream-attainment but from being merely a virtuous bhikkhu, to

---

1. Transl. by Mrs. Rhys Davids in *Indian Religion and Survival* p. 64, as "just 'happening', not of parents."

arahanship (*S.* III. 168 *ff.*). Pondering with method means concentrating upon the five grasping groups (or groups of fuel for existence) as being, among other things, full of desire and pain, impermanent, empty and not of the self.

Thus there is a continuity between the Ways. Having fared along one and shed the wrong states which pertain to it, a disciple may pass on to another. This occurence may be spread over more than one rebirth. For example, Dīghāvu, a lay-disciple, was called a stream-winner in this life, and after he had died Gotama is reputed to have said that Dīghāvu would not rturn from that world where he was reborn. (*S.* V. 344 *ff.*). On the other hand we hear of disciples, who became stream-winners in this life and who shortly afterwards became arahans—also in this life. In such cases it is probable that attainment in this life to the two intervening ways was not thought to be omitted. For otherwise full purification could not be entailed. Again it is said that two boys (*Pss. Breth.* p. 10, 61) realised the four ways in succession in the very act of having their curls cut off. Such rapidity of realisation is suggestive of preparation in previous rebirths, a person achieving the utmost in this becoming because his or her destiny "was fully ripe" for this.

But in drawing up the scheme of the four Ways it was the majority, the less highly developed and cultivated that early monastic Buddhism had in mind. If these could not attain arahanship in this rebirth, they might at least gain one of the lower fruits. But here we are faced with a difficulty. For as Buddhism developed the winning of arahanship became tied down to the here and now. It is to my mind not easy to reconcile to this concpt the concept of the Way of No-return as a stage on the way to this same arahanship. For if, after a person has left this earth, he is not to return to it, if he is to pass utterly away in the realm where he is reborn after his bodily death here, how can he become an arahan as that is ordinarily conceived by the texts, with their insistence on *diṭṭhe va dhamme* (here and now, lit;, in these very seen conditions)? The Way of No-return in fact appears as a cutting short of the development implied by the four-Ways-group, which hence presents a curious anomaly. For the gulf between the non-returner and the arahan is physically unbridgeable, and therefore the inclusion of the third Way is out of place if it is thought that the attainment of arahanship here and now is the ideal of those on the Way of No-return.

Yet theoretically it must have been held to be possible for a non-returner to reap the fruit of arahanship. Or was it that the arahanship thus thought of did not fulfil the "here and now" condition? It is true that in the Piṭakas there is nothing approaching a decisive record of a person who was declared to be first a non-returner in this life and then an arahan, also in this life. But it is true that the Commentaries on the *Theragāthā* and the *Therīgāthā* speak of some of these unusual people, of one Thera and of four Therīs, that having been setablished in the fruition of no-return, they not long afterwards attained arahanship, and in this life.[1]

If for some reason the present moment, or as we should say "opportunity," could not be exploited so as to gain arahanship, it was perhaps because not enough effort had been put forth. In the *Majjhima* (I. 436) it is said that the attempt to get rid of the five Fetters which belong to this world, their elimination being considered necessary for non-return—may end either in the extirpation of the āsavas, which is virtually the same as arahanship, or in the destruction of the five Fetters and a state of non-return. Thus the effort to achieve non-return may overreach itself, and end in arahanship; *or* it may accomplish exactly that which it set out to do. But the disciple who put forth the effort has not won both states, but the one or the other. Indeed in this passage the two appear to be mutually exclusive.

Again, this alternative result may depend upon the presence or absence of any substrate for existence. In the *Sutta-Nipāta* (p. 140) is a phrase which has been much repeated in the Suttas. It says, "For a bhikkhu who is zealous, ardent, the self established you may expect one of two fruits: either *aññā* (perfected knowledge) here and now, or if his stuff of existence be not wholly spent, the condition of a non-returner."

At first sight it looks as if the presence of a remainder of the stuff of existence (*sa-upādisesa*) or the absence of it (*anupādisesa*) were meant to denote alternative consummations. But this is not so. Either the bhikkhu has *añña,* which would mean that he has no substrate remaining, or he has not quite achieved *aññā* (here). The *Dhammapada Commentary* (II. 163) distinguishes two forms of *parinibbāna*, utter waning out. It says that *parinibbāna* means there is a substrate remaining after the attainment of arahanship by the destruction of the *kilesas*; and there is no substrate remaining after

1. We do not know on whose authority these bold assertions were made.

the destruction of the *khandhas*. The *Itivuttaka* (p. 38) and the *Sutta-Nipāta Commentary* (I. 350) identify these two conditions (*sa-upādisesa* and *anupādisesa*) with the nibbāna-state (*nibbāna-dhātu*). Nothing spatial is meant by this: it is defined (*s.* v. 8) as destruction of passion, hatred, delusion and the āsavas.

These considerations show, not the irreconcilability of *anupādisesa* (called *aññā* in the *Sutta-Nipāta* pasage) and *sa-upādisesa*, but the existence of a close connection between them. But when it came to be thought that arahanship was to be won here and now, logically the third Way should have been eliminated from the group of the four Ways; for it suggests an alternative achievement to arahanship, so long as insistence is laid on gaining this inthe present rebirth. But the third Way was not eliminated. Yet something very like it appears to have been attempted in an Aṅguttara passage (IV. 378). It is said of all those on the three lower Ways that when they have done their time here they are with a substrate remaining, but will not be rebornin any state of woe. The arahan is not mentioned in this passage: neither is *anupādisesa*. Does this joint exclusion of the arahan and *anupādisesa* intend to imply that this state was the monopoly of the arahan?

There is not so much perplexity about the state of a *sakadāyāmin* as there is about the *anāgāmin* after he has deceased from this body. It is clearly stated, in both the Commentaries on the *Majjhima* and on the *Puggalapaññatti*, that he is to return once to this earth and to spend the intervening time in the deva world.

One point in this passage of the *Majjhima Commentary* calls for some notice. It is concerned with the meaning which it intends to ascribe to the term *magga*, way. For this passage says that the once-returner "having here made to become the Way of once-returning, wanes utterly here.........or making to become the Way here........." It is open, to question, I think, whether the Way here means the way of once-returning as it is explicitly called the first time it is mentioned; and whether it is called simply *magga* in subsequent allusions to it for the sake of brevity (which is not however as a rule a virtue of the Commentator); or, whether the one sole Way is intended. Either interpretation would be possible. Once-returning might be as easily entailed by cultivation of the Way itself as by cultivation of the Way of Once-returning. For the latter was a part or stage of the former. It is said that whoever is blessed with the ariyan eightfold Wayis a stream-winner (*S.* V. 347). And the once-returner although at a higher stage on the Way than was the stream-winner was not on a different way, for there was not a second one by which a disciple could progress. This mention of the (one) Way may have been due to a lingering memory of the earlier teaching which became "left-in" in the Commentary. At all events nothing can now fortunately alter the fact that, in this Commentary, the Way is called by its simplest designation, *magga*.

And I think that there are good grounds for the hypothesis that by *magga* the *Majjhima Commentary* means the way, and nothing less. The Way was for making to become, and later, meant going to nibbāna; and these were the aims of those on the fourfold Way. In addition various Commentaries (*MA*. I. 162; *S*. I. 196) call *sota*, stream, a name for the Way. Again, in the *Dīgha* and *Saṃyutta Commentaries* (*DA*. I. 313=*SA*. II. 73) *sotāpanna* is defined as "having attained the stream of the Way."

Descriptions of those who are on the four Ways are descriptions of those who are progressing on the Way shown by Gotama to all his disciples and followers. Declarations of knowledge pertaining to these Ways are manifestations of the extent ot which the training has been variously fulfilled, or of the different states to which it will conduce while it is being fulfilled to a greater or less degree. So far we have found that the greater or lesser amount of destruction of the fetters is the criterion for measuring those on the four Ways. Another, and possibly late, means of discrimination is also used (*S*. V. 375). This includes, besides elimination of the Fetters, four endowments: faith in the Buddha, in Dhamma, in the Saṅgha, and joyousness and swiftness in insight. The first three of these remain constant, being ascribed to those on each of the four Ways, while their other achievements vary with their progress. But in other passages (*D*. II. 93; III. 227=*S*. II. 69), possibly earlier, the first three of these endowments with the possession of virtues dear to the Ariyans (instead of joyousness and swiftness in insight) are called the four possessions of the stream-winner only, and not of those on all the four Ways.

There are records that others besides those who had entered the Orders became arahans. It is therefore only to be expected that others also were capable of entering the lower Ways.

Gotama is recorded to have said that the most backward bhikkhu is a steam-winner (*Vin*. III. 10=*D*. II. 155). Of women he is reputed to have said that they might become (*bhabba*) those to realise the fruits of the first three Ways and arahanship if they would go forth from home into homelessness (*Vin*. III. 254). This last clause seems to be in contradiction of the view that lay-people may be stream-winners, and looks like a piece of later editing. For it is highly probable that Gotama would not have tried to discriminate between a lay-man and a lay-woman in the matter of stream-entrance. He is reputed to have told the Sākyan lady Kāḷgodhā that she had won the fruits of stream-attainment and that that was a gain for her; and there are various records of laymen who are said to have won this state. Thus Dhammadinna affirmed that he had the four limbs of the stream-winner intact. Moreover Gotama is recorded to have instructed Mahānāma that these four limbs are to be used by one lay-disciple who is a stream-winner to comfort another who needs their assurance because he is ill (*S.* IV. 408 *ff.*). Again, he is recorded to have declared that any white-frocked house man who observes the first five *sīlas*, and who is possessed of the four endowments of the stream-winner may declare the Self by the self (*attanā va attānan*) by uttering the formula of stream-attainment.

These *attā* couples of sayings which occur especially in the *Aṅguttara*: may declare the Self by the self (*A.* III. 211), the Self upbraids the self (*A.* I. 57), the self conceals the Self (*A.* I. 149), are redolent of the old Upaṇiṣadic outlook, and are a priceless indication of the bond which was then held to exist between the Highest Self and the individual self, the lesser being able by its own nature to declare its share in the nature of the All and its union with it. These couples are a fragment of original Sākya, and belong to a time before *nibbāna* as a waning of the self of man had intervened as a natural corollary of the growth of the *anattā* doctrine.

There is a very interesting passage in the *Aṅguttara* (III. 351) which states that various classes of devas who possess perfect faith in the Buddha, in Dhamma, in the Saṅgha and who have the virtues dear to the Ariyans, are stream-winners. Such devas include the Four Firmament Devas, the Devas of the Thirty, of Tusita, those who delight in creating and those who have power over the creations of others. The devas of Brahmā's company are not mentioned, for they were, so it is thought, non-returners. Neither are the devas "beyond that" (*tatuttariṃ*) included.

We turn now to those who may becomeonce-returners and non-returners. In all the canonical records which I have come across of women who are saiid to be on one or other of these Ways, they are only said to be so after they have left this earth. The same is not true for men. For there are at least three passages all in the *Saṃyutta*, where a man is called an *anāgāmin* while he is alive. A Brahmā belonging to the independent class of Brahmās (*paccekabrahmā*), of which we have no traditional knowledge, was asked by some bhikkhus on his appearance to them after he had passed hence, "Were you not called *anāgāmin* by the Lord?" But if he had been so called, we do not know whether he won this title before or after he had left this world.

In the *Aṅguttara* (II. 159) it is said that if both the once-returner and the non-returner have here and now attained to the realm of neither-perception nor non-perception, deceasing hence they will pass to the company of the devas who have attained this realm. But the once-returner will come back to this state of things because he has not destroyed the Fettens which pertain to this world. In another passage (*A*. I. 63 f.) the sole difference between a non-returner and a once-returner is that the former "having attained to a certain calm freedom of mind dwells therein."

There is a puzzling passage in the Lohicca Suttanta of the *Dīgha*. Here Gotama is made to say that if any samaṇa or brāhmaṇa were to put obstacles in the way of those clansmen who have won distinction in Dhamma and the discipline, as for example the fruit of stream-winning or the fruit of one or other of the Ways, he would be putting obstacles in the way of those who are making embryos fit for devas (*dibbā gabbhā*) ripe for rebirth in becomings fit for devas. This curious little passage appears to mean that attainment to any of the four Ways might lead to rebirth among the devas. Or does it actually mean this? Had it meant literally this, would it not have said *devesu*, among the devas? Is the use of *dibba* meant to imply tht one might be merely deva-like, without necessarily joining their company? I do not think so. I think that before *arahatta* (arahanship) came to be identified with *nibbāna*, and before that came to mean the waning of the self, and not merely of *rāga, desa* and *moha,* (passion, hatred and illusion), the arahan was regarded as having some bourn beyond, when this life was over; and that before *nirodha*, making to cease, came to assume prime importance, the arahan was allowed to fit in with the essentially Indian belief in the running on and faring on of beings. This was *saṃsāra,* whose "beginning and end are alike unthinkable." Who is more worthy than the arahan for the bliss of the deva-realms? Who is more worthy for a myriad oppotunities for self-betterment? He was as certainly fit for these as he was for cessation.

Chapter - 17

Growth of Not-Man in Buddhism

C.A.F. Rhys Davids

Since Indian teachers began to make central, not just 'man,' not just the visible, bodily expressed man, but the inner, the spiritual man—the 'man-in-man,'—their teaching became and has remained the most notable word on the subject that the world has seen. To say of each man: 'Thou, the inmost thou, art That!'—Highest Reality, Spirit, Divinity!—may be, nay, must be but a groping-after; it may be amplified in ways more or less unworthy. It was so amplified. But to utter it, to hold to it, as cults come and go, is to have got in the wedge-end of the true. With anything less there is surely no right wording of this that is very man. With it we set out towards further coming-to-know in a way that will at long last lead each one to 'That.'

But there came a day when India wavered in her vision. This was when she began to consider man in a new way of analysis, man not only as having body, not only as thinker and doer, but as 'having mind': *cetanā, cetanavant.* It was as 'having intelligence among intelligences' that the 'man' entered into body and became its driver.[1]

We have to get out of our modern standpoints to understand the new, strong fascination which this analysis exercised on the Indian imagination. Yet are we ourselves novices—crude novices at that—in our own recent detachment of mind-study from man-study. And were it not that we are too near to see ourselves in true perspective, we should discern with sympathy that old-world development.

As we know, the founder of the new analysis is said to have been one Kapila, and his secular or non-Brāhmaṇical school became known as Sāṅkhya or Computing. The word includes both numbering

---

1. Cf. *Maitrī Up.*, 2, etc.

and naming. As analysis, its effects became articulate long after in a temporary name given to Buddhist ecclesiastics.[1] There was in Kapila's teaching no lessening the reality or worth of the 'man,' no resolving of man into mind. The novelty was in considering the ways of him, other than physical ways, as *natural process*. Process could be xamined; the proceeder as *sui generis* was not examinable.

The teaching appealed to the newer time-spirit astir in North India, and infected the Brahmin teachers. As a school it was not yet taken over; that came later. But computing mental phases, valuing in terms of mind came strongly into vogue, as is betrayed in the Chāndogya, Bṛhadāraṇyaka and Aitareya Upaniṣads. And a sense of nascent danger is also betrayed:—'Seek not the thinking, the feeling.......seek the thinker, the feeler'.......[2] Later as we know, Vedāntism absorbed the worth and work of Sāṅkhya, and the 'man-in-man' survived the danger,—a danger of which we here and now know something—of being submerged in mind.

But among other teachings the Sāṅkhya influence worked with a more potent and lasting leaven. Centres of religious reform arose after Kapila, committed from the start to a new emphasis on the greater religious importance of *the life* as compared with the ritual, of the will in choice as compared with the prescribed act. Herein they were implicitly, if not explicitly, anti-Brahmin—implicitly, since we do not hear of any anti-Brahmin crusade. Brahmin ideals of man's nature and worth were at first accepted. And the saintly man as spiritual entity was still called 'Brāhmaṇa.' That this spiritual entity was real, the real of reals, *did not come into question*. Had a teacher said 'The man (*puruṣa, ātman*) is not', it would have been to show himself a madman.

Nevertheless with the fading importance of ritual offered to placate, there was bound to arise examination in current values of That concerning whom and what the rites were performed. That was imperishable (*akṣara*) and, as such, immutable and not becoming. Ws the very man indeed one with That? Was he as 'having intelligence' really independent of the infirmities of intelligence? Could he as entity persist, with self-expression by way of mind, which analysis showed to be a succession of units far more brief-lived than body? Could it be maintained that, clogged with burden of body and mind, he was most inwardly one with consummate all-

1. Vibhajjavādins.
2. *Kauṣītaki Up.*, 3, 8.

being? The Śākyan (i.e. Buddhist) mandate had placed man as wayfarer in a Way, signifying both choice and growth in the Better, whereby in many ages and many words he might attain to That. But there was supervening another vogue, the monk-vogue of an enlargd escape from worldly hindrances even during youth. In that vogue the patient wayfaring by way of life's countless opportunities towards that perfection, of which the inner man was but the germ, was depreciated; the idea of 'becoming'[1] became dreaded as so much rebirth. The perfect man, with consummation into That cut off, dwindled into a 'worthiness,' to be attained in earth-conditions—a perfection, to us, clearly unobtainable in that it was limited by its conditions. In this vogue of monasticism the Indian conception of the man-in-man as inchoate divinity, which might under the concept of the Way (*mārga*) have deepened the religious thought of India, wilted and died. The man became merged in his ways, a stream of bodily and mental events.

I tried to trace this evolution of the not-man in Buddhism four years ago.[2] There is not enough evidence perhaps to make the truth of it patent to our Indologists, who are compelled to study Pāli literature as only an adjunct to more central studies. But there are evidences sufficient to make a case *not to be brushed aside.* Now as yet the brushing aside is just what has been done. Books still appear referring to a tenet of not-man, or not-I, or not-self, or not-soul, as fundamental in the original teaching of what came very late to be called 'Buddhism.' This would matter less if the early mandate were called, as Asoka called it, 'Saka' or Sākyan, and not Buddhist. It never was called Buddhist till the founder's teaching had been twisted and smothered in monasticism. But by modern writers, *either* the Sākyan gospel is iddentified as the monastic elaboration—in this case the Piṭakas are taken at their face-values, i.e., monk-values—*or* the disentangling of a wholesomer gospel for 'Everyman' from these values is stated to be impossible.

So I am trying here to state the case for evolution once more, and to say it better, if all too briefly.

Among the teacher-dicta ascribed to the Founder as His earliest are these: (1) *Is it not better that you should seek the 'man'*[3]? and the negative warning: (2) *The 'man' is not body, not mind.*

---

1. *Arahattaṃ.*
2. Buddhist Psychology, 2nd. ed., London, 1924, ch. xiii.
3. *Attānaṃ.*

(1) In that day the words 'man' and 'self' were equivalents. When the injunction just cited came to be written down, 'self' (*attānaṃ*) was used, not 'man' (*puriṣaṃ,* or *puggalaṃ*). But 'man' was probably the word actually used, since this, and this alone gives point to the injunction which was a counter-question:—'Is it a *woman* with stolen property you ask me about? Were it not better for you to be seeking the '*man*,' the very 'You'?'

(2) In the other saying, the wording which came to be selected, by repeaters, by editors, or both, has been singularly unfortunate, and has doubtless played its part in the growth of error. Instead of the negative syllable being attached to body or to mind, it is prefixed to the man (or self): 'body is not-self,' *rūpaṃ anattā*, and so on. Had the saying been worded in the books: *Puggalo*, or *attā*, *na rūpaṃ*, etc., the need of this crusade might never have arisen. That it actually was so worded originally I believe to be highly probable. There was, I repeat, no question, when the Founder taught, of the 'man's' reality. And whereas later editing has inserted the fourfold grouping of the mind, there is no parcelling out of the one responsible individual into such 'groups' or events when his very salvation is in question. It is: 'Verily I say unto *you*!'...'I tell *thee,* sire, I declare to *thee,* sire, *thou* hast no time to dally'...'Verily not by another has this been done; *thou* hast done it and by it shalt *thou* now be judged.'

It is the very man we see as the 'burden-bearer' of body and mind, laying down one body at death, taking up another, wayfaring through the worlds—'you and I'—the man remembering, where there is abnormal gift, how 'I' was so and so in a former life; the man who has lately left the earth appearing clairvoyantly to one abnormally gifted on earth and recognized *as the some time friend* of past years.[1]

All such, as teaching or as told experience, the books ascribe to the Founder. Nor is there anywhere imputed to him that later quibble: 'I use these words by way of common speech-usage, but in their ultimate meaning they are but labels for fictitious unities.'[2] Has there ever been a Helper of the Many who dd so speak? Or who taught concerning the very man and his welfare and his coming-to-be in negatives?

But when the books were finally redacted, when at length the books in a non-Indian environment, were written down, much had changed. To careful critical reading this is fairly evident. That parable

---

1. E.G. Bimbisāra, the king, Anāthapiṇḍika, the merchant, Ajita, the warrior, appear severally after death to Gotama.

2. I do not find this distinction clearly worded before the Milindapañho, p. 160.

of the Jeta wood:—is it not obvious that there has been a dropping out? They are clearing kindling-wood out from the trees: 'are the faggots the wood?' asks the Teacher...'No more are body and mind really *you*'.[1] Body goes to the funeral pyre; the man stands as stands the wood, putting forth new verdure and blossom with each spring...with each access of new will...But in the books the application of the wood to the man has somehow fallen out, and all point in the parable is gone!

The omission is fairly obvious. Was it made, involuntarily or voluntarily, in consequence of a changed standpoint? Was that standpoint changing during the Founder's lifetime? I should say it certainly was, especially during his old age, when we may gather he toured less, and resided mostly in the Sāvatthi Jeta Wood, in his 'Fragrant-wood Hut.' His wor went on, for his community had become numerous and influential. And there will have been much work at Sāvatthi of comparing repetitions of Sayings, and deciding on standardized versions and, in cases of leading tenets, fof a reduction to brief formulas and labels. But in all this, and the more aged he grew, there will have been ample opportunity for the growing pre-occupation with *mind* rather than with the *man* to assert itself among energetic younger men representing a newer vogue. The man as way-farer among the worlds, earth as but one of them, on his long way to That, belonged already to the thought of yesterday. It was that body and mind which had been declared to be 'not the man,' it was the human congeries or, in modern jargon, 'complex' which was proving of interest. It was this world more than the long world-way that was the central problem. It was the new idea of consummation in 'worthiness' (*arahatta*) here, before the human complex broke up, that took the place of a goal only to be attained by life-developments elsewhere.

Thus the simpler *caveat* of the earlier 'what the man is not' was elaborated into the formula of the 'person-group': "the wise man does not look upon body or any mental 'group' as the self, nor the self as having body or mind, nor upon either as being in the self, nor the self as being in either."[2] Again we know how the 'advanced' woman's term for living being as a 'mere bundle of complexes'[3] recorded among the older sayings, eventually captured the imagination of the scholastics, together with its singularly inapt

1. Saṃyutta, iii, 33; iv, 82.
2. E.g. Majjhima, i, 300.
3. *Suddha-sambhāra-puñja*, S., i. 135.

chariot simile, bringing to Vajirā, the nun, undreamt of posthumous fame.

The second century of the Buddhist Sangha probably witnessed the compilation of the first half of the Abhidhamma books. In these the most noteworthy feature is the growth of mental analysis, and of the habit of banishing the the 'man,' and of discussing merely the ways of him, bodily and mental. Of such discussions there are interesting anticipations in the Sayings of the preceding century, notably the two catechetical Suttas of the Majjhima. And here too the 'man' who enjoys what the senses bring, but 'mind.' In the past, with little vision, I welcomed her a harbinger of our own old 'sensus communis.' The commentary might have served as warning; with no psychological insight it illustrates simply, directly, more truly, with aparable of five *rentiers,* receiving an income small or large, and the *king*, to whom all the five villages pay taxes. It is the 'man' who tastes, the 'man' who values. How much editing, I wonder, could that Sutta tell us of, were it too 'man'?

Of the first, earlier half of the Abhidhamma Piṭaka, one books is called *Puggala Paññatti*. But so far is this from making good on the subject of the evicted 'man' (*puggala*), that the translated title 'Designation of Human Types'—types, classes, not individual entity, men, not the man,—fits very accurately? With the fading out of the realityof the 'man,' the study of men in sets, of mind in class and category was gaining ground enormously.

But this vogue had not prevailed without dissentients. It was only natural that Indian culture, when and so far as it was taken up into Buddhism, should not easily make such a *volte-face* as to go back on the veryaxis of its religious view of life. Upholders of the reality, the ultimate truth of the 'inner controller' (*antarayāmin*) had formidable arguments. It is in the 5th, the concluding book of the *first* canonical Abhidhamma Piṭaka, the *Rathā-vatthu*, that we can see, in the precedence and the length of the controversy on the 'Man' and in the points, often unmet, of his upholder, what a crisis the Sangha had been going through, before the orthodox purging at Patna under Asoka became possible. There is no space here to go into the series of debates between the Mantheorist (*Puggalavādin*) and the Vibhajjavādin, representing the prvailing orthodoxy. Despite the absence of any adequate psychological terms, or of writing, the points raised amount none the less to a searching and comprehensive inquiry. Virtually theyare in a two-fold group: the nature of man as judged by our own immediate experience here, and the need of a hypothesis of that nature as tenable in a belief in passing at death to other words. Is man the sole ultimate, *sui generis*? Or what sort of *co*-ultimate is he? Is he ultimate in virtue of self-consciousness? Then *is* he when not self-conscious? Is he agent where agency and locus of agency are indicated:—seer in sight, etc., like villager in village, king in kingdom, jailer to jail? Does he persist in virtue of his faculty of becoming (*bhava*), or is not becoming itself non-persisting?

No explanation of this notable effort, taken in relation to the rest of the book itself and to the values in earlier books on the one hand and later books on the other, is to me possible save in the light of such a changed standpoint as has been put forward.

Nor should it be overlooked—I say it here and now again—that nowhere in the Kathāvatthu does the orthodox Analyst bring forward in defence the distinction between popular and philosophic meaning in doctrinal teaching on the 'man' (*puggala*). Yet it is just here that he needs it, and would surely have referred to it. It is only in the Commentarial peroration that use is made of it—a fairly good proof that it came only later into use.

Let us now take later milestones to that change.

In that other remarkable book of debates, the *uestions of King Milinda,* the date of which is placed in the first century of our era, the standpoint of the 'not-man', based, be it noted, solely on Sister Vajirā's simile, is hurled by the senior speaker—the monk—at the junior (the king), or ever he asks about it. 'My name, sire, is a label for the parts of me; nothing more, no 'me'-ness. And to the fiction 'man' is now given a new name: 'experiencer' (*vedagu, vedako*[1]). Not as other-world hypothesis is the 'man' most hard to kill. It was becoming as easy to put the other world on one side as it would seem to be even at this time of day. It is as 'that-who-is-conscious'—the unanalyzable agent in the analyzed mind-events—that 'the man' made his last stand. That, *e.g.*, the seeing is not either willed or enjoyed by the mindless eye-organ, but is an act byand for Some-one:—this is answered quite childishly by the 'Sage.' As a Sāṅkhyan argument it was still valid later in the manual *Nyāyabindu*.

As to that in the man-complex who *reacts on the impressions*, in attention and other forms of will, here there is no teaching and no wonder; for where will is both discerned and worded at all worthily, the *willer* must of necessity be also discerned and worded.

---

1. *Miln.*, p. 54, etc.

Our second milestone is the Pāli Commentaries of Buddhadatta and Buddhaghosa. In them scholastic Buddhism has reached the summit of its negative standpoint. It may not sound a negative position, when we note the divisions of the latter's famous treatise *Visuddhi-magga*:—Morals, Concentration, Wisdom. Butas we read, we see that these are discourses on the ways of a Subject who is perpetually declared to be a nonentity. We hear about events happening to, and mental states arising about 'a self, a doer, an experiencer' who is expressly said not to be. That 'he' is spoken of 'is merely, as the wise know, by way of common usage......' 'Only the events, the states occur: this is right view.'[1] Arugment about it is no longer needed. All the teacher has to do is to say it over and over dogmatically, much as a child might be told in the dark that there are no bogies.

Or if, with Buddhadatta, we ask:—can there be mental states without the minder? He tells us, that just as buḍs appear owing to the elements and the seasons, so do mind states appear from the confluence of causes.[2] He too and Buddhaghosa no less, trot out the little Sister's foolish simile, equating the 'man' with a man-made apparatus (a chariot) to aid his movements. But Buddhadatta fathers her folly on to the Founder himself: 'was it not said by, etc.?' To equate 'the man' with physical process is perhaps a less glaring error.

Now to the best of my knowledge this not-man position has remained a cardinal tenet in South Asian Buddhism till the present day. From the days of the writing down of the Canon it forms with two other equally sinister negations the axiomatic trinity in the religious philosophy of monastic Buddhism: 'impermanence, ill, not-man.' It is true that there would seem to-day to be symptoms within the fold, that the last of the three, as worded in Canon and Commentary, is felt to be untenable. *An-atta*, I hear, is now, by at least one divine, asserted to mean 'dependence', 'non-absoluteness'. It is good to note a moving in very still waters; but the assertion surely finds no support in Seriptural sources. It is at most but *one aspect* of the old general assumption.

It will be cast at me, that while later 'minds', together with the tardily introduced art of writing, have resulted in developed affirmation and more fluent expression, the not-man dogma is already emphatic in the Suttas of the Canon. Have we not, beside those

---

1. P. 602 of my edition.
2. *Abhidhammāvatāro* : 'Kārakapaṭivedho'.

cited, the Alaggaddūpama (No. XXII) and the Aggi-Vacchagotta (No. LXXII) of the Majjhima Nikāya, not to mention much else, where in the wording of the senses etc. as "neither the self nor 'selfic'," and so forth, the consideration of the very man is, if not denied in so many words, shown as no fit subject for careful thought?

I grant that this is so, and that, in the much edited Canon as it has come down to our day, we see that the later developments are but a natural outcome of the standpoint taken up in and by thta editing. The mistake we make today is that of yesterday; that is, in accepting the opinions developed and developing in those Pāli scriptures *as the original teaching*; in accepting them without question, without constantly reminding ourselves that we are dealing, even in the portions deemed to be oldest, with palimpsests, compiled and recompiled during centuries of oral tradition from the voices of repeaters, by monks and for monks.

I say, 'for monks'. It is not realized, by those especially who red at second-hand only, how true this became, how absorbed in its inner monastic world the Sangha became, how nugatory in religion the opinion of the laity was, how ignorant was the laity of the contents of the oral, and then of the written literature, *how ignorant the laity still is*. In the beginning the teaching of Gotama the Sākya was a mandate for Everyman, placing his feet in a truer Way to his eternal welfare. Gradually that mandate became worded as not for Everyman but for the Half-man (witness the word 'pabbajitena' in the first 'sermon'), for theman who had cut the knots of life's problems instead of working by his natural life at the solving of them. That short-cutting was, in conditions fleeting and woeful, to erase the 'man' who was way-faring through them, who was valuing them as such, and was seeing in them *opportunities* for becoming more and more That Who he really was; and to build, out of the fleeting flux of observed results, bodily and mental, a creature of precocious 'worth', the ideal monk (*arahaṃ*).

There is evidence that, in these mobile repeatings, where no books were, rectifications were needed from time to time, and were made. For the relative perfection of trained memorizing, on which we too readily fall back, was a Brahmin monopoly; the Buddhists were mere amateurs in it. And no repeater, probably no one centre, ever knew more than a section, never knew *all* the records as we can now. The rectifying meant this and only this: adapting varying versions to accord with the view held, at a given time, by the rectifiers. And thus, and inevitably the 'Sayings' edged further and further from the teaching, grown antiquated, of the days of the mandate.

I do not say that we can 'recapture the first fine rapture' of that. We can try. But it is worthier of our new science of historical criticism to try, and to confess we are trying, than to accept at their face-value the monk-dicta of Asokan or Sinhalese editors as the primary message. Worthier is it to remember Kern's conclusion: "The more we try to remove the difficulties, the more we are driven to the suspicion that original Buddhism was not exactly that of the canonical books."[1] Made over thirty years ago, that conclusion is still too little heeded.

Probably our own 'man'-less psychology hinders us from seeing how irrational is the deadlock into which Buddhism had fallen when the Pāli Commentaries were written. We do not quite deny the 'man'. But we call him 'soul', 'metempirical self', and shelve him. We then analyze events, results, complexes, like any Buddhist. The result is, we are losing the individual in the 'herd'. Herein we are off the vantage-ground whence we can judge the mandate of a new world-religion. This has ever been the telling man of a fuller, not an emptier life, the telling him that there is more he can be and become as very man, not less. Such a message never was, never could be a message of negatives.

1. *Indian Buddhism* (1896), p. 50.

Chapter - 18

Interpretation of the "Anatta" Doctrine of Buddhism:

A New Approach

R.P. Chowdhury

The importance of the "Anatta" doctrine in Buddhism needs no emphasising. With Anicca and Dukkha it forms the corner-stone of Buddhist philosophy. Therefore, a correct interpretation of the term is essential for a right understanding of the teachings of the Buddha. "In the whole history of Buddhist philosophy there has perhaps never been a more debated and more misunderstood term than anatta."[1] The *Buddhist Dictionary* remarks "It (Anatta) is the only specific Buddhist doctrine with which the entire Buddhist structure stands or falls."[2]

The Anatta doctrine is presumed to mean that there is no soul. It is taken as the opposite of attavāda. Does the word "Anatta" mean "not-Self" or does it mean "soulless", "without a soul?" Should the Anatta doctrine mean that everything is non-Self or should it mean that there is no soul? Not-Self or no soul—is the question.

To avoid possible confusion, it is necessary to mention at the outset that it would be better to use capital 'S' to denote "Attā" (Ātman), the (universal) Self, and small 's' to denote "attā" the individual soul or individual self. It is better, I suppose, to use the word "soul" in the sense in which it has been employed by the Eternalists (Sassatavādins).

The accepted meaning of "Anatta" is that there is no permanent entity in anything, be it a mental state or a physical object. Things are without a soul, "natthi etesaṁ attā." This kind of interpretation, though commonly accepted is open to serious objection.

---

1. *"The Self and its Complications"*—by W. Stede (Bulletin of the School of Oriental Studies, 1948).
2. p. 11.

Anicca and Dukkha are pure adjectives, and so they do not present any difficulty, but "Anatta" is a noun, the negative of "Attan", and yet it can be used as adjective as in a Bahubbīhi compound, like "ajjhattaṁ sukhadukkhaṁ", "sabbe sattā bhavantu sukhitattā" etc., and so a double interpretation of the term is possible. The difficulty is enhanced by the fact that the word "Attā" is used not only to mean the individual soul but also the universal Self. The Pali commentators, followed by modern writers, take the word "attā" only in the sense of an individual soul and "anatta" only as an adjective meaning "soul-less", whereas in reality "Anatta" is that which is not the universal Self, and the word is never used as an adjective. The distinction between "not-Self" and "soul-less" may not be clear in the English garb, yet, as we shall see, there is a world of difference between the two, and the difference is unfortunately overlooked or ignored.

In the first place, the accepted interpretation of the term "Anatta" as "without a soul" "without (durable or separate) self", "soulless"[1] is ruled out by grammar. "Matter is soul-less" cannot be the correct translation of "rūpaṁ Anattā" which should be changed into "rūpaṁ anattaṁ" to yield that meaning. But nowhere is such a reading found. The same remark applies to "viññāṇaṁ Anattā", "cakkhu Anattā", "cakkhusamphasso Anattā", "yam p'idaṁ cakkhusamphassapaccayā uppajjati vedayitaṁ sukhaṁ vā dukkhaṁ vā adukkhamasukhaṁ vā tam pi Anattā." If the accepted sense of the word is correct, they should read "viññāṇam anattaṁ"[2], "cakkhu anattaṁ" etc. The fact is that here the compound "Anatta" is not a Bahubbīhi which behaves as an adjective; it is a Kammadhāraya in which the word remains a noun. "Rūpam Anattā" cannot but mean "form is not-Self" according to the rules of grammar. But "Vedanā Anattā", "Saññā Anattā", "Sankhārā Anattā","Sabbe dhammā Anattā" may be taken also to mean "feeling is self-less" etc; "all things are self-less"; though grammatically correct, such is not the import of the words. On grammatical grounds alone the popular interpretation falls to the ground. It is only by mangling grammar that the traditional interpretation can be upheld, but no student of language can support such an interpretation.

It is strange that this aspect of the question so obvious has so far escaped the notice of Pali scholars. Even Coomaraswamy wrote

---

1. It is so taken also in Sanskrit Buddhism—*Systems of Buddhist Thought,* p. 24f.
2. It is interesting to note that there is a solitary instance of a variant reading—"viññāṇm anattaṁ" in Majjhima I, p. 549.

in 1916 in explaining "Anatta", "there exists no changeless entity in anything, and above all, no 'eternal soul' in man,"[1] and yet he added later on "the coining of the term anatta to imply absence of a perduring individuality is a triumph of ingenuity."[2]

That the translation of the word "Anatta" as "soul-less" is incorrect becomes clear when the word "Attā" is used without the negative prefix "an"—e.g., "saṅkhāre parato disvā na ca Attato" which means "looking upon things as foreign and not as one's own Self." The word "Attā" simply means "Self"; it cannot be made to mean "having a self or soul." How then can the negative "Anatta" occurring in such contexts mean "not having a self?" It can only mean "not-Self."

Moreover, where the positive term "Attā" actually occurs side by side with "Anatta" in the Canon, the meaning of "Anatta" becomes further clear. The sentence "Anattasambhūtā dhammā kuto Attā bhavissati?" means "how can the states that are the product of non-Self be the Self?" Again, "Cakkhu Attā yo vadeyya . . .iti cakkhum Anattā"[3] cannot but be translated as "he who should say that the eye is the Self . . .the eye is not-Self." If, however, it is translated as "the eye is soul-less" it does not fit into the context. Then again, the sentence "yad Anattā taṁ n'etaṁ mama, n'eso'ham asmi, na me'so Attā" can only be translated as "that which is not-Self that is 'this is not mine, I am not this, this is not my Self." In the Anattalakkhaṇa Sutta too "Attā" and "Anattā" are found used together—"Rūpaṁ bhikkhave Anattā" (O monks, the body is not-Self) . . .rūpañ ca h'idaṁ bhikkhave Attā abhavissa (if, O monks, the body were the Self). The same is the case with the other factors vedanā, saññā etc. Here "rūpaṁ Anattā" cannot be translated in any other way except as "the body is not-Self"; it cannot be translated as "the body is self-less." If the word "Anatta" cannot be rendered in any other sense in the above contexts, how can it be otherwise rendered in other places? We cannot give a double translation according to our pleasure, in some places as "non-Self" and in others as "self-less." But this has actually been done by the scholars. One cannot have it both ways. Although the title of the Anattalakkhaṇa Sutta has been interpreted in both ways the word "Anatta" occurring in the text of the Sutta which explains the subject-matter has not been translated by any scholar as "soulless." Jennings who translates

---

1. *Buddha and the Gospel of Buddhism,* p. 198.
2. *Ibid.,* 206.
3. M, III. 282.

"rūpaṃ bhikkhave Anattā" as "the material form, mendicant brothers, is not a permanent-self" translates the title as "Discourse on the absence of signs of [permanent individual] Self."[1] He also translates "sabbe dhammā Anattā" as "All things in nature are without permanent soul."[2] It is surprising that Rhys Davids who rendered "rūpam bhikkhave Anattā" in the body of the above Sutta as "O monks, body is not the "self", should describe the Sutta as one "on the non-existence of the soul."[3] With reference to the Sutta E.J. Thomas says "Buddha then preached to them on the non-existence of the soul. The soul (ātman) which is denied is not the self of actual experience, but a theory of the permanent nature of the soul, a reality held to be behind all the physical phenomena."[4] Dr. N. Dutt is also of opinion with regard to the Sutta that "Buddha denied the existence of "Attā", i.e., of any permanent substance apart from the khandhas."[5] U Ottama remarks that the Anattalakkhana Sutta "explains the most fundamental philosophical standpoint of Buddhism that there is no abiding permanent factor behind the phenomena either animate or inanimate known as the "Anatta theory."[6] These conclusions, however, are not warranted by the text which simply says that rūpa is not the Self, vedanā is not the Self etc. The Anattalakkhaṇa Sutta is a much-misunderstood sermon.

To come back to the interpretation of the word "Anatta"—if the word is taken as "soul-less" translation under certain contexts becomes odd. The sentence "Yo kho bhikkhave Anattā tatra vo chando pahātabbo,"[7] if translated by "you, monks, should give up your desire for that which is void of a permanent (individual) soul would mean by implication that you should not give up your desire for the soul!—a position which is exasperating. How again, should we translate "dukkhe Anattasaññā"—as "no-soul sense in suffering"—which is a meaningless expression; should it not rather be translated as "considering suffering as non-Self?"—the nature of Self being bliss? "Anatta" which means "non-Self" can never yield the meaning "without soul." Non-Self prompts the query "what is Self?" but then what is the opposite of "soulless?"

---

1. *The Vedantic Buddhism of the Buddha*, pp. 42, 48.
2. *Ibid.*, xliv.
3. *The Buddhist Birth Stories*, p. 113.
4. *The Life of the Buddha*, p. 42.
5. *The Early Monastic Buddhism*, p. 92.
6. The Anatta-lakkhaṇa Sutta published by the Mahabodhi Society Introduction.
7. S. III. 77.

From the translation of non-canonical literature too examples can be quoted to show that the word "Anatta" has been used sometimes as "non-Self" and sometimes as "selfless." Prof. U Pe Maung Tin in his translation of the *Visuddhimagga*, for instance, translates "saññā saṅkhāre ca Anattato passanto" as "he who sees perceptions and complexes as self-less";[1] "sayaṃ ca assāmikabhāvato Anattā" as "not-self because it is under no master"[2] and "Anattani Attā ti vipallāsaṁ pajahāti" as "abandons the perverted view that there is self in the selfless."[3]

The rendering of "Anatta" by "soulless" has led to a search for the school or schools which believed in a soul in things and against which the Anatta doctrine is supposed to have been addressed. It is worthwhile repeating that according to the accepted sense of the term "anatta" there is no immortal soul not only in man and other sentient creatures but also there is none in the objects of Nature. E.J. Thomas remarks "To what form of the Anatta theory the Buddhist canonical position was originally opposed is not clear. It might refer to some form of the Sāṅkhya or to the Jains."[4] Jennings echoes the above opinion when he says with more confidence that Anatta "seems clearly to have been intended to deny the Jain doctrine of indestructible souls or spirits pervading all matter."[5] Of course, Jainism, unlike the Sāṅkhya, believes in souls in every object, and the buddhists also believe that there is no permanence in anything animate or inanimate; it is therefore, possible that the anatta doctrine was directed against the Jains. It is however, difficult to accept the view that the Buddha should have cared to controvert a particular doctrine (the existence of souls) held by a school whose influence was quite limited, as it must have been. Moreover, this particular doctrine of the Jains is nowhere clearly stated in the Pali canon; on the other hand the *Majjhima Nikāya* contains an account of the discomfiture at the hands of the Buddha suffered by one Saccaka, a Jain who held that the body is the Self, feeling is the Self, etc.[6] It is quite clear from what we have tried to establish that a search for a school against which the Anatta doctrine was directed, is bound to be futile. "Tesaṁ . . .appāṭihīrakataṁ bhāsitaṁ sampajjati."

It was not any tenet, Brahmanical or otherwise that the Buddha sought to counter by his Anatta doctrine. He warned one and all not

1. *The Path of Purity,* 480.
2. *Ibid.*, p. 739.
3. *Ibid.*, p. 567.
4. *The Life of the Buddha,* p. 203.
5. *The Vedantic Buddhism of the Buddha,* p. xliv.
6. M. I., Cūlasaccaka *Sutta*, No. 35.

to regard the khandl as or a part thereof to be the Self. They are not-Self—an-Atta; they are the others (*para*) as in the sentence—saṅkhāre parato disvā, na ca Attato. It is a failing of the human kind, and for that matter, of all sentient beings to regard the body or the mind or the body cum mind as the Self. The Self is the 'I' but the mind and body complex is nor the real 'I' or Self. When I say "I am healthy," I identify the Self with my body, when I say "I am worried," I identify the Self with my mind. This identification is universal; it prevails among men and women, young and old; it prevailed in the past; it will prevail in the future and in all countries. The Ātman forgetting its real nature believes itself to be the ego. The ego arises when the Self is identified with the khandhas. Ego and individual self are more or less convertible terms. Of all the identifications, "I-am-the-body" idea (dehâtma-buddhi) is the most widely prevalent. It is the distorting power of Avijjā which does all this. It is those who have destroyed Avijjā know their disembodied universal existence.

The quest for the Self has been the quest of mankind in every country. "Know thyself" was the sentence inscribed on the ancient temples of Greece. In India too "Know thy self"—Ātmānaṁ viddhi in Sanskrit and Attānāṁ gaveseyyātha in Pali was the primal question that the philosophers tried to tackle. We can deny everything but not the self. Even those who deny the self imply its existence by their very denial. The question, however, is—what constitutes our self? The Buddha repeatedly said that the five khaṇdhas which sum up all the phenomena, mental and physical are not-Self—Ānattā. If a man were to collect the faggots in the Jetavana grove and set them on fire, it would be absurd if we should say that he is collecting us and setting us on fire, similarly the khandhas we are made of are not us; we are not they.[1] When Mithila was burning Janaka declared "nothing of me was burnt"—Mithilāyaṁ ḍayhamānāya, na me kiñci aḍayhatha.[2] We take ourselves to be what we are not. An oft-repeated expression of the Buddha is "an unregenerate man views body, feeling etc. as the Self or the Self as consisting of body, feeling etc. or body, feeling etc. in the Self, or the Self in body, feeling etc.[3]—this is the famous Sakkāyadiṭṭhi, the so-called "theory of soul" which really is viewing the non-Self as Self. Śaṅkarācārya observed, in the

---

1. M. I. 300.
2. Jāt. VI, 54.
3. M. I. 140f. These famous and frequently occurring words are interpreted by taking the word "Attā" to mean (according to their wont) the individual self but the meaning is not clear if the word is not used as universal Self.

same way "give up the idea of Self in the non-Self" which is quoted below. The Buddha advised us to give up that which is not ours—yaṁ na tumhākaṁ taṁ pajahatha, and what does not belong to us?—the five khandhas. How can we understand the passage without the Self being understood? There is a profound truth regarding us which the Buddha meant to convey by these words.

Different conceptions of what constitutes the Self prevailed, ranging tfrom the crude body-am-I idea to the self in the highest stage of formless meditation—the sphere of neither-perception-nor-non-perception. See, for instance, the *Brahmajāla Sutta* pages 34 to 38. All these were not the Self—Anattā. In the *Chāndogya*[1] and the *Taittīriya Upaniṣads*[2] both of which are pre-Buddhistic, progressive definitions of what constituted the Self according to Indra and Bhṛgu respectively are described. Śaṅkarācārya in his commentary on the Brahma Sūtra I also gives a list of the different conceptions of the Self. What many of the philosophers regarded as Attā, the Buddha considered to be Anattā.

The negative is the only valid way of describing the Ātman. In the Bṛhadāraṇyaka Upaniṣad the Ātman is described as "not this, not that" (neti, netyayam Ātmā). Śaṅkarācārya too said "I am not the body, not the 1-sense, nor the vital principle etc."[3] "All phenomena are not-Self. With regard to the khandhas, the Buddha announced "this is not mine, this I am not, this is not my Self." All description being description of qualities, that which is devoid of qualities can only be denoted by negatives, but that does not make Reality a negation.

When the Buddha asked a band of aristocratic youngmen (bhaddavaggiyas) whether it was not better to divert their search from a missing woman to the Self, he used the singular number. In fact Attā is always used in the singular number except in grammatical declension. That which is one appears as many. There are no selves but Self. The pure Attā has been imprisoned in a body, (and this we are accustomed to regard as not only a natural but also a desirable state). On account of Avijjā that which is universal appears as particular, that which is free as bound, that which is eternal as temporal, that which is infinite as finite, that which is unconditioned as conditioned. It is remarkable that the Buddha taught the above mentioned young men the path leading to Nirvāṇa. The search for the Self is the same as the quest of Nirvāṇa.

---

1. VIII. 7-12.
2. III. 1-6.
3. *Ātmaṣaṭka* I. See also his *Daśaślokī* I *and Tattvopadeśa,* 9.

The Pali canon also speaks of the Big Self—Mahattā and the little self—appâtumā.[1] The difference between the Big Self and the small self is really one between the true Self and the false self. Are there then two selves—the false which is the ego and the real Self? No, there is only one Self which appears as many due to primal ignorance. The many selves are false and fictitious. They have no existence of their own. The ego-self is a fraud. Enquiry reveals its falsity and the reality of the universal Self. The obvious is not necessarily the real.

The universal Self is utterly different from the individual self. It is limitless. It is the true nature of all men and beings (sarvabhūtântarātmā). This Self pervades all creation. It is indivisible. This universal Self is the real self of man. There is no personal distinction between I, you, and he stremming from it. There is not one shred of individuality, no subject-object relationship whatever in the Self. The difference in selves is superficial. The Self that remains after the ego is destroyed is the universel Self. The Ātman "is neither born, nor does it die."[2] The same epithets are used for Nirvāṇa.[3] The epithets being the same the Reality of which these are the epithets must necessarily be the same. Names are labels which are attached to that which is nameless.

Historically speaking, the word "Anātman" is seldom found in pre-Buddhist literature. A probable reason was that that which the other teachers regarded as Attā was not so, at least so far as the Buddha was acquainted with the views of the contemporary philosophers as recorded, for instance, in the Brahmajāla Sutta. The references in the Vedic literature to Anatta are found in the *Śatapatha Brāhmaṇa*—anātmā hi martyaḥ.[4]—that which is subject to death is not-Self. The *Taittīriya Saṁhitā* too refers to the word.[5] In the post-Vedic literature the Bhagavad Gītā contains the word in VI. 6. In the Vedānta literature the term is frequently met with. Never in the Vedānta the word has been used as "without a soul." Śaṅkarācārya wrote a work entitled "Anātmaśrīvigarhaṇaprakaraṇa" and also another book "Ātmânātmaviveka" by name. Some of his references

---

1. S. 140, and A I, 249. See Yamakami's "*Systems of Buddhist Thought* p. 24f. for "Mahātman" and "hīnātman".
2. *Kaṭha Upaniṣad.* Aja, unborn, ajara, undecaying, amara, immortal, amṛtyu, deathless, abhaya, fearless are some of the epithets of Ātman given in the *Bṛhadāraṇyaka Upaniṣad*, IV. 4. 25.
3. See the Ariyapariyesana S, M. I. 161f. See also the Gītā II. 20.
4. II. 2. 3.
5. VII. 12. 36.

to "Anātman" are given here—Viśvam avyaktaparyantam idaṁ hyanātmā—this Universe up to the unmanifested is non-Self.[1] Ātmânātmavivekaḥ kartavyo bandhamuktaye viduṣā[2]—to remove bondage the wiseman should discriminate between the Self and the non-Self. Ātmânyanātmamatiṁ jahi[3]—relinquish the idea of Self in the non-Self. Na câtmâyam Anātmā syād Anātmâyaṁ na ca Ātmakaḥ[4]—this Self cannot become non-Self, and this non-Self cannot become the Self. Ātmānam api dṛṣṭvā tvaṁ tyaja Anātmānam ādarāt[5]—(as a wise man who sees both poison and nectar even so) seeing the Self you discard with care the non-Self. Anātmanyātmadhīr bandhastannāśo mokṣa ucyate[6]—bondage consists in regarding the non-Self as Self, and its destruction is known as Liberation. Dṛśyaṁ sarvam Anātmā syāt[7] all things perceived are non-Self. Ātmânātmavicāraḥ kartavyaḥ[8]—one should discriminate between the Self and the non-Self. The Anātman is defined as anṛta—false, jaḍa—inert and duḥkha—suffering in the same book.[9] It seems that the word used by the Buddha was appropriated by the Vedantists.

The above examples from Sanskrit make the meaning of the word Anatta abundantly clear. Buddhaghosa defines Anattā as that which is characterised by the denial of soul (attapaṭikkhepato—*Visuddhi-magga,* 668). He always uses the word Attā in the sense of a permanent individual soul. Absence of control is a characteristic of Anatta (avasavattanâkaro Anattalakkhañaṁ—*ibid.*, 640); it is that which is under no master (assāmiko—*ibid.*, 612); which cannot be brought under order (avidheyya—*ibid.*, 479) and that which is without essence (asāra). Buddhaghosha uses the adjective asāra (essenceless) in explaining the Anattalakkhana Sutta (...idampi Anattā asāratthena—*ibid.*, 613). In what sense is it asara? On account of the absence of soul-essence in the Atta conceived as a controller, doer, percipient and self-willed (asāratthenâti attā nivasī, kārako, vedako, sayaṁvasī ti evaṁ parikappitassa atta-sārassa abhāvena—*ibid.*, 610).

The meaning of Anattā was quite clear to the audience the Buddha addressed yet He sometimes chose to make the meaning

---

1. *Vivekacūḍāmaṇi,* 119.
2. *Ibid.*, 152.
3. *Ibid.*, 269.
4. *Advaitânubhūti,* 29.
5. *Ātmaprakāśikā*, 13.
6. *Ajñānabodhinī,* 158.
7. *Ātmânatmaviveka*, 1.
8. *Ibid.*, 61.
9. *Ibid.*, 118.

clearer by means of similes of which one was absence of control (vasa) that is characteristic of Anatta (Vattati te tasmiṁ rūpe vaso—evaṁ me rūpaṁ hotu, evaṁ me rūpaṁ mā ahosi?—M. I. 230). Buddhaghosha took up the simile. The ultimate Reality described as Ātman is our very own, and so we have perfect control over it, just as, on the contrary, we have none over the khandhas which constitute Anattā. The simile, however, must not be pushed beyond the point that Anattā being foreign to us is beyond our control. Attā is not a thing that we can fashion it in any way we like. The *Paṭisambhidā* (p. 37) says "Anattā asāratthena." Buddhaghosha too defines Anattā as asāra. The ultimate Reality, Ātman is meant here. That is the vastu; all else is avastu.

It looks as though, as a result of avoiding the use of Attā in the correct sense which is clear, the necessity of emphasising the characteristics arose, and the word came to be interpreted and understood more and more in terms of sāra, vasa etc. and, all the time they had at the back of their mind the concept of the immortal jīva. Attā itself never means sāra or vasa.

Mahāyāna too had developed the no-soul idea. Beside sarvam anityam and sarvaṁ duḥkham they have the formula sarvam anātmam (All is "without soul," "lacking a self"). This is significantly different from its Pali equivalent sabbam Anattā (on the analogy of rūpam Anattā). And they coined the term nairātmya to denote absence of soul. The word nirātma, however, occurs frequently in the *Maitrī Upaniṣad*, as pointed out by Mrs. Rhys Davids (*Sakya,* 378). Nairātmya is of two kinds—pudgala nairātmya (no soul in man) and dharma-nairātmya (no soul in things).

Buddhaghosha observes in the *Visuddhimagga* (p. 628) that Anatta is held to be Attā (Anattā pana Attā ti gahīta (?). The Buddha had contrasted Ātman, the Reality with Anātman nāmarūpa, but Buddhaghosha instead, contrasts Attā taking it to mean Jīva conceived as a permanant entity with Anatta which does not share the characteristics of such a soul. The sense is distorted and unclear. Buddhaghosha gave a lead in the interpretation (rather misinterpretation) which was followed by later writers including modern authors. Anattâ ti attanā, jīvena, puggalena rahito—so says the Commentary on the *Kathāvatthu* (J.P.T.S., 1889, p. 33). A modern author translates rūpaṁ anattā as material form is not "a permanent self" as quoted above. A contrast with sassatajīva is not involved here. It is not to be taken as repudiation of sassatavāda.

This change in the shift of the meaning of Attā from the Universal to the particular is a remarkable development of Buddhist thought. As a result the distinction that the Buddha had made between Ātman the sole Reality and Anatta the false, was lost sight of, and attā being taken as immortal individual soul, Buddhist thought eventually tended towards neglect and even denial of a transcending Reality. The study of the development of Buddhist philosophy is no doubt interesting but we are here concerned with what the Buddha had actually taught. The nairātmya idea is not to be found in the utterances of the Buddha which alone are authoritative. We are apt to interpret the teaching of the Buddha in terms of later development of ideas. This is the wrong way of trying to understand Him.

It may be argued that the Buddhists used the word in the sense of "without a soul" even though it is grammatically open to objection. But words convey ideas, and then the ideal too would automatically change from one of preaching of the Absolute that is the Ātman to that of preaching the doctrine whether there is or is not the immortal soul in man and Nature, which is an utterly different proposition. The change of connotation would involve a corresponding change in the quest of life.

The fact that there is no permanent substance in physical states is amply indicated by the words "nijjīva"—lifeless (rather than "soulless"), "nissatta"—unsubstantial (rather than "not a sentient being"), and the use of the word "Anatta" in this sense is wrong. Moreover, the adjective "anicca" conveys the idea that there is no permanence in phenomena. Impermanence connotes lack of substance. The distaste for attā was possibly the reason for the kind of interpretation put upon the word "Anatta" despite the anomalies involved in doing so. We do not know how the distaste grew. It is possible that as Buddhism spread people who firmly believed in a soul were converted and hence emphasis was laid on the point.

It is remarkable that the difference between "not-Self" and "selfless" does not worry the scholars, as pointed out above. The one is naively changed into the other without a feeling of compunction. Reason demands a uniformity of interpretation one way or the other, but here there is only one way. Scholarship is not to be swayed by preconceived ideas or tradition, however ancient.

The fact is that opposition to the doctrine of Ātman is due to a misunderstanding of the implications of the term. The word "Ātman" means the universal Self and not the individual self. There is only one Self common to all, and the different selves arise due to wrong identification of the Self with the non-Self. The individual self is not the real Self. The Buddha's criticism is directed against the wrongly conceived Attā and not against the Ātman in the truest sense. The wrong conception arises when the individual self is regarded as the real Self. The ego is not the Self but passes itself off for the Self. The ego separates us from our real Self. The Buddha's attitude towards a wrong conception of the Ātman is being used against the reality of the Ātman. That wrong views regarding the Ātman were held to represent the real Self, was the Buddha's objection. So long as primary ignorance persists so long the individual selves also exist. There is no ego for the Arahat; for us, however, it is real. Anatta acquires a meaning only with reference to Attā, just as darkness does with reference to light. The negative invariably indicates the positive, the shadow the archetype. If we say—this is not gold, that is not gold, we do not mean that there is no gold. When the Buddha said in respect of the five khandhas "this is not mine, this I am not, this is not my Self," the question automatically arises "what is mine, who am I and what is my Self?" The band of five disciples understood that what is left after the khandhas are completely eliminated is that of which it could be truly said "this is mine, this am I and this is my Self." Surely Anicca, Dukkha and Anatta involve the existence and reality of their opposites. "If there is not the Unborn, how is escape possible from that which is subject to birth."[1] The opposites of Anicca and Dukkha—Nitya and Sukha are mentioned as epithets of the Reality in Sanskrit.[2] In Pali, however, instead of nicca the adjective "dhuva", "accuta" are found as designations of Nirvāṇa. Primal ignorance may make us regard any state as nicca. Compare in this connection the bragging of Baka, a Brahmā god who regarded his impermanent state to be permanent, and his wrong notion was knocked out by the Buddha.[3] A potent reason for avoiding the use of the adjective nicca to denote the Ātman was that the word "nicca" was much associated by the Eternalists with the concept of a permanent individual self, and so the word was naturally avoided to designate the ultimate Reality. It is significant that nibbāna is described at least in one place as nicca (*Paṭisambhidāmagga* I, 238). Nibbāna is, of course, also described as sukha.[4] In regard to Anattā its opposite is also necessarily indicated;

---

1. *Udāna* II. 20; Pāṭaligāmiya Vagga. 3.
2. Cp. the epithets of the universal Self mentioned in the Gītā; unborn (aja), permanent (nitya) and eternal (śaśvata).
3. M. I. Brahmanimantanika S. "idaṁ saccaṃ idaṁ ḍhuvaṁ idaṁ sassataṁ idaṁ kevalaṁ idaṁ acavanadhammaṁ."
4. Nibbānaṁ paramaṁ sukhaṁ.

there is no escape from this. If the meaning of "Anattā" is twisted, what would be the positive state to which the word would refer?—that which is devoid of individual soul would have as its opposite that which has such a soul (as indicated before). Moreover, unless the positive is assumed how can we explain, for instance, the parting advice of the Buddha exhorting us to take refuge in the Self (Attasaraṇa)—this is interpreted as the Buddha's exhortation to be self-reliant. Did the Buddha ask us to take refuge in the individual self which is unreal, illusory and non-existent as it verily is? Of what avail is catching at a straw, taking refuge in a falsity? Mr. Murty, however, thinks that the empirical self is here denoted (*The Philosophy of Radhakrishnan*, p. 574). We cannot have it both ways—deny on the one hand that there is an individual self and on the other make it our refuge. Much of our estimate of Buddhism is vitiated by an inherent contradiction. It would not have been necessary to labour the point which is so obvious but for the fact that many people have no idea of the complexities of "Attā" by which they invariably mean the individual soul in which the soul-theorists of different categories believe. According to the testinony of the sages Ātman is Brahman, the Absolute of Philosophy.

Should the accepted interpretation be justified simply because it makes a distinction between Brahmanism and Buddhism? It looks as if a distinction must be made somehow between the two systems of thought, and so a distinction has been made on the basis of the interpretation of the Anatta doctrine. But the ultimate Truth is one, and the Truth discovered by the Upaniṣadic sages cannot be different from what the Buddha had discovered, and for that matter any sage (not saint) to whatever country he may belong. It is out of the question that the Buddha borrowed from the Brahmins. The same Truth was discovered by the Buddha independently, and the expressions were similar because of common environment. There is a remarkable similarity between the two peaks—the orthodox (non-dual) Vedānta and heterodox Buddhism. Spiritual truths are not different from scientific truths in that they hold good in all countries and for all times. Even other teachers separated in time and space have spoken, though in a different way of the same ultimate Truth. Christ said rather paradoxically "Whosoever shall seek to save his life shall lose it; and whosoever shall lose his life shall preserve it."[1] The ego must be destroyed before the reality of the egoless state can be attained. Research into comparative religion has

1. St. Luke 17.33.

established this fact that there is a transcending Reality which is expressed in different ways in different faiths according to the difference in historical processes. There is no room for proclaiming a new Truth. The formulation of the Truth may be different—that is all. The sages have all gone beyond the range and power of primal ignorance and arrived at the supreme Truth, and therefore their description of Reality agrees in fundamentals, but the ideas in which that Reality is formulated and the language in which those ideas are couched must necessarily differ. On the other hand, those who have not been able to cut the Gordian knot of the Heart (hṛdayagranthi) arrive at different conclusions about the Truth, for they take nāmarūpa to be real, moving as they do, within the orbit of Avijjā. It would be amusing should anybody suggest that the highest Reality is Brahman and not Nibbāna. Brahman is equated with Ātman in the *Upaniṣads*,[1] and in the *Bhagavad Gītā* the two terms Brahman and Nirvāṇa are combined.[2] Things which are equal to the same thing are equal to one another. Therefore, Brahman is not other than Nirvāṇa. The highest Reality is one but sages give different names to it.[3] That does not make the Reality different. Nor is the Reality affected by our interpretation thereof. Imperfect interpretation does not make the Reality less real.[4]

Finally, as regards the bearing of the doctrine of Anatta on Liberation—the Anattalakkhaṇa Sutta which is found repeated again and again in the Canon gives us the secret of Deliverance. The bonds are first described—the assumption that the khandhas constitute our Self, and release from bondage is only possible by de-identifying the Self from the non-Self. When each of the non-Self khandhas is realised as "this is not mine, this I am not, this is not my Self"—n'etaṁ mama, n'eso' ham asmi, na me'so Attā—indifference to it automatically grows; indifference leads to dispassion, and dispassion results in deliverance—nibbindati, nibbidā virajjati, virāgā vimuccati. Thus did the band of five disciples attain Liberation. This is the sequel to the Anatta Lakkhaṇa Sutta. We can here compare the words of Sankaracharya quoted above "to remove bondage the wise man should discriminate between the Self and the non-Self." The non-dual Vedanta diagnoses the cause of bondage in the same way and prescribes the same method of release from it. Truth being the same,

1. "Ayamātmā Brahma.
2. II. 72. (Brahmanirvāṇa).
3. Ekaṁ sat, viprā bahudhā vadanti.
4. Cp. "Truth is one, there is no second" *Suttānipāta*, 848 (Ekaṁ hi saccaṁ, na dutiyam atthi).

the process of realising it must also be the same, at least it is the same in both Buddhism and the non-dual Vedanta. Now if "Anatta" is taken to mean "soulless" what would be the nature of the bonds that bind us and the means to bread them? Bondage, then, would consist in the wrong view that there is a permanent substance in everthing, psychical or physical, and emancipation therefrom would lead to Liberation. Would the knowledge that there is no permanent soul in things and beings lead to indifference, and ultimately to Liberation? But where is the canonical support for such an assumption?

There is no parallel in the history of Philosophy to this confusion based on the misunderstanding of a single word (Anatta) that gave a turn to the teaching of a Religion which was not intended by its founder. The word Anattā has been used in violation of its intention. The Buddha did not deny the reality of the Ātman but pointed out that it was wrongly indentified—what was not Ātman was mistaken for Ātman.

Chapter - 19

Scientific Background of the Buddhist Tantras

B. Bhattacharyya

Usually, it is the habit with uninformed people to decry a thing because it is not understood. The rule applies with equal force to the science and practice of the Tantras. Many scholars have dubbed the Tantras as magic, blackmagic, necromancy, unscientific and psuedo-scientific, and decried the teachings and findings of the Tantras as being worthless and worthy of nothing but unqualified condemnation on this or that ground. It will, therefore, be a shock to many to learn that theTantras are based on solid scientific facts, and that their followers derived and utilized cosmic power which is freely floating around.

The Tāntrics were conversant with the theory of tele-communication like radio and tele-vision, and that they could transmit sound and power through space without elaborate appliances. Dūraśravaṇa (hearing distant sounds), Dūradarśana (seeing distant visions), Dūracikitsa (distant healing) and similar powers were listed as Siddhis (super-normal powers) as a direct outcome of Tāntric Sādhana. In the Tāntric works there is a clear indication that heat and cold could be transmitted through space to the desired object or person, and influence it or him from a distance. The process of Śānti (propitiation) could be performed from a distance, and thereby bring about the cure of a disease.

In the Tantras cosmic colour plays a most important part. Every deity hasan individual colour, every direction has a colour; the Dhyāni Buddhas were made up of one colour or another. The Tāntrics were conversant with the power of cosmic colours and employed them for multifarious purposes. The Tāntrics of the Buddhist faith considered Śūnya as the creator of the universe, limitless, omnipotent and omnipresent, and the repository of infinite wisdom, infinite knowledge, infinite sound and infinite light. The Tāntrics intuitively knew that the world of matter in its ultimate state is nothing but rays and radiations, and this knowledge is reflected in their writings and in their many and varied practices of bewildering intricacy.

The Tāntrics formulated that all letters, words and sentences, with or without meaning, are nothing but Śūnya in essence, that is to say, they are condensations of cosmic power, and therefore, these letters, words and sentences have certain definite vibrations, and these vibrations can be employed for good as well as evil. The deities are the beings of the invisible world just as we are the beings of the visible world. The deities have their definite vibrations because they are nothing but Śūnya in essence, that is to say, the deities are condensations of Śūnya, the ultimate cosmic force. The Mantras for the deities have the same vibrations as their presiding deities; they are able to attract the deities and make them visible to the mind's eye, and when Sādhana reaches its final point they become visible even to the naked eye. The worshipper and the deity become one by the process of complete identification, and the Sādhaka derives all the powers residing in the deity.

The Tāntrics knew the power of the mind which according to them was Śūnya in essence. The mind has one peculiar power, and with the help of this power the human mind could adjust itself to the different vibrations and become one with them. In modern scientific language the mind has the power to adjut itself to the same wave-length as that of the deity or anything, high or low. Low thoughts lower down the wave-length of the mind while higher thoughts raise its level. Even Śūnya can be conceived and realised if the mind is properly attuned to the highest wave-length of the Śūnya or the Absolute Limitless Cosmic Substratum.

Further, the Tāntrics were acquainted with the fact that certain syllables had the same wave-length as those of the five Skandhas (elements), and that the utterance of the syllables gave rise to the same set of vibrations as those of the five Skandhas (elements). The five Skandhas, it may be remarked, are the counterparts of the five *Tanmātras* or 'subtle substances' as formulated in the Sāṁkhya system of philosophy. Behind the Skandhas are the five cosmic colours which by condensation give rise to the five Dhyāni Buddhas and their numerous offspring. The five Dhyāni Buddhas, their cosmic colours and the five Skandhas or cosmic principles represented by them are given in the Table below for ready reference:

Dhyāni Buddhas	*Skandhas*	*Colours*
Vairocana	Rūpa	White
Ratnasambhava	Vedanā	Yellow
Amitābha	Saṁjñā	Red
Amoghasiddhi	Saṁskāra	Green
Akṣobhya	Vijñāna	Blue

The Tāntrics recognised no difference between name and form, and believed rightly that the name is not different from form, and that even a syllable can represent the Skandhas, and all the power the Skandhas possess, is contained in the syllable itself. These syllables are known as the Bījamantras or Seed-syllables, usually consisting of one syllable with an anusvāra. There were syllables for the ultimate cosmic principles such as Earth, Air, Water and Fire. The seed LAṂ, for instance, stands for the Pṛthvī principle, VAṂ for the Ap principle, RAṂ for the Fire principle and YAṂ for the Air principle. This indicates that there is no difference between RAṂ and Fire, and that by constant meditation on the seed RAṂ the Fire principle can be brought under control, manifestly because the wave-length of the two happen to be the same.

In the same way, by patient research they found out the germ syllables and the Mantras of the deities of the Vajrayāna system. The germ syllables were the deities themselves and the Mantras formed the call-signs for the different deities. In other words, the Tāntrics discovered the supreme truth that Bījamantras are endowed with the same vibrations as those of the eities, and by employing the Mantras the corresponding deities can be attracted, visualised and realised. In terms of modern science, the Mantras and the Bījamantras have the same set of vibrations or wvae-length as the deities of the invisible world, and that the human mind was capable of changing and tuning its vibrations to the wve-length of the deity by constant meditation.

The difference between the Bīja and the Mantra is something like this: The Bīja represents the deity in a subtle form while the Mantra is for the gross form. The syllable TĀṂ, for instance, is the Bīja of the popular Vajrayāna deity, Tārā. This Mantra is required in the beginning of meditation, and the mind should concentrate on its Yellow Rays spreading out to the firmament and illumining the invisible worlds and there discover the form of the deity. The longer Mantra of Tārā is: OM TĀRE TUTTĀRE TURE SVĀHĀ which is to be constantly repeated and meditated upon in order to bring the deity nearer to the worshipper by the process of attraction. According to the Buddhist Tāntrics different Mantras have different powers although they may relate to the same deity. The different Mantras have to be utilized for different purposes. Everywhere it was conceded that the Bīja, Mantra and the rest had the same set of vibrations as the deity worshipped, because they recognised no difference between the deity and its various symbols—all having the same measure of vibrations.

The method of propitiation and realisation of the deities or the radiant beings of the invisible world was elaborated in the Sādhana which may be called the WHO'S WHO of these radiant beings. But more interesting and instructive is the story of how the Tāntrics used to transmit power through space to distant objects either for good or for evil. In the Mahākāla Sādhana at the end part of the famous Tāntric work, the *Sādhanamālā*,[1] this story is related in detail. The details of the process of distant influencing became the starting point of the unique and the most practical system of healing by Tele-Therapy or the Cosmic Ray Therapy which seeks to cure patients from a distance without medicine, personal attendance or examination. The process described in the Sādhana, therefore deserves special attention.

In the Mahākāla Sādhana, it is said that in order to influence a person at a distance an effigy of *Kuśa* grass should be made for the person aimed at, and thereon the Mahākāla Mantra should be repeated continuously. Then *Viṣarājikā* seeds and pungent condiments like black pepper, dry ginger and *Pippalī* should be powdered, mixed and prepared into a paste. This paste should be liberally applied to the effigy while repeating the Mantra already cited. Then on each and every limb thorns should be pierced. Thereafter, a fire should be made with *Khadira* wood, and on that fire the effigy should be baked while repeating the Mantra. When this is done, the person aimed at is suddenly overtaken by high temperature and his consciousness is lost.

When, however, it becomes necessary to counteract the effect of the process just described, the Sādhana adds that the effigy should be removed from fire, and milk should be poured on the effigy until fever subsides.

In terms of the present day science, it can be easily understood why Mantras have to be repeated in order to bring the effigy in tune with the vibrations of the victim aimed at. Mantras are repeated

---

1. *Sādhanamālā*, GOS. Vol. II, p. 589.

continuously in order to raise the wave-length of the inanimate effigy of *Kuśa* grass to the level of the person to be influenced by adding word vibrations. And unless the wave-lengths of both the effigy and the person are tuned to the same length, the cosmic forces will not recognise the person, just as a Radio set will not give any programme until it is tuned to the same wave-length as that of the station radiating the programme. When after continuous muttering of the Mantra the vibrations of the effigy and the person are brought to the same level, the Tāntric is able to transmit the fire principle through space by heating and baking the image. As the wave-lengths of the two ends are the same the heat applied to the effigy is immediately transmitted through space to the person at a distance. No wonder the heat of the fire-principle brings about fever and delirium.

To reverse the effect of the earlier process is to bring normalcy in the victim by sending out cold vibrations by the same wireless method. For this purpose the effigy is taken out from fire. By this, heat is first eliminated, and then when milk is poured incessantly on the effigy cold vibrations of milk is transmitted through space to the victim. Milk represents the Water (Ap) principle, and moreover, being white in colour, it is doubly cooling. The healing process takes effect almost immediately and in a short time the victim is well.

Taking the cue from the Mahākāla Sādhana, a new system of healing, called Tele-Therapy is developed which seeks to transmit hot and cold forces or the forces of the five elements (Earth, Air, Water, Ākāśa and Fire) through space to patients at a distance, and make them well without medicine and without examination or external applications. It is not possible to prepare effigies for particular persons and raise their wave-length, because that is a very cumbrous process now in the present century when photography is so well developed. It may be noticed that the photograph has the same set of vibrations as its owner, and therefore, the wave-lengths of both the photograph and its owner are the same. The cosmic forces recognise this identity of wave-length. On the photographs certain jewel vibrations produced from an electric motor are released for several hours a day, and this has yielded remarkable results in a number of acute and chronic diseases. The experience of the last three years in the line has shown great promise, and it is now possible for us to foresee a time when the work of healing will be done with the help of photographs from an office or a laboratory. Whether we like it or not, we are enveloped in cosmic rays, call them either

Mahābhūtas or the planets as it pleases. They are not at a distance, they are right in the midst of our bodies and our sense-organs. This will be shown when a person is examined through a prism byany common inquirer. When the Rays become malefic, illness supervenes, and again when they are altered, that illness disappears. In spite of our researches into the subject of disease and medicine, we have progressed very little and have not been able to find out the true cause of even the principal diseases. Once the cause is known, eradication becomes easy and simple. Let us remember that the diseases are in their ultimate state, nothing but rays and radiations. The so-called *virus* of modern medicine is the Ray Malefic.

The doctrine of the Buddhist Tāntrics that everything in this world has for its substratum the limitless Śūnya, and wherever there is a manifestation of Śūnya, a colour is attached to it. This gives a clue to find out the true colours of all tangible objects through a prism. With the help of a prism true colours of gems have been ascertained, all the VIBGYOR rays have been individualised and their powers have been pretty well fixed. And what is important, all the seven cosmic colours have been produced with the help of gems and an electric motor, and transmitted through space to numerous patients over their photographs with gratifying results. The gems are cosmic colour concentrates, they are Śūnya in essence, and their brilliance shows that they are not only rich in cosmic colours but also can readily discharge their rays when under the influence of an electric motor. The Rays travel with the speed of thought, and they are omniscient, omnipresent and omnipotent like their substratum—the Śūnya. The gems release hot and cold vibrations, e.g. the Green rays discharged by Emeralds send out cold vibrations, and the Red rays released by brilliant Rubies transmit hot vibrations; and they know exactly their mission, and unerringly reach their destination and start their healing work. Their working ways are as mysterious as those of the Creator himself.

It is high time, in spite of what the uninitiated or the ignorant may think or write, to divert our close attention to the Tantras, the repositories of higher scientific knowledge. The Tantras should not only be studied and treated with respect they deserve, but also scientific facts should be gleaned from them, and put into practical use through scientific institutions. Still there is much for modern science to learn from the Tantras. When the knowledge of the scientific aspect of the Tantras becomes the general property of mankind, the scientists will come face to face with the real substratum of the

Universe, the Śūnya or Brahman, as it may be called, and start playing with the Cosmic Rays even as the great creator, endearingly called The Grandfather, does. When that stage is reached, the latest scientific developments are likely to pale into insignificance, because we are as yet ignorant of the cosmic elements, the cosmic rays and the great cosmic powers that are freely floating around. When we come to know what the Tāntrics knew, the difference between Magic, Philosophy and Science will disappear.

It is ignorance that makes a person think that he can do sinful acts in secret without a chance of their being detected by any visible or invisible agency. When true knowledge dawns on mankind a person will think several times before doing any improper action, because he is surrounded and enveloped in the ever-vigilant, omniscient, omnipresent and omnipotent cosmic rays which are watching him by dayand by night, limb by limb, and examining him thought by thought. True knowledge of a scientific nature may still lead mankind to the high principles of Right Living and Right Thinking, as Graciously formulated by Lord Buddha Two Thousand Five Hundred years ago!

Chapter - 20

Saṁsāra or Buddhist Philosophy of Birth and Death

Narada

That birth precedes death, and death, on the other had, precedes birth, is one of the principal tenets of Buddhism. The constant succession of birth and death in connection with each individual life-flux constitutes what is technically known as Saṃsāra (together wandering). Several renderings are given of this enigmatic formula of Buddhist thought. One of the least correct as regards the wording, and the most misleading as regards the meaning, is "Metampsychosis," which in reality implies a transmigration of *something* or, to be more precise, an *immortal soul*. The Vedāntists will perhaps readily agree with this translation, as it only confirms the teachings of Upaniṣads, which say "just as the worm from leaf to leaf, even so goes the Ātman, the self, from existence."

Buddhists, on the contrary, strongly object to such a rendering for, according to Buddhist philosophy, there is no *goer* but a mere *going*, no *doer* but a mere *doing*. Since there is no proper English equivalent that fully conveys the meaning of the Pāli terms, it is preferable in every way to retain the original and so avoid all misconceptions.

What, then, is the absolute beginning of Saṃsāra or, to put it in other words, what is the primal origin of life? This is a question which perplexes many a profound thinker. The expected answer has not yet been obtained, despite the fact that it has received the attention of all thinking men and it is not too much to say that in all probability it never will be.

The Indian Ṛṣis who are venerated for their colossal intellect have expended an enormous amount of labour and energy in order to comprehend this riddle of life. Deluded by the web of illusion, they have deduced all their so-called facts from the unwarranted thesis of an imaginary "self," and have concluded that life has for its origin the mystical Paramātman.

Christianity also professes to give an explanation. Citing the analogy of the clock, it attempts to trace everything to the fiat of an Almighty God. With due deference to the teachings of Christ, suffice it merely to state in the words of Schopenhauer that "the birth of an animal as arising out of nothing, and accordingly, its death as an absolute annihilations, whilst man who has also originated out of nothing has yet an individual existence, is really something against which the healthy mind revolts, and which it must regard as absurd."

Unfettered by any religious belief, freed from all dogmatic assertions, but solely relying on *common sense*, modern science steps in and endeavours to tackle the problem with her usual accurate investigations and ingenuity. In spite of her systematised knowledge she may fairly be compared to a child making its first observations in natural history. Nevertheless we gladly welcome her into our midst for she neither claims to be perfect, nor does she deem it a sacrilege if one has the audacity to contradict her views. To an age, or rather to people who strongly believe in the creation of an omnipotent God, the scientific theories that life has had a beginning in the infinite past and that man is evolved from the ground ape, are indeed very valuable substitutes.

Buddhism interposes and pertinently says "*without beginning and end is Saṃsāra. A beginning of beings, encompassed by nescience,* who, fettered by the thirst for life, pass on to ever new births, verily is not to be perceived." It seems further to address the enthusiastic seekers after truth and say: Young friends, worry not in vain, seeking for a beginning in a beginningless past. It life is an *identity*, it must necessarily have a primal origin. Life, strictly speaking, is a flux or force like electricity or gravitation, and, as such it necessitates a beginningless past. Whether you are descended from an arboreal or a ground ape, created by God or Brahman, birth, death and suffering are inevitable. Seek therefore the cause of his 'faring on' that concerns all humanity, and utilise every ounce of your valuable energy to transmute this life-stream to the unchangeable, unconditioned state, the Nibbāna.

To a materialist who loves to speculate for the mere sake of argument these words will, of course, be of no avail. Well, it makes no great difference to Buddhism. The word of Buddha is intended only for those sorrow-afflicted brethern to whom the Dhamma has become a necessity. "The Dhamma is like some painful cure which no rational person would undergo on its own account but because necessity compels."

Accordingly, in the search after to cause of birth and death Buddhism takes for its starting point the *being as he is*, here and now, and traces back the causes of his conditioned existence. From the Buddhist point of view all men and animals are composed of inter-related mind and matter (Nāma and Rūpa), which constantly change with lightning rapidity, not remaining for even two consecutive moments the same. Though all are identical inasmuch as they possess the two common factors, mind and matter, yet they are all so varied that, leaving animals aside, even amongst mankind no two persons are found to be alike in any respect, each person having his particular traits of character.

One might say that the variation is due to heredity and environment. No doubt they are partly instrumental; but surely they cannot be solely responsible for the subtle distinctions that exist between individuals. Otherwise we fail to understand why twins often physically alike, sharing equal privileges of up-bringing, are often temperamentally, intellectually, and morally totally different. Tracing back the individual, therefore, to the fœtus in the womb to see where lies the cause, we discovered two other common factors the sperm-cell and the ovum-cell. Now a question might arise as to whether these two are the only materials for the production of the fœtus. We must perforce answer the question in the negative. For we cannot comprehend why precisely "he" should spring from the particular sperm and ovem-cell in question and not another, since one as equal claims to the other. Buddhism makes the matter clear by attributing this appropriation of cell-matter to the existence of a *third element*. "By the conjunction of three things, O, Bhikkus," runs a passage in the Mahātaṇhā Sankhaya Suttanta (No. 38) of the Majjhima Nikāya, "does the formation of a germ of life come about. If mother and father come together, but it is not the mother's proper period, and the 'exciting impulse' (gandhabbo) does not present itself, a germ of life is not planted. If mother and father come together, and it is the mother's proper period, and the 'exciting impulse' also presents itself, then a germ of life is there planted." This newly discovered element is, in the words of Abhidhamma, termed Paṭisandhi-viññāṇa (linking-consciousness).

We have now found out the first term of life's progression, but our limited knowledge does not help us to proceed further and determine the cause of this 'exciting impulse.' The Buddha, however, developing a supernormal sense, so a to penetrate into realms beyond the reach of normal sense, comprehended also the root of this third element. He tells that the coming-into-being of the linking consciousness is dependent upon the passing away of another consciousness in a past birth, and that the process of arising and passing away is the result of an all-ruling powerful force known as Kamma. One might call for proofs. It must frankly be admitted that this proof cannot be furnished by an experiment upon the lecture table. Whether we believe in a past existence or not, it forms the only reasonable hypothesis which bridges certain gaps in human knowledge concerning facts of every day life. Our reason tells us that this idea of past birth and Kamma alone can explain the degree of differences that exist between twins, how men like Shakespeare with every limited experience, are able to portray with marvellous exactitude the most diverse type of human character, scenes, and so forth, of which they could have no actual knowledge, why the work of the genius invariably transcends his experience, the existence of infact precocity, the vast diversity in mind and moral, in brain and physique, in conditions, circumstances, and environments observable throughout the world, and so forth.

There is yet a further cause besides Kamma, continues the Buddha. Not knowing the four realities (Saccāni), allured to life by the wholly illusory inclination to sensual pleasures, one does good and evil, which constitute what is known as Kamma-energy that materialises in multifarious phenomena. Unknowningness (Avijjā) is therefore the cause of birth and death; and its transmutation into knowingness or Vijjā is consequently their cessation. The result of this Vibhajja method of analysis is summed up in the Paṭiccasamuppāda. The Paṭṭhāna succinctly expresses the same in the following words. In virtue of unknowningness (Avijjā), Craving (Taṇhā), Activities (Saṅkhāra) Attachment (Upādāna), and Volition (Cetanā), arise Rebirth-Consciousness (Paṭisandhi-viññāṇa), Mind and Matter (Nāma, Rūpa), Six Senses, (Saḷāyatana), Contact (Phassa), and Sensation (Vedanā).

The first set of five causes produces the second set of effects, which, in their turn, play the part of cause to bring about the former five. Thus the process of cause and effect continues *ad infinitum*. The beginning of the process cannot be determined, nor the end either *if the life flux is encompassed by nescience*. But when this nescience. But when this nescience is turned into knowledge, and the life-flux diverted into Nibbāna-Dhātu, so to say, then the end of process or Saṃsāra comes about.

Briefly expounding the cause of Saṃsāra set forth in these enigmatic formulas of thought, and dealing with the not less interesting problem of life's last episode, we find Buddhism assigning death to one of the following four causes:—

(1) The exhaustion of the force of Reproduction (Janaka-Kamma) that gives rise to the birth in question (Kammakkhaya). The Buddhist belief is that, as a rule, the thought, volition, or desire, which is extremely strong during life-time, becomes predominant at the point of death and conditions the subsequent birth. In this last thought-moment is present a special potential force which may be either weak or strong. When the potential energy of this Reproductive Kamma is exhausted, the organic activities of the material form in which is corporealised the life-force, cease even before the approach of old age.

(2) The expiration of the life term (Āyukkhaya). What are commonly understood to be natural deaths due to old age, may be called under this category. There are various planes of existence according to Buddhism and to each plane is assigned a definite age limit. Irrespective of the Kamma force that has yet to run one must however succumb to death when the maximum age limit is reached. It may also be said, if the force is extremely powerful the Kamma energy rematerialises itself in the same plane or even in some higher realm as in the case of Devas.

(3) The combination of both Kamma and Āyu (Ubhayakkhaya).

(4) The action of a stronger arresting Kamma (Ubhayakkhaya) that suddenly cuts off the Reproductive Kamma before the expiry of the life term. A more powerful opposing force can check the flying arrow and bring it down to the ground. Just in the same way a very powerful Kammic force is capable of nullifying the potential energy of the last thought-moment and destroy the psychic life of the being. The death of Devadatta, the Buddha's cousin was due to an Upacchedaka-Kamma. The premature death of the Crown Prince of Russia may also be instanced as an example of this class.

The first three types of death are collectively called Kāla-maraṇa (timely death), and the last is known as akāla-maraṇa (untimely death).

Explaining the cause of death in the foreging manner, Buddhism tells us that there are also four modes of birth, viz:—Egg-born creatures (aṇḍaja), womb-born creatures (jalābuja), moisture-born-creatures (saṃsedaja), and creatures having a spontaneous birth (opapātika). This broad classification embraces the entire range of beings that possess life.

Birds and reptiles that are born of eggs belong to the first division.

The womb-born creatures comprise all human beings, some Devas inhabiting the earth, and those animals that take their conception in the mother's womb.

Those that take moisture as material for their growth, such as mosquitoes, are grouped in the third class.

Creatures having a spontaneous birth are general invisible to the naked eye. They are said to be born with a form as if of fifteen or sixteen years of age appearing suddenly, independently of parent. Since they do no pass through the embryonic period which cause the total oblivion of the memories of the past, they are capable of recollecting their past births. 'Passing thence he was born as a deva and glanced into the past to see what good act conditioned him to be born thus,' are passages which often recur in the Suttantas. Brahmans, Devas of heavenly realms, Petas, and the miserable once who are subjected to torments and suffering in the wicked states (Nirayas) belong to this last division.

It must be mentioned here, before, we come to deal with the actual process of re-birth, that Darwin's theory of evolution finds no place in Buddhism. Buddhists do not believe in a succession of physical forms. The new physical vehicle is not the successor of the past, through it must be admitted that the coming-into-being of the present is conditioned by the passing away of the past. The multifarious forms are merely the manifestation of Kamma-force. "Unseen it passes whithersoever the conditions appropriate to its visible manifestation are present here showing itself as a tiny grant or worm, there making its presence known in the dazzling magnificence of a Deva or an Archangel's existence. When one mode of its manifestation ceases it merely passes on, and where suitable circumstances offer, reveals itself afresh in another mode or form."

It is common to say after witnessing an outbreak of passion or sensuality in a person whom we deemed characterised by a high moral standard, "how could he have committed such an act, or followed such a course of conduct? It was not the least like him. It was not the least like what he appeared to others, and probably to himself." What did it denote? It denoted, Buddhists say, a part at any rate of what he really was, a hidden but true aspect of his actual self, or, in other words, his kammic tendencies.

Dormant but undestroyed and with an ever-present possibility or rising again there lie in us all according to Buddhism five natures viz., Divine (Dibba), human (Mānusika), brutal (Tiracchina) ghostly (Peta) and hellish (Nerayika). These natures, however civilised we may be, may rise in disconcerting strength at unexpected moments so long as we are worldlings (Puthujjana). We live for one thought-moment just as the wheel rests on the ground at one point, and are always in the present. The present is constantly slipping into the irrevocable past. Now we sow the seed of the future. Now, even now, we are creating the hells that we shall be hurled into. Now, even now, we are building the heavens that comfortably accommodate us. What we shall become is determined by this present thought-moment. In just the same way according to Buddhist philosophy the impending birth is determined by the immediately preceding thought, which is generally the thought volition, or desire that was extremely strong during our life-time. Therein, therefore, lies the possibility for the Kamma force that manifested in the forms of a human being to remanifest itself in the shape of a brute, ghost, deva or a human being, or, in other words, for a Kammic descent in one bound in the so-called evolutionary scale of forms.

As there is possibility for a Kammic descent so there is also the possibility for the contrary—a Kammic ascent. When the animal is to die, for instance, it will experience a moral consciousness that will ripen into a human birth. This last thought-moment does not wholly depend on any action or thought of the animal, for generally it is dull and incapable of morality. It depends on some ancient good deed it has done in the round of existence, and, which for a long time has been prevented form producing its result. In its last moment the animal therefore cherishes idea, desires or images which will cause a human birth.

Poussin, a French writer, illustrates this fact well by the law of heredity. A man may be like his grandfather but not like his father. The germs of a disease have been introduced into the organism of an ancestor; for some generation they remain dormant; they suddenly manifest themselves in actual disease. So intricate is the living complex, so mysterious the law of heredity, a Westerner says. So intricate is the law of Kamma, so mysterious is the effect of Kamma, Buddhists would say.

And now, to come to the most interesting and extremely subtle point of our subject;—

Suppose a person is about to die. From the seventeenth thought-moment reckoned backward from the point of death no renewed physical functioning recures. Material qualities born of Kamma (Kammaja Rūpa) arise no more, but those to which came into being before the static phase of that thought-moment persists till the time of the dying thought and then case.

This critical stage may be compared to the flickering of a lamp just before it is extinguished.

To this dying man is presented Kamma, Kamma-nimitta, or Gati-nimitta. By Kamma here is meant some action of his whether good or bad. It may be a weighty action (garuda Kamma) such as Samādhi (established one-pointedness of the mind) or Parricide, and so forth. These are so powerful that they totally eclipse all others and appear very vividly before the mind's eye. If experience has afforded nothing weighty, he may take for his object of thought a Kamma immediately before death (Āsanna Kamma). It would not be far wrong to say that most of the soldiers who die fighting would be having a death-proximate Kamma, such as the killing of their fellowmen. Consequently their re-birth can in no way be desirable. In the absence of an Āsanna Kamma a habitual meritorious or Jemeritorious act (Āciṇṇa Kamma) is presented, such as stealing in the case of a robber, or the curing of the sick in the case of a physician. Falling all these, some casual act, that is one of the cumulative reserves of the endless past (Kaṭattā Kamma), becomes the object of thought.

By Kamma-nimitta is meant any sight, sound, smell, taste, touch or idea which was obtained at the time of the commission of the Kamma, such as knives in the case of a butcher, patients in the case of a physician, an object of worship in the case of a devotee, etc.

Gati Nimitta is some sign of the place where he is to take birth, a thing which invariably happens to dying individuals. When these indications of the future birth occur, and if they are bad, they can be turned into good. This is done by influencing the thoughts of the dying man, so that his good thoughts may now act as the proximate Kamma, and counter act the influence of the re-productive which is about to effect in the next re-birth.

Taking for the object one of the above, a thought-process (Citta-vīdhi) then runs its course even if the death be an instantaneous one. It is said that the fly which is being crushed by a hammer on the anvil also experiences such a process of thought before it actually dies. Abhidhamma enumerates twenty types of re-birth, processes, but as space does not permit of their description here, let us imagine for the sake of convenience that the dying person is to be reborn in the human kingdom and that the object is some good Kamma. The process of decease-consciousness (cuti-cittā-vīthi) is as follows.

His Bhavaṅga consciousness is interrupted, it vibrates for two thought-moments and passes away. After which the mind-door consciousness (Manodvārā-vijñana) rises and passes away. Then comes the psychologically important state—Javana process, which here runs only for five thought-moments by reason of its weakness instead of normally seven. As such it lack all reproductive power, its main function being the mere regulation of the new existence. The object in the present case being desirable, the consciousness here experiences is probably a moral one—automatic or volitional, accompanied by pleasure, and connected with knowledge or not, as the case may be. The Tadālambana consciousness which has for its function a registering or identifying for two moments of the object so perceived may or may not fellow. After this occurs the death-consciousness (Cuti-citta) the last thought-moment to be experienced in present life. There is a misconception among some that the subsequent birth is conditioned by this thought. What actually conditions re-birth, let it be said, is not this decease-thought, which in itself has no special function to perform, but that which is experienced during Javana process.

With the ceasing of the consciousness of decease, death actually occurs. Then no more material qualities born of mind and food (Cittaja and Āhāraja Rūpa) are produced. Only a series of material qualities born of heat (Utuja) goes till the corpse is reduced to dust.

By death is here meant, according to Abhidamma, the ceasing of physic life of one's individual existence or, to express it in the words of a western philosopher, the temporal end of a temporal phenomenon. It is not the complete annihilation of the so-called being, for, although the organic life has ceased, the force which hitherto actuated it is no destroyed. As the Kammic force remains entirely disturbed by the distintegration of the fleeting body, the passing away of the present consciousness only conditions a fresh one in another birth. In the present case the thought experienced whilst dying being a moral one, the re-birth-resultant consciousness takes for its material an appropriate sperm and ovum-cell of human parents. Simultaneous with its rising spring up the body-decad, sex-decad, and base-decad the seat of consciousness-(Kāya-Bhāva-Vatthu-Dasaka). The re-birth consciousness then lapses into the sub-conscious state (Bhavaṅga).

"The new being which is the present manifestation of the stream of Kamma-energy is not the same as has not identify with the previous one in its line; the aggregations that make up its composition being different from, and having no identify with, those that make up the being of its predecessor. And yet it is not an entirely different being, since it is the same stream of Kamma-energy, though modified per chance. Just by having shown itself in that last manifestation, which now is making its presence known in these perceptible world as the new being (Na ca so na ca añño)."

The transition of the flux is also instantaneous and leaves no room whatever for any intervening stage (antara bhava). The continuity of the flux at death is unbroken in point of time. The time duration is equal to the time occupied by one thought-moment i.e. less than the billionth part of the time occupied by a flash of lightning. The only difference between the passing of one thought-moment to another, so to say, or the dying thought-moment to the rebirth consciousness, is that in the latter case a marked perceptible death is visible.

One might say here that a subject cannot exist without an object. What then is the object of this sub-conscious state? The reply is: self-same object which was presented to the mind's eye immediately before death.

One might further ask:—Are sperm and ovum-cells always ready waiting to take up this re-birth-thought? As Doctor Dahlke says in his "Buddhism and Science," this taking hold is not something that has law, that runs its appointed course according to definite laws, but it is law itself, A point on the ground is always ready to receive the falling stone.

Thus does this process of birth and death ever recur as long as this inexorable law of Kamma prevails.

Chapter - 21

Buddhist Controversy over the Five Propositions

Et. Lamotte

At an ancient time to which we refer, five propositions derogatory to the dignity of Arhats were discussed in the Buddhist Communities of Ceylon as well as of the Indian continent.[1] They are explained both in the Abhidharma of Sarvāstivādins (*Jñānaprasthāna* of the IIIrd century after the Nirv., T. 1543, k. 10, p. 819 b; T. 1544, k. 7, p. 956b)[2] and the Ceylonese Abhidhamma (*Kathāvatthu*, II. 1-5, pp. 163-203). They were taken up later again and discussed in the *Vibhāṣā* (T. 1545, k. 99, p. 510 c), *Kośa* (I. p. 2), the glosses of Paramārtha and the Treatise of Ki-tsang on the sects.[3] In these are found the enunciation of those propositions and the references furnished by the authors and in the ancient sources to the date of their invention and the name of their inventor. On the whole the references are not concordant.

The Five Propositions: In the sources enumerated above, the five propositions (*Pañcavastu*) are formulated in the following manner:

(a) The Arhat can be seduced by others and may have seminal losses while asleep.

(b) Though they are freed from sullied ignorance (*kliṣṭa-avidyā*) they remain meanwhile subject to unsullied ignorance (*akliṣṭa ajñāna*), the residue of their old impurities.

---

1. Les texts pāli sout cités d'après les éditions de la *Pāli Text Society* de Londres; les textes chinois d'après l'édition du *Taisho Issaikyo* de J. Takakusu et K. Watanabe (T).

2. Sur ce texte, voir Ś. Śāstri, *Jñānaprasthānaśāstra retranslated into Sanskrit*, vol. I. Santiniketan, 1955.

3. P. Demiéville. *L'origine des Sectes bouddhiques d'apre's Paramārtha*, Mélanges Chinois et Bouddhiques, I, 1932, pp. 15-64. On trouve dans cet ouvrage la traduction du Traité de Ki-tsang et des fragments du commentaire de Paramārtha au Traité de Vasumitra.

(c) Though free from doubt with regard to the three doors of deliverance (*vimokṣamukha*) they remain subject to doubt with regard to the external things, and even the four holy truths.

(d) They can be taught by others and owe them their salvation.

(e) The exclamation: "Oh sorrow" may be regarded as a means destined to initiate the appearance of the Way.

These propositions aim at nothing less than dethronement of the Arhat from the enviable position enjoyed by them from the very beginning. These appear to be the characteristics of the commoners (*pṛthagjana*) instead of the perfects (*ārya=arhat*), of laxity in place of austerity, nay, in fact, the laymen sought equality with the religieux in spiritual attainments. The heresy, if there be any, endured for a long time and served within the community as a mischievous leaven: it is concerning this that the Buddhist schools were set against one another and became divided among themselves.

When did the heresy appear and who was its inventor? Here are the answers given in the sources:

1. Vasumitra: In 116 PN during the reign of Aśoka, among the Nāgas and their partisans.

2. Vibhāṣā and Mahāyānist authors supporters of the Vibhāṣā: During the reign of Aśoka as a result of the activities of Mahādeva.

3. Saṃmitīya tradition: In 137 PN, among the Sthaviras Nāga and Sāramati, and the Bahuśrutas.

4. Bhavya: In 160 PN, during the reign of Aśoka.

VASUMITRA: Vasumitra, a Sarvāstivādin teacher, who lived 400 years after Parinirvāṇa and who was posterior by a century to Kātyāyanīputra, author of the Jñānaprasthāna, wrote a book on the Buddhist sects entitled Samayabhedoparacanacakra.[1] The book was translated into Chinese by Kumārajīva between 385 and 431 (f. 2032), by Paramārtha between 557 and 569 (T. 2033) and by Hiuan-tsang in 662 (T. 2031); it is commented in Chinese by K'ouei-ki in 662 (TKS.A. LXXXIII, 3) and translated into Tibetan in the IXth century by Dharmākara (Tanjur, Mdo. XC, 11).

---

1. Sur Vasumitra voir J. Masuda, *Origin and doctrines of early Indian Buddhist Schools*, Asia Major, II, 1925, pp. 1-78; E. Teramoto et T. Hiramatsu, *Samayabhedoparacanacakra...*, Kyoto, 1935; A. Bareau. *Trois traités sur les sectes bouddhiques attribués à Vasumitra, Bhavya et Vinitadeva*, Journal Asiatique, 1954, pp. 229-266.

The book opens with a reference to the five propositions (T. 2032, p. 18 a 9-14; T. 2033, p. 20 a 15-25; T. 2031, p. 15 a 15-23): "One hundred and sixteen years after Parinirvāṇa of Buddha, there was a town called Pāṭaliputra. Then king Aśoka reigned over Jambudvīpa, ruling over the universe. At that time the Great Community (*mahāsaṃgha*) was divided into schools and made variations in the law. There were then the bhikṣus: (1) the first called *Neng,* Nāga (variant: *Ta-Kouo*. Mahārāṣṭra; *Long-kia,* Nāga); (2) the second called *Yin Yuan,* Pratyaya (variant: *Wai-pien,* Prācya; *Pien-pi,* Pratyantika); (3) the third called *To-wen*, Bahuśruta; (4) the fourth called *Ta-to*, Sthavira. They discussed the five propositions (*pañcavastu*) instituted by the heretics. It is in this way that for the first time after Buddha, two schools came into being, one called Mahāsāṃghika and the other Sthavira."

Among the translators, Hiuan-tsang alone precisely states that the originator of the Five Propositions was Mahādeva, the information being taken from the Vibhāṣā. According to Vasumitra and his first translators, names of the heretics were yet unknown. The comparison of the versions clearly reveals that the Pañcavastu was criticised by the Sthaviras but adopted by these Saṅghas of the Nāgas, of the Prācyas or Pratyantikas, lastly of the Bahuśrutas. We may ignore entirely the first two Saṅghas. According to the comments of K'ouei-ki (l.c), the Nāgas whose name implies an irresistible power and an obdurate obstinacy, were the chief organisers of the dispute and of the schism that followed; the Prayantikas sided with the heretics, and without being the originators of the disputes not possessing the irresistible power, followed and supported the heresy; lastly the Bahuśrutas comprised the commoners (*pṛthagjana*) still occupied with study (*śaikṣa*), but observing the prohibitions and acquiring vast knowledge.

Personally in the first two names we notice ethnical: heresy originated with the Nāgas whose primitive habitat was, according to the tradition of the Purāṇas, the region of Narmadā, a tributary of Mahārāṣṭra to which the version of Paramārtha refers; thence it was extended to the neighbouring regions designated by Vasumitra under the vague denomination of "Frontier Regions" (Pratyantika).

As far as the riverine residents of the Gangetic basin and of Yamunā are concerned, the Mārāṭhā country was situated in Southern India. Now, according to the Aśokāvadāna (T. 2042 k. 5, p. 120 c

11-121 b 1; T. 2043, k. 9, p. 162 a 1-162 c 8)[1], the Sarvāstivādin community of Mathurā under the leadership of the famous patriarch Upagupta at the time of Aśoka, was put in a flutter by the visit of a monk who hailed from Southern India, but no notice is taken of his name. Before his admission into the religion, this monk committed fornication with a woman of another family. He killed his mother for having reproached him for his conduct. He then sought the hand of his beloved. Being repulsed by her he retired from the worldly life, learnt by heart the text of the Tripiṭaka and gathered around him a number of disciples. He then betook himself to Mathurā to discuss with Upagupta, but the latter being aware of what crime he had been guilty, refused to have a discussion with him and so the monk returned to his native country taking with him the band of his disciples.

It would be tempting to find in that religious person a champion of heresy of the Five Propositions which the holy patriarch Upagupta, chief of a school of Arhats, could only condemn. But the religious man had already exercised an ominous influence over those disciples of Upagupta, who remained still in the stage of commoners (*pṛthagjana*). They remonstrated with their master for his impoliteness to a foreigner and Upagupta, in order to appease those critics, was compelled to appeal to his master Śāṇavāsa.

This anecdote referred to in the Aśokāvadāna bears remarkable resemblance to the version of the Vibhāṣā.

THE VIBHASA: This great book on the Abhidharma of the Sarvāstivādin compiled in the 2nd century of our era by the Kashmirian Arhats, devotes quite a chapter (T. 1545, k. 99, p. 510 c. 23-512 a 19) to the heresy of the Five Propositions. It attributes the invention to a certain Mahādeva about whom it narrates a long story though less edifying and tries to paint his character in a black manner.

Mahādeva was the son of a merchant of Mathurā. His father went abroad, leaving his son at home. At the age of twenty, the son became fine in appearance; and his mother fell in love with him and had secretly intercourse with him. During more than six years, the son did not know that his mistress was his own mother, then though he came to know of it, he did not give up his passion. The father

1. Cf. J. Przyluski, *La légende de l'empereur Aśoka,* Paris, 1923, pp. 366-369.

came back from abroad, having acquired great wealth; little before his arrival, the mother being afraid of his getting scent of this affair persuaded her son to administer poison to him. Mahādeva administered the poison and killed his father; then he secured his wealth and continued to live with his mother. But in the long run, when he was found out, he felt ashamed and ran away and concealed himself with his mother in Pāṭaliputra. He met there the Arhat monks whom he had previously revered in his own country, and he murdered them also lest they might betray him. Then he killed his own mother fining that she played false with him. Having thus committed three *ānantarya*-sins, he realised the evils and felt deep remorse; and in order to wash out those sins he gave up his family life. He then entered into the monastery of the Kukkuṭārāma where he heard a monk recite a stanza on the redemption of sinners by good conduct; this monk ordained him by giving him *pravrajyā*.

Mahādeva listened to and studied the Tripiṭaka and collected several followers. The king of Pāṭaliputra (whose name is not given) when got to know of this, invited him to his palace and bestowed on him his offerings. Returned to the monastery, Mahādeva formulated by turn the five heretical propositions explained above. On account of the controversies which the heresies raised, the king sought advice of Mahādeva to settle the dispute. The latter told him that, according to the Vinaya, it was the majority that decided the controversies. The king then put two parties in two sides, and as the party of Mahādeva was greater in number, he decided in his favour and condemned his adversaries. It is thus that the religious people of the Kukkuṭārāma were divided into two schools: the school of the Sthaviras and the school of the Mahāsāṃghikas.

The Sthaviras however wanted then to quit the monastery. Being apprised of their intention, the king ordered to put the Sthaviras on a rotten boat and to throw them into the river Ganges, and then it would be known who was an Arhat and who was a commoner. At the critical moment five hundred Arhats exercising their magical powers rose in the air and went to Kasmir where they scattered themselves up hills and down dales. Having received the news the king sent to them a messenger to bring them back to his capital, but they declined his invitation. The king then made a gift to the church of the whole kingdom of Kasmir and built there five hundred monasteries for the residence of the saints; these monasteries received the names of the various forms taken by the saints when escaping from Pāṭaliputra, for example: Garden of Pigeon (*Kapotārāma*) etc., and the Vibhāṣā adds "It is reported that these monasteries are still flourishing." The king of Pāṭaliputra then conferred his favours upon Mahādeva and his disciples who lived near him. Mahādeva passes away after being held in high estimation by the people but, when they wanted to burn his dead body in the cremation ground, the fire could not be ignited and it was necessary to use as fuel the excrements of dogs; his body was then burnt, but suddenly a violent wind arose and dispersed the ashes of the heretic.

Now according to Vasumitra, the enunciator of the Five Propositions, remained anonymous. The Vibhāṣā, a century later, finds him a name and attributes to him quite a history. It treats him definitely as an adversary, laying against him the charge of all the unatonable crimes and invents for him an unhappy end. It should be noted that the Mahāvibhāṣā only (T. 1545) takes notice of Mahādeva and that it is not similar to that found in the Vibhāṣā of Buddhavarman (T. 1546).

But once introduced the legend died hard. Adopted with enthusiasm by the Sarvāstivādin, it received valid recognition from the Mahāyānist teachers. But as these latter did not lose their sympathy for the Mahāsāmghikas whom they regarded as their distant precursors, they endeavoured, otherwise to clear up the memory, at least to attenuate the wrongs committed by Mahādeva, the initiator of the Mahāsāṃghika schism.

Mahayanist Authors and Supporters of the Vibhasa:

1. In the VIth century, Paramārtha (557-569) in his criticism of Vasumitra (summed up in T. 2300), and his pupil Ki-Tsang (549-623) in his Treatise on the sects (T. 1852) reproduced the account of the Vibhāṣā after introducing therein substantial modifications:[1] Upto 116 PN there did not appear heterodox opinions within the Saṅgha. After the 116th year appeared Mahādeva, of the Kauśika family, son of a merchant of Mathurā. Having committed three *ānantarya*-sins, he gave up his worldly life and went to Pāṭaliputra by confering ordination upon himself. He received entrance into the palace of Aśoka where he had secret intercourse with the queen. He entered again into the monastery. He took up the Mahāyāna sūtras and incorporated them into the Tripiṭaka. He fabricated, on his own

1. P. Demiéville, *L'origine...*, pp. 33-40.

authority, many sūtras wherein was formulated the quintuple heresy and summing them up in a stanza, he recited it after the recitation of the śīlas in the Uposatha ceremony. Many controversies having arisen in the monastery, King Aśoka on his own authority, took recourse to voting to settle the dispute. The partisans of Mahādeva were then greater in number. The Arhats, who were in minority, frightened the community by exhibition of some magical powers. The queen exercised her influence and had the Arhats thrown into the Ganges in boats of broken staves. The Arhats took flight and went away to Kasmir, some transforming themselves into fishing-float pigeons, others into birds. After arriving at the destination they took again their ordinary forms. Meanwhile the queen realising her error repented and was converted. After the death of Mahadeva, Aśoka looked for the Arhats of Kasmir and invited them to return to Pāṭ aliputra. As Mahādeva had introduced the Apocrypha into the Tripiṭ aka, the Arhats gathered together in Council (the third since the beginning) and recited once more the canon of the scriptures. It was at that time that the divergences of opinion among them took place ending in the formation of two separate schools; that of the Mahāsāṃghikas and that of the Sthaviras.

It will be noticed that Paramārtha quickly passes over the sins of Mahādeva, seeks to acquit Aśoka of finding fault with the queen, attributes to the heretic a scriptural activity which the Vibhāṣā did not mention at all, and poses a third Buddhist council with a new compilation of the Tripiṭaka; after which only the schism was ultimately placed.

2. In the VIIth century, the master of the Law, Hiuan-tsang, sums up once more the story of the Vibhāṣā, but with more faithfulness than that of Paramārtha. The passage is found in the Si-Yu-Ki (T. 2087, k 3, p. 886 b. 11-22)[1]:

A hundred years after Parinirvāṇa, Aśoka king of Magadha extended his power over the whole world; he revered the Triratna and loved all beings. There were in his capital among the religious Buddhists, 500 Arhats and 500 commoners (*pṛthagjana*) whom the king patronised impartially.

The religious commoners included in their ranks a certain Mahādeva "a man of great knowledge and of great talent, keen

1. Cf. T. Watters, *On Yuan Chwang's Travels,* London, 1904, I, p. 26f.

investigator of the Nāmarūpa" (sic) who put in treatise his personal views and his heretical observations. The controversy having burst forth, Aśoka took the side of Mahādeva and the commoners, and tried to drown the Arhats in the Ganges. But the latter fled away to Kasmir where they established themselves up hills and down dales. The king at once became repentant for their departure and himself set out to invite them to return to his capital. On their refusal to return, the king built for them 500 saṃghārāmas and made a gift of Kasmir to the Church.

Hiuan-tsang agreeing with the Vibhāṣā, affirmed that the persecuted Arhats remained in Kasmir and refused to return to Pāṭ aliputra. In these conditions there could be no question of the session of the third Buddhist Council, which, according to Paramārtha, had taken place at Pāṭaliputra after the return of Arhats. However, in another passage, where describing his visit to the Kukkuṭārāma of Pāṭaliputra, Hiuan-tsang (T. 2087, k. 8, p. 912 b)[1] states that King Aśoka after his conversion to Buddhism convoked in his monastery a saṅgha of thousand members "comprising of two communities: one of the saints (*ārya*), the other of the commoners (*pṛthagjana*)." In it there is a reference to the Sthaviras and the Mahāsāṃghikas but nothing is said that they held a council and proceeded with a fresh recitation of the Tripiṭaka.

Though accusing his Mahādeva of heresy, Hiuan-tsang does not make at all any mention of the Five Propositions to which people refer generally. He praises his knowledge and his talent and described him as a sublte investigator of the "Nāma-Rūpa" otherwise known as the five Skandhas. But the question of the Nāma-Rūpa preoccupied more the Sarvāstivādins than the Mahāsāṃghikas. It may be asked whether in the opinion of the Chinese master, Mahādeva was not a Sarvāstivādin teacher; but, if so, it would be contrary to the whole tradition, according to which the heretic was the initiator of the Mahāsāṃghika schism.

It seems that the great Hiuan-tsang did not try to harmonise the informations which he collected carefully from his readings, notably from the Vibhāṣā, and the many oral traditins gathered by him locally to which he refers "in bulk." His account about the settlement in Kasmir of five hundred Arhats thrown by Aśoka into the Ganges followed immediately the story of the covnersion of the

1. *Id.*, II, p. 89.

Kasmir in the year 50 PN. by Madhyāntika and his five hundred Arhats (T. 2087, k. 3 p. 886 a 19-886b 11). Obviously it referred to an identical event, but divided into two for some chronological reasons.

3. K'ouei-ki (632-682), disciple of Hiuan-tsang, in his criticism on the Yogācāryabhūmī of Asaṅga (T. 1829, k. 1 p. 1 b) tries to rehabilitate Mahādeva by presenting him as a victim of calumny: "High was his reputation, great his virtue; though young he had realised the Fruit; he was respected by kings and nobles and venerated by monks. And that is the reason for which were imputed to him the three *ānantarya*-sins to which were added the Five Propositions...". It is not the only text favourable to Mahādeva. There was already an earlier commentary on the Ekottara, half-Mahāsāṃghika half-Mahāyānist, the Fen-pie-kong-to-louen, translated into Chinese between 25 and 220 A.D. which spoke of a saintly king Mahādeva endowed with four *brahmavihāra* and qualified him as *Ta-che*, or great Bodhisattva (T. 1507, k. 1, p. 32 c 8-10).

Mahadeva II: In order to complete the record it should be noted that besides Mahādeva I, the initiator of the Five Propositions and instigator of the schism, the sources point out the existence of a second Mahādeva, a Mahāsāṃghika teacher who lived 200 years PN, continued to teach the Five Propositions and provoked new secessions inside the Mahāsāṃghika sect. This Mahādeva II[1] is well known to Vasumitra who it is seen did not make any mention on Mahādeva. I. Here are some references:

1. *Vasumitra, tr. Kumārajīva* (T. 2032 p. 18 a 17-20) "Then in two hundred years Mahādeva a heretic (*tīrthika*) gave up his worldly life and resided in the Caityaśaila. In the Mahāsāṃghika sect developed anew three sub-sects: Caityika, Aparaśaila and Uttaraśaila."

2. *Vasumitra, tr. Paramārtha* (T. 2033, p. 20 b 2-4): "When two hundred years had elapsed, there was a heretic called Mahādeva who eschewed the worldly life and joined the Mahāsāṃghika school; he resided alone in Mount Śaila and taught to the Mahāsāṃghikas the Five Propositions. Thence there were two new secessions: school of Caityaśaila and school of Uttaraśaila (and according to the Tibetan version, school of Aparaśaila)."

---

1. Sur l'existence de deux Mahādeva ou d'un Mahādeva rédoublé, voir déja N. Dutt, *Early Monastic Buddhism*, Calcutta, 1945, II, p. 120; P. Demiéville, *A propos du Concile de Vaiśālī*, T'oung Pao, XL, p. 268.

3. *Vasumitra, tr. Hiuan-tsang* (T. 2031, p. 15 b 1-4): "When two hundred years had elapsed there was a heretic who left the worldly life, gave up falsehood and reverted to the correct mode; he was called also Mahādeva. Being recluse of the Mahāsāṃghika sect he received full ordination; he was erudite (*bahuśruta*) and energetic (*vīryavān*); he resided in the Caityaśaila. To the community of this sect, he explained again the Five Propositions which provoked discussions and sub-divisions into three sects: Caityaśaila, Aparaśaila and Uttaraśaila.

4. *Śāriputraparipṛcchā*, tr. by an anonymous writer between 317 and 420 A.D. (T. 1465 p. 900 c 6-12) "In the Mahāsāṃghika school, two hundred years after my Nirvāṇa, there will appear as a result of disputes the schools; Vyavahāra, Lokottara, Kukkulika, Bahu-śrutaka, Prajñaptivāda. Two hundred years after the discussions, will be added to those Five schools, the school of Mahādeva, that of Caityika and that of Uttaraśaila."

5. *Paramārtha and Ki-tsang*: When two hundred years had completed, an upāsaka-king of Magadha (according to K'ouei-ki, king *Hao yun* "Loving the clouds") propagated widely the Law of Buddha, and in order to take advantage of his bounties, all the heretics took to religious life. Mahādeva who was ordained by himself took upon himself their headship, received new disciples and ordained them in his own saṅgha. The king made a selection among those monks who were "parasites" (*steyasṃvāsika*) and authorised only one party among them, the three hundred more intelligent ones, to live in Magadha. Mahādeva being no more tolerated by them left the place and established himself separately in the mountain with his partisans. Then among those mountain-dwellers themselves, arose certain differences of opinions and thus were formed the two schools called Caityaśaila and Uttaraśaila.

Should one see in this Mahādeva II localised by all the sources in the mountainous regions of Andhra an arbitrary division into two Mahadevas? or should one reject the historicity of the two Mahādevas and see only in them an expedient intended to show the progress of a heresy originating in Southern India among the Nāgas of Mahārāṣ ṭra, and spreading from Saṃgha to Saṃgha, ending ultimately in Mahāsāṃghika schism, and after many advancements it finally triumphed over some churches, notably the Caityika and Śailas of Andhra? We leave to the reader the responsibility of answering these questions.

MAHADEVA IN THE PALI SOURCES: The Ceylonese school was firmly pronounced against the Five Propositions which it exposed and refuted in the Kathāvatthu II, 1-5 (p. 163-203), but did not furnish any reference to their author. The commentary restrained itself by stating precisely that the heretical propositions were taught by the Pubbaseliyas, Aparaseliyas and others.

Among the numerous Mahādevas known to the Pāli tradition, Professor Malalasekera has pointed out no less than nine[1], none of whom makes a good heretic figure. Two among them were contemporaries of Aśoka: One Mahādeva minister of Aśoka who took measures for despatch to Ceylon a branch of the *Bodhivṛkṣa* (Mahāvaṃsa XVIII, 20); a Mahādeva Thera who played a considerable role at times as a religious master and as a Buddhist missionary. In fact he conferred the ordination (*pabbajjā*) on Mahinda, son of Aśoka (Dīpavaṃsa, VII 25; Mahāvaṃsa, V, 206; Samantapāsādikā p. 51); then after the council of Pāṭaliputra, in 236 PN, he set out to preach the Good law to Mahisamaṇḍala where he converted 40,000 souls and conferred ordination on 40,000 young men (Dīpavaṃsa VIII, 5; Mahāvaṃsa, XII, 3 and 29; Samantapāsādikā, p. 63, 66). In Mahisamaṇḍala, Andhra and the region of Dhānyakaṭaka where the Pubba and Aparaseliya sects had their seat, some authors think that Mahādeva was founder of those schools which issued out of the Mahāsāṃghika stock and which adhered to the Five Propositions.[2] But if the Mahādeva in question had been a heretic, it becomes difficult to explain how the Ceylonese Chronicles make him a disciple and confidant of a very orthodox monk like Moggaliputta Tissa, a declared Vibhajyavādin, and could count him as one of the great propagators of the True Law. Then Mahisamaṇḍala is not certainly the country of Andhra, but may be Mysore, may be and still more probably Māhiṣmatī or country of the Mahiṣakas, associated by the Purāṇas with Mahārāṣṭra which had as its capital Māhiṣmatī on the Narmadā.[3]

---

1. GP Malalasekera, *Dictionary of Pāli Proper Names,* London, 1938, II, pp. 505-506.
2. Voir notamment E. Frauwallner, *Die buddhistischen Konzile,* Zeitschrift der Deutschen Morgenländischen Gesellschaft, CII, 1952, pp. 240-249.
3. Cf. D.C. Sircar, *Text of the Puranic List of Peoples,* IHQ., XXI, 1945, p. 307. Voir aussi B.C. Law, *Geography of Early Buddhism,* London, 1932, p. 22; *India as described in Early Texts,* Londres, 1941, p. 74, 104.

THE SAMMATIYA TRADITION: It is mentioned for the first time in the VIth century by Bhavya or Bhāvaviveka, author of the Tarkajvālā (Mdo XIX, p. 162 b c-163a 3; cf. Mdo XC, No. 12)[1], reproduced later with some modifications in the XIVth century by Bu-ston (tr. Obermiller, II p. 96), in the XVth by Gzon-nu-dpal (Roerich, *Blue Annals*, I, p. 96), and in the XVIIth by Tāranātha (tr. Schiefner, p. 52). According to this tradition, in the year 137 after Nirvāṇa, under the King Nanda and Mahāpadma (sic), an assembly took place at Pāṭ aliputra in which participated the Sthaviras holding the same view as Mahākāśyapa, Mahāloma, Mahātyāga, Uttara, Revata etc. A monk (of the name of Bhadra) taught the Five Propositions and because of them a great schism was produced in the assembly. The sthavira Nāga and Sāramati—or better Nāgasena and Manorathaā—adopted the five Propositions and conformed them to their teaching. Now the religious men were divided into two schools: Sthavira and Mahāsāṃghika, and the quarrel between the two groups lasted for 63 years. Then in the year 102 (correctly in 200) after Nirvāṇa, the sthavira Vātsīputra revised the doctrine correctly.

It is here no more the question of Mahādeva but of a Bhadanta whose heretical views were supported by a Nāga or Nāgasena, whose name recalls the Nāgas, already pointed out by Vasumitra. The schism broke out, not under Aśoka in the year 100 PN (short chronology) but formerly under Mahāpadma of the dynasty of the Nandas in 137 PN (long chronology). The Saṃmatīya tradition follows in fact an identical computation or very near the Ceylonese chronology which counts 218 years between Nirvāṇa and the coronation of Aśoka and which attributes the reign of Nandas from the year 140 to 162 PN (346-324 B.C.).

BHAVYA: In his Tarkajvālā, Bhavya just referring to the Saṃmatīya tradition summed up above, ascribed in his own account to the Mahāsāṃghika schism a later date: "One hundred and sixty years after the Parinirvāṇa, while king Dharm-Āśoka reigned over Pāṭaliputra, a great schism arose in the Saṃgha after some controversies, and the saṃgha was split up into two schools, Mahāsāṃghika and Sthavira.[2]" But the proposed date: "160 in the reign of Aśoka" does not respond to any known computation and does not tally either with the short chronology which places Aśoka in 100 PN or with the long chronology that makes him reign from

1. M. Walleser, *Die Sekten des alten Buddhismus,* Heidelberg, 1927, p. 81-82.
2. Td., *ibid.*, p. 78.

219 to 256 PN. However the same date, 160 PN, is still mentioned by other authors and notably by Bu-ston (II, p. 96) who attributes the origin of the schism not only to the advent of the Five heretical Propositions but also to the fact that the Arhats "read the speech of Buddha in four different languages: Sanskrit, Prākrit, Apabhraṃśa and Paiśācika."

CONCLUSIONS: The Scrutiny of the records has brought to light the doubts and the chronological contradiction concerning:

1. *The date of schism*: in 137 PN during the reign of the Nandas; in 100, 116 or 160 during the reign of Aśoka.

2. *The instigator or instigators of the schism*: the Nāgas of the Southern India helped by their neighbouring Pratyantika and the Bahuśrutas; a monk called or surnamed Bhadanta; lastly Mahādeva. The last one is presented either as a culpable criminal of the three ānantaryas, or as a man full of knowledge and of talent, unjustly slandered, or lastly as a Sarvāstivādin, "a subtle investigator of the Nāmarūpa."

3. *Causes of the schism*: the controversies provoked by the appearance of the Five Propositions, the introduction of Mahāyānist sūtras in the Tripiṭaka or even the translation of the Scriptures in four different languages.

4. *The consequences of the schism*: Having taken refuge in Kasmir the Sthavirian Arhats established themselves there finally or again after a short sojourn returned to Pāṭaliputra where they convoked a new council. As to the instigator of the schism (Mahādeva) either he lived at Pāṭaliputra till his death or he went to the mountainous regions of Andhra where he continued to teach his thesis to the Pūrva, Apara and Uttaraśailas. But some sources regard Mahādeva the teacher of the śailas as a personage different from Mahādeva, the originator of the schism.

The contradictions lead us to reject the chronology as apocryphal. Moreover it is of very little importance. It matters little whether the heresy originated under Aśoka or century earlier, whether its author is called Nāga, Mahādeva or Bhadanta, or whether the Sthavirian Arhat took refuge temporarily or permanently in Kaśmir. The fact seems certain that, between the death of Buddha and the reign of Aśoka the Maurya, the Buddhist community had been subject to centrifugal forces which must have brought about finally the secession. The causes of dissension were multiple. Some religious men in possession of the Fruit of Arhat claimed to monopolise the sanctity; they roused the jealousy of the commoners (*pṛthagjana,*) and the latter invented the Five Propositions for the sole purpose of humiliating the Arhat and of outraging their honour. Some monks who, whether assembled again in councils or not, had recited in common the words of Buddha, gave themselves out as the only depository of same and wanted to impose on their colleagues the canon of their compilation which they had just put together. But the latter resisted the imposition; they had themselves memorised the words of the Master or did not consider the canon as closed and found out the introduction therein of new compositions more or less conformable to the primitive teaching. At least there was no unanimity in regard to the secondary points of doctrine and discipline: in the matter of Vinaya notably the laxist tendencies were manifest in some communities (Vaiśālī, Kauśāmbī). The dispute brewed for a long time before resulting in a secession. If an old evidence is to be believed, we mean that of the Mahāprajñā-pāramitopadeśa or of its translator Kumārajīva (T. 1509, k 2, p. 70 a), the Great Community remained intact till the time of Aśoka; "When Buddha was dead, when the Law was recited for the first time, it was still like the time when Buddha lived. A hundred years after, King Aśoka called a big quinquennial assembly (*pañcavarṣapariṣad*) and the great masters of the Law held discussions. Because of their differences, there appeared some distinct sects (*nikāya*), each having a name, which eventually became developed."

The fact is that the division of the Saṃgha did not at all put an end to the polemics, and that the Five Propositions continued to be discussed. The Theravādin and the Sarvāstivādin combatted them in the Kathāvatthu, the Jñānaprasthāna and its Vibhāṣā respectively. The Saṃmatīya, the Vātsīputrīya and the Mahīśāsaka rejected them in the same manner. As a set off, they found some defenders among the Mahāsāṃghika and their sub-sects Bahusrutīya, Caitya and Śaila, and were even adopted by a school of the Sthavirian stock, that of the Haimavata.[1]

---

1. A. Bareau, *Les Sectes bouddhiques du Petit Véhicule,* Saigon, 1955, p. 291.

Chapter - 22

Śaṅkara's Reference to a Buddhist Passage

Vidhushekhara Bhattacharya

In vol. VI, p. 141 of the *IHQ.*, I referred to a Buddhist passage quoted in Śaṅkara's commentary on the *Brahmasūtras*, II. 2. 24, which I could not trace back to its source.

Here is another Buddhist passage, and so far as my information goes, it has also not yet been traced. It is cited by Śaṅkara in his commentary on the *Brahmasūtras*, II, 2. 22:

api ca vaināśikāḥ kalpayanti *buddhisbodhyaṃ trayād anyat saṃskṛtaṃ kṣaṇikaṃ ceti.*

Undoubtedly here the italicized portion is one half of a kārikā, there being only one syllable (presumably *tat*) left out of the end.

The word *traya* in the kārikā refers to *pratisaṅkhyānirodha, apratisaṅkhyānirodha,* and *ākāśa.*

Chapter - 23

Śaṅkara's Reference to a Buddhist Passage

Vidhushekhara Bhattacharya

According to the Vaibhāṣikas *ākāśa* is a reality (*vastu-sat*), and in support of it they quote (*Abhidharmakośavyākhyā*, I. 5, p. 16) the following passage which reminds one of the Upaniṣadic style.[1] It is introduced there with the words: uktaṃ hi bhagavatā:

pṛthivī bho gautama kutra pratiṣṭhitā/ pṛthivī brāhmaṇa abmaṇḍale pratiṣṭhitā/ abmaṇḍalaṃ bho gautama kva pratiṣṭhitaṃ/ vayupratiṣṭhitaṃ/ vāyu bho gautama kva pratiṣṭhitaḥ/ ākāśe pratiṣṭhitaḥ/ ākaśaṃ bho gautama kutra patiṣṭhitam/ atisarasi mahābrāhmaṇa, atisarasi mahābrāhmaṇa, ākāśaṃ mahābrāhmaṇa apratiṣṭhitam, anālambananam iti vistaraḥ/

In order to maintain the existence of *ākāśa* Śaṅkara in his commentary on the *Brahmasūtra* II. 2-24, refers to the same passage in the following words:

saugate hi samaye p ṛ t h i v ī b h a g a v a ḥ k i ṃ s a n n i ś r a y a ity asmin praśnaprativacanapravāhe pṛthivyādīnām ante v ā y u ḥ k i ṃ s a n n i ś r a y a ity asya praśnasya prativacanaṃ bhavati v ā y u r ā k ā ś a s a n n i ś r a y a iti.

It seems that these lines in Śaṅkara's commentary are an abridgement of the Buddhist passage quoted abvoe, and not a direct quotation. Therefore, the difference between the two texts is of no importance.

What is the book in which the passage is originally contained?

---

1. See *Bṛhadāraṇyaka Up.*, III, 9. 20-24.

Chapter - 24

Society for Buddhist Lore

(Gesellschaft für Buddhismus Kunde)

founded at Heidelberg

M. Walleser

I am glad to give some details about the said Society, not so much in the hope of evoking some interest in the effective work done or to be done by it, as with the intention of raising a question and of giving a definite answer to it—besides the answer given already by the founding of the society itself.

The question is this. Presuming that Buddhism is (what nobody will earnestly deny) not only a cultural movement of the deepest influences on the life of more than two thousand years and on the moral as well as spiritual development of the greater part of Asia, but that even to-day it is vigorous enough to stir the attention of the most advanced spirits in the old and in the new world, one may ponder over the problem: how is it to be explained that an aspect of life, professed in a rather popular and almost illogical style, could win over not only the hearts of millions of simple people without shedding a drop of blood, but also subjugate the most refined representatives of old and civilised cultures (the Indian and Chinese ones) under the sway of its idea,—yea, which even to-day puts the most advanced Western philosophy and science to the necessity of defending their arguments and consequences against the inexplorable results of its logic and epistemology. Of course, the struggle is not, in its proper sense, between Christ and Buddha—one might rather think that the thoughts of these two most spiritual representatives of mankind moved, at least for the ethical and practical view of life, in the same direction—but between the deeper spiritual instincts by which they were instigated and led. And this chief difference or even antagonism lay, as it seems to me, in that the one—Buddha—is the first great expounder of the sovereignty and independence of human mind, while the other was the most prominent herald of human dependence on transcendental·forces. As in all generalisations, there may be a certain one-sidedness and exaggeration in such an anti-thesis, the more so, as the theoretical side of the problem was rather far from both of them, but if we are induced to circumscribe a very complicated matter by a single word, I really do not see how to do it in another way.

Now, let us take it for granted that we can understand these two powerful streams of spiritual development by the supposition of two antagonistic tendencies of the kind mentioned above, and we shall concede that, if the principle of the "want of supposition" or "Voraussetzungslosigkeit" has been carried to its highest pitch and its ultimate consequences by Buddhism, we shall have all inducements to search in the development of these unrestrained doctrines—unrestrained in so far as they are not regulated by the regard for a trans-human essence or power—for the last consequence of pure human. In other words, if really Buddhism continued to adhere to the words of its Master who had preached the sovereignty and independence of human mind in the most impressive manner, it must in the course of its inner development have attained those limits which to independent human mind it is allowed to reach. And I am convinced, it has,—not in the purport that Buddha himself would have had an insight into all the logical outcomes of his principle of independence, but rather in that the most clever of his followers and successors were driven by the logic of facts to certain results which were not to be outstripped but by breaking with the principle of "Voraussetzungslosigkeit" itself. I dare not assert that this point has ever been reached in the history of spiritual Buddhism (although I should understand if any one did in view of the fact that Buddhism has succumbed in India itself to the stronger might of Brāhmaṇic revelation), but I only repeat: if ever in the world the last and ultimate consequences of the autonomous human faculty of mind have been drawn, it must have been in the huge philosophical, especially of later Indian Buddhism, which flourished in the last centuries before the rise of Śaṅkara and Kumārila.

This vast literature has for the most part been lost. What has not been destroyed in these struggles got astray during the bloody invasions of Mahomedanism and in the prodigious exuberance of the literary activity on the side of the Brāhmaṇical systems. But a very few documents of those last but, in their subtlety, admirable achievements of Buddhist acuteness have survived in India itself (as e.g., Śāntirakṣita's Tattva-saṃgraha with Kamalaśīla's commentary which has recently appeared in the Gaekwad's Oriental Series) in their original Sanskrit grab; almost the whole of it has been preserved to posterity only in Chinese and Tibetan translations, and even the few original Sanskrit texts, which have been transmitted to us, would scarcely be quite intelligible, had we not in their translation into those foreign languages the means of correcting the errors which have crept into the manuscriptural tradition. Thus it will be clear that the study of Sanskrit must be supplemented by that of, at least, Tibetan and Chinese, if the scientific exigencies are to be supplied as to the exploration of those venerable documents of the most acute thinkers whom, perhaps, the world has ever seen.

Now, a lot work has been done already in the direction of reconstruction of the ideas and arguments of those ancient philosophers. It may be permissible to mention the names of L. de la Vallée Poussin, F. Stcherbatsky, G. Tucci, and the splendid work done by these and other pioneers in the vast field of later Sanskrit Buddhist literature. But there is still a lot of work left to be done, and I hope, the author of this short article will be pardoned, if he implores the help of all those who are interested in this task of combining Sanskrit, Tibetan and Chinese philology to assist anyhow the exertions of those savants who, as workers in one or other of the aforesaid ranges of Buddhist literature, will in the first line bear the burden of editing and translating those texts which will contribute to a more exact knowledge of the philosophical aims of expiring Buddhism on the Indian soil. But herewith the work is not done: not only the older strata of Buddhist thought, delivered to us chiefly in the Abhidharma of the northern schools will have to be earnestly searched through, but also the commencements and even later developments of Buddhism in China and Tibet (to name only the most important domains) are of the utmost importance for the reconstruction of that state of cultural and scientific development which Buddhism has reached in India and which may be considered to be its purest manifestation.

Now, this task is the one which the "Gesellschaft für Buddhismus Kunde" should like to promote. And this in three ways:

First, an Institute for research has been established, by presenting to the student and scholar a locality where he can compare at ease the different collections in which the Chinese, Tibetan and Indian Buddhist literature is available. As to the latter, the editions of the Pali Text Society are at hand together with the Ceylonese and Siamese editions of the Pali commentaries (the latter, a present from the late king of Siam and other members of the royal family to the author of this note). Besides, a number a manuscript-copies of almost all the existing Sanskrit Mahāyāna Sūtras are at hand together with the editions of the Bibliotheca Buddhica (Leningrad), as well as the bibliographical and encyclopœdic material which is indispensable for philological work in those different languages.

Secondly, for publishing the scientific work which may be expected either from the members of the Society who will take the opportunity of studying in the Institute or from foreign members; a "Year-book" letters can be used, although in a limited number.

Thirdly, an attempt will be made to introduce a certain formal correspondence in the scientific work by the permanent superintendence or rather mutual assistance given by the members of the Institute. If it is scarcely to be presumed that one single scholar will be fully conversant with the different idioms in which the Buddhist literature presents itself, in a degree that he will have an accomplished mastership of all the difficulties ever ready to rise, it will not be thought deprecatory for anyone of the collaborators to consult a worker in a neighbouring field who himself in other questions and respects may be dependent on a third. In every case, the task is generally of such a complicated kind that with the *consensus omnium* which we demand and pray for, the ordinary and usual method of scientific work, which elsewhere requires the entire responsibility from the single worker, will be supplanted by another which, in the main lays the ultimate responsibility on the editor, without depriving the special worker of the care consisting in the legitimate liability to do his best in order to bring the object of his endeavours and exertions to its highest accomplishment. So, the Society will reckon it an honour, as well as a pleasure, to invite cordially the collaboration and assistance on the part of all those who think highly of the performances and attainments of Buddhist philosophy as to require for it a special kind of treatment and, consequently, a special kind of workmanship.

The Rules of the Society may be had on application to the Society at Heidelberg, Goethestr. 12. The annual subscription for which the Year-book will be delivered post free has been fixed at 12 marks (12s.) to be paid in on the account of the Society at the Rheinische Creditbank Filiale Heidelberg.